THE GOLDEN GIRLS

THE CULTURAL HISTORY OF TELEVISION

Breaking Bad: *A Cultural History*, by Lara Stache

Cheers: *A Cultural History*, by Joseph J. Darowski and Kate Darowski

Frasier: *A Cultural History*, by Joseph J. Darowski and Kate Darowski

Friends: *A Cultural History*, by Jennifer C. Dunn

Gilmore Girls: *A Cultural History*, by Lara Stache and Rachel Davidson

The Golden Girls: *A Cultural History*, by Bernadette Giacomazzo

In Living Color: *A Cultural History*, by Bernadette Giacomazzo

Mad Men: *A Cultural History*, by M. Keith Booker and Bob Batchelor

Northern Exposure: *A Cultural History*, by Michael Samuel

Seinfeld: *A Cultural History*, by Paul Arras

Sex and the City: *A Cultural History*, by Nicole Evelina

The Simpsons: *A Cultural History*, by Moritz Fink

Star Trek: *A Cultural History*, by M. Keith Booker

THE GOLDEN GIRLS

A Cultural History

BERNADETTE GIACOMAZZO

ROWMAN & LITTLEFIELD
Lanham • Boulder • New York • London

Published by Rowman & Littlefield
An imprint of The Rowman & Littlefield Publishing Group, Inc.
4501 Forbes Boulevard, Suite 200, Lanham, Maryland 20706
www.rowman.com

86-90 Paul Street, London EC2A 4NE, United Kingdom

British Library Cataloguing in Publication Information Available

Library of Congress Cataloging-in-Publication Data

Names: Giacomazzo, Bernadette, 1979– author.
Title: The golden girls : a cultural history / Bernadette Giacomazzo.
Description: Lanham : Rowman & Littlefield, [2023] | Series: The cultural history of television | Includes bibliographical references and index. | Summary: "A fun and meaningful examination of the beloved 1980s sitcom The Golden Girls, including how it tackled progressive social issues of its time and forever changed the way audiences view older women"—Provided by publisher.
Identifiers: LCCN 2022056054 (print) | LCCN 2022056055 (ebook) | ISBN 9781538166550 (cloth) | ISBN 9781538166567 (epub)
Subjects: LCSH: Golden girls (Television program)
Classification: LCC PN1992.77.G58 G53 2023 (print) | LCC PN1992.77.G58 (ebook) | DDC 791.45/653—dc23/eng/20230315
LC record available at https://lccn.loc.gov/2022056054
LC ebook record available at https://lccn.loc.gov/2022056055

TO MA

Thanks for not dropping me off at the orphanage even when I made you crazy, for being the Sophia to my Dorothy (even though you're Neapolitan and not Sicilian), and, most of all, for being there when I needed you the most.

I don't say it enough—in fact, I don't say it at all, but that's because I'm Sicilian, not Neopolitan. But just because I don't say it doesn't mean I don't feel it: I love you, Ma.

CONTENTS

INTRODUCTION

On December 31, 2021, an era came to an end—and the world seemed to simultaneously stop in every time zone.

Betty Marion White—who was just a few weeks short of her one hundredth birthday—died in her sleep in her home in Brentwood, California, after suffering a stroke on Christmas Day.

The outpouring of grief from fans all over the world was both remarkable and singular in its messaging. Although many celebrities leave complicated legacies behind, White was one of a rare few whose charm, effervescence, and humor not only surpassed the test of time, but crossed generational lines.

Celebrities from every corner of Hollywood—everyone from Ryan Reynolds to Steve Martin, from Jennifer Love Hewitt to Viola Davis, and from Seth Meyers to Steve Aoki[1]—paid tribute to this incomparable legend, all echoing the same heartbreaking sentiment: White was a woman who was larger than life, who simultaneously grew older but never grew old, and who—in so doing—became timeless in her lifetime.

But with White's passing came another, much larger realization for the pop culture zeitgeist, one that would "hit different" once the enormity of its impact was truly felt.

The last of the Golden Girls had died.

Sure, no one thought that the actresses who played the titular Girls would live forever.

Death is really the only guarantee in life.

Fans of the show first felt a loss in 2008, when Estelle Scher Gettleman, professionally known as Estelle Getty—who played the feisty Sicilian mother and grandmother Sophia Petrillo on *The Golden Girls*—lost her battle with Lewy body dementia in 2008, at the age of eighty-four. Just one year later, Bernice Frankel—professionally known as Beatrice Arthur, and the once and forever Dorothy Zbornak—lost her battle with cancer at the age

Betty White, a television pioneer, died in 2021—just a few weeks shy of her one hundredth birthday. She was the last surviving cast member of *The Golden Girls*—Estelle Getty died in 2008 of complications from Lewy body dementia, Bea Arthur died in 2009 of cancer, and Rue McClanahan died in 2010 of a stroke.

of eighty-six. And in 2010, a stroke claimed the life of the beautiful Eddi-Rue McClanahan—known professionally as Rue McClanahan, who immortalized Blanche Devereaux on *The Golden Girls*—at the age of seventy-six.

So fans of the Girls knew that it was a question of *when*, not *if*, White would join her three former TV roommates in the great lanai in the sky.

Death is really the only guarantee in life.

But that didn't make the actual passing of White any easier for people all over the world.

If anything, the knowledge that Betty White was no longer among the living—and thus, the knowledge that the last of the Golden Girls had died—made it even more difficult to accept, because the last beacon of hope—that final tie to our past, which didn't really feel like "the past" at all thanks to the magic of syndication, not to mention the countless tributes and encomia from people from every corner of the entertainment industry—had finally dimmed for the final time.

During the course of seven years—and 180 episodes—*The Golden Girls* changed the television landscape. For the first time in history, Americans (and, later, the rest of the world) were watching sexagenarians—and one feisty octogenarian—leading active, vital lives as complete, full women.

These women weren't defined by the men—or, in Dorothy's case, the lack thereof—in their lives. These women weren't viewed through the lens of their children. And these women certainly weren't doddering old grandmothers staying home and baking cookies all day (though, certainly, Sophia could make a mean rum cake—even if she drank all the rum while she was making it).

Rather, these were women—widowed and divorced—who had careers, who had families, who enjoyed adventures both together and with other friends, and who had lovers (and, in the case of Blanche Devereaux, "many, many lovers").

But more than just being gals about town—the precursors to *Sex and the City* and *Desperate Housewives*, among other shows—this sexagenarian (and octogenarian) fab four weren't afraid to tackle the "tough stuff," the social and political issues of the late 1980s and early 1990s, topics that were once considered taboo to even discuss, let alone in a mature and loving fashion—topics that continue to resonate throughout our society in the twenty-first century, further cementing the Girls' timeless nature—which, perhaps, made it all too easy to forget that the Girls, or at least the actresses who played them, were mortal, just like the rest of us.

For *The Golden Girls* creator Susan Harris, there was no question that these four women would be cemented into the pop culture zeitgeist. In an interview with *Out*—a magazine dedicated to LGBTQIA issues—Harris explained that creating these four iconic characters served as a salvo for both young *and* old and helped us to change our perception of getting older—and, more specifically, of *women* getting older—in the United States.

"I think everybody—including younger people when they reach an age when they feel alienated—the thought of being alone, and spending your life alone, is terrifying," she said.[2] "These women were at an age where they were alone and were likely to stay alone until they found each other. They encouraged each other and had a life together. It showed that you didn't need the customary, traditional relationship to be happy. It paints a picture of all the possibilities for family."

Thanks to Dorothy, Rose, Blanche, and Sophia, the "family" extended to people all over the world. And the "family" was ours no matter our race, religion, creed, or sexual orientation—though it was the latter that would prove, ultimately, to be the show's most endearing and enduring quality, especially when it was revealed that the *Girls* were advocates for the community in real life, too.

Thanks to Dorothy, Rose, Blanche, and Sophia, the voiceless now had a voice—everyone from "illegal" immigrants to the poor and the elderly were seen as the complex, inextricably *human* people that they were.

And thanks to Dorothy, Rose, Blanche, and Sophia, the healing power of friendship—and community and sisterhood—cannot be denied. They were living, breathing proof that you can get through anything life throws your way when surrounded by the love and support of good friends and family—who are sometimes one and the same.

And a slice—or many slices—of cheesecake.

CHAPTER ONE

A BRIEF HISTORY OF THE GIRLS

To understand the true history of *The Golden Girls*, it's important to understand how the concept for the show began in the first place.

In 1984, Warren Littlefield—who was, at the time, NBC's senior vice president of comedy development—was watching what he told *EW*[1] was "some bullshit sketch" that advertised NBC's upcoming programming slate.

The "bullshit sketch" in question was a promotion for *Miami Vice*, a blockbuster smash "buddy cop" show that starred Don Johnson as Sonny Crockett and Philip Michael Thomas as Rico Tubbs—a show that was wildly successful in its day and still a bit of a pop culture phenomenon in modern times (albeit also seen, correctly, as a product of its time).

Dubbed "Miami Nice," the sketch starred *Night Court* star Selma Diamond[2] and future *Everybody Loves Raymond* star Doris Roberts,[3] two sexagenarians who kept mistaking *Miami Vice* for "Miami Nice."

"Bullshit" or not, the sketch amused the executives at NBC, who held onto the concept, hoping that an inspired television writer would eventually run with it and turn it into the million-dollar hitmaker that every television executive dreams of green-lighting.

They didn't have to wait too long: not long after the infamous sketch premiered, Paul Junger Witt and Tony Thomas—a production team with a series of hits under their belt, including *Soap* and *Benson*—were in a pitch meeting with Littlefield, hoping to get their show about "a female lawyer" picked up for production.

Littlefield rejected their pitch—whose details have been lost to the annals of time, so it's not clear if it was a comedy or a drama—but told Witt about the "Miami Nice" sketch and asked Witt to tell his wife—Susan

Harris—about it, hoping that she'd write a show around it. Harris initially refused.

"Paul came home and said, 'There's this idea, but you're not going to want to do it,'" she told *EW*.[4] "And I said, 'That's right. I don't want to do anything. But what is it?' He got me when he said the words 'old women.' It was a demographic that had never been addressed."

While Witt and Thomas were part of a husband-wife team that was about to make history, Tony Thomas had showbiz cred all his own as the product of a prominent Hollywood family. His father was legendary actor Danny Thomas and his sister is the actress Marlo Thomas. He is also related to talk show legend Phil Donahue by marriage.

In fact, a Danny Thomas joke made its way into season 2, episode 5, "Isn't It Romantic?" when Dorothy's high school friend reveals that she's a lesbian—and that she might be in love with Rose. When Sophia reveals Jean's "coming out" to Blanche, she takes it rather blithely: "I've never known any personally, but isn't Danny Thomas one?" This prompts Dorothy to utter a line that can be found on many a pro-LGBTQIA shirt today: "Not Lebanese, Blanche! Lesbian!"

For her part, Harris had earned the right to sit back and relax for a little while. Born Susan Spivak in Mount Vernon, New York, Harris—who had taken her first husband's last name upon marriage and kept it professionally after they'd divorced—had written for a string of successful television shows, including *Love, American Style*, *All in the Family*, and *Maude*, an *All in the Family* spin-off, which starred Beatrice Arthur in the titular role of Maude Findlay, a brash, no-nonsense, liberal-minded middle-aged woman living in the wealthy Westchester County enclave of Tuckahoe, New York. Tuckahoe was located less than ten minutes from Harris's hometown, so she knew more than a little bit about how they thought.

Harris, in fact, was one of three writers on the infamous and controversial "Maude's Dilemma" episode of *Maude*, in which the titular character decided on a late-in-life abortion at the age of forty-seven in a pre-*Roe v. Wade* world, a time when more Americans were against the practice than for it.[5]

So perhaps it was no surprise that Harris's initial notes for one of the characters that was tentatively (and, eventually, permanently) named Dorothy on the show that would become *The Golden Girls* was a "Bea Arthur–like character."

But more on that shortly.

Incidentally, Harris's initial pilot script also included a character named "Coco," who was a gay male waiter who made it to the pilot episode. But

Susan Harris's notes about the character that would become Dorothy Zbornak included ruminations that she should be played by a "Bea Arthur–like character."

in the initial pilot, which aired on NBC on September 14, 1985, Coco—portrayed by Charles Levin, best known for his role on *Hill Street Blues*—became a "gay male houseboy." He lasted only one episode, however, which was ultimately for the best, as *The Golden Girls* wouldn't have had the same flair with Coco as a permanent fixture.

Ultimately, and despite her initial protestations about making the show in the first place, Harris turned in the pilot script to Littlefield. The executive loved her treatment on sight and green-lit the series for production.

With the show ready to go, the casting calls began.

There is some debate as to which Girl was the first to be cast. What each account makes clear, however, is that Arthur—the one Harris had the clearest vision for—was the last to accept her role.

The other three—Getty, McClanahan, and White—all seemed to be cast simultaneously.

For the purposes of this cultural history, however, we'll take the first-hand word of McClanahan, courtesy of her memoir *My First Five Husbands . . . And the Ones Who Got Away*,[6] which was published just two years before she died of a stroke in 2010, and her 2006 interview with the Television Academy.

According to McClanahan, she was the first to get cast—though initially she was made to read for the role of Rose. This, naturally, would not do for the elder ingenue.

"I can't play Rose, I've got to play Blanche," she told her agent, according to her interview with the Television Academy.[7]

Her agent, however, informed her that the role of Blanche was promised to Betty White—and McClanahan could either read for Rose and be in *The Golden Girls* or "forget it."

So McClanahan reluctantly read for Rose. But at the next table read, she sat with Betty White, and director Jay Sandrich told them to switch roles. White, he said, was to read for Rose, and McClanahan was to read for Blanche. This suited both ladies just fine—White would later claim that she "loved" the character of Rose when she first read it—and thus, legends were born.

"I didn't have a handle on Rose," McClanahan said to the Television Academy in 2006.[8] "I didn't know how to play Rose."

That, perhaps, seems like a bit of a stretch—fans of the Girls will recall that prior to becoming known as the man-eating vamp Blanche Devereaux, McClanahan was best known for her role as the well-meaning but dizzy Vivian Cavender Harmon on *Maude*, who was a precursor to Rose, if you will. Meanwhile, before White was the once and forever Rose Nylund, she was known as the vampy Sue Ann Nivens on *The Mary Tyler Moore Show*—a precursor to Blanche, if you will.

Perhaps the ladies didn't want to be typecast in their careers—especially this late in life. Perhaps they just didn't feel like reading for the characters they were originally cast for. Or, perhaps, they just wanted to challenge each other as actors—after all, the ladies had worked together before on several occasions.

And there were no better women to play Blanche Devereaux and Rose Nylund than Eddi-Rue McClanahan and Betty Marion White, respectively.

A native of Oklahoma, McClanahan lit out to the East Coast to pursue an acting career in the 1950s after she graduated from the University of Tulsa with a dual degree in German and theater. She got her start in plays in Pennsylvania—specifically, *Inherit the Wind* in 1957—before eventually making her way to the New York City circuit, wowing audiences with her 1969 Broadway performance of *Jimmy Shine*, where she played opposite Dustin Hoffman.

By the 1970s, McClanahan had worked her way up to the soap opera circuit—a big deal, at the time, for working actresses, though the influence of soap operas among modern-day actors is slowly fading from memory as the dramatic serials become a distant relic of a bygone time—and landed the role of Caroline Johnson on *Another World*, where she stayed for a year.[9] She followed that with a role on *Where the Heart Is* before landing the role of Ruth Rempley on *All in the Family*, which led to the role of Vivian Cavender Harmon on *Maude* and Aunt Fran on *Mama's Family*. Just before landing the role of Blanche Devereaux, she landed guest spots on comedies like *Gimme a Break!* (featuring the legendary Nell Carter), *The Love Boat*, and *Charles in Charge* (opposite future Trump supporter Scott Baio, who was a "teen dream" actor and one-time Pamela Anderson paramour for much of the 1980s).

White, meanwhile, was not only a veteran of the stage and screen, but a pioneering performer on television. As the first woman to produce a sitcom on television, White was one of the few women of the time who knew her way around both sides of the camera. As such, she'd earn the moniker "First Lady of Television," successfully transitioning to the television medium after a successful career in radio.

Contrary to popular belief, White—not Lucille Ball—was the first woman to produce a sitcom on television. Though Ball co-owned the production company that put out the legendary *I Love Lucy*, she was not credited as a producer on the show. Jess Oppenheimer was the producer of *I Love Lucy*, and Ball's first husband and *I Love Lucy* costar Desi Arnaz was an executive producer. White, however, was credited as the producer of 1953's *Life with Elizabeth*, earning her the honor of being the first woman to produce a sitcom on television.

What's more, White's successful transition from radio to television was no easy feat. As difficult as it is to comprehend today, with so many visual mediums—both analog and digital—dominating the landscape, many radio stars of the 1940s struggled to find fame when television became the predominant medium beginning in the 1950s, in part because many of them had a "face for radio" (a polite way of saying they were ugly).

White also became known as a popular game show panelist, appearing on such shows as *Password* (where she frequently starred opposite her third husband—and the love of her life—Allen Ludden, who was the host of the show) and *Match Game*.

But it was her roles on *The Mary Tyler Moore Show* (as Sue Ann Nivens) and *Mama's Family* (as Ellen Harper Jackson—a character she originated on *The Carol Burnett Show*) that garnered White the most acclaim—and recognition—prior to *The Golden Girls*. And, like McClanahan, White also starred on a few episodes of *The Love Boat*.

The next character cast was Sophia, the tart-tongued Sicilian-by-way-of-Brooklyn octogenarian who was the mother of the equally sardonic Dorothy.

Estelle Getty won the role after earning rave reviews in *Torch Song Trilogy*,[10] Harvey Fierstein's classic three-act play focusing on an unrequited gay love affair. Getty originated the role of Mrs. Beckoff ("I'm the mother!") at the Actor's Playhouse in Greenwich Village, New York, though she would take the proverbial show on the road, eventually landing in Los Angeles, where she caught the attention of one of the casting directors for *The Golden Girls* and won the role that would come to define her career.

During the audition process, though, Getty wasn't sure if she'd be able to secure the role of Sophia. Sure, she'd earned some recognition on the New York City theater circuit in bit parts throughout her life, and *Torch Song Trilogy* was nothing if not a cultural milestone—but unlike her future co-stars, television fame eluded her, save for a few bit parts in TV shows like *Hotel* and *Cagney & Lacey*, and such films as *Mask* and *Tootsie*. But in early 1985, she got permission from her manager to return to California to audition for Sophia, thinking it would be her "last chance" at finding film and television work at her age. She promised to return to New York if she didn't land the role—and ultimately returned to New York more than a decade later, after *The Golden Girls* (and its various spin-offs including *The Golden Palace* and *Empty Nest*) was finally over.

Unfortunately, by the time Getty returned to New York, the Lewy body dementia that eventually would claim her life had taken hold of her mind. Save for a few bit parts in television shows like *The John Larroquette Show* and *The Nanny*—as herself—for nostalgia purposes, her appearances on television were all but over.

Despite this tragedy, however, it's safe to say that Getty successfully secured her television legacy.

Estelle Getty's big break came when she starred in Harvey Fierstein's groundbreaking play, *Torch Song Trilogy*.

With three of the Girls in place, the last—but by no means the least—Girl needed to fall in line.

Enter the one and only Bea Arthur.

Bernice Frankel—as she was known when she was born in Brooklyn, New York, on May 13, 1922—didn't start out as an actress.

Instead, after a year of studying at the Blackstone College for Girls, she answered her nation's call of duty in 1943, when she enrolled in the U.S. Marines, which had established the Women's Reservists division, making them the last branch of the U.S. military to allow women to join their ranks. Their first advertisement went out in February 1943, with the tagline "Be a Marine . . . Free a Man to Fight." In essence, the idea was to put women in noncombat roles so that men could be shipped off to Europe to fight on the World War II battlefields.

And Private Frankel was one of those women. Initially serving as a typist in the Washington, D.C., headquarters, Frankel went on to the Motor Transport School at Camp Lejeune, North Carolina.[11]

In addition to making her name as a marine, Frankel made her name in another way: in 1944, she filed a name change request form with the marines when she married fellow cadet Robert Alan Aurthur, who also would later go on to work in the entertainment industry. Though they divorced after three years of marriage, Frankel kept her married name but changed the spelling to *Arthur*—and it was the name she would keep for the rest of her life.

What was, perhaps, most interesting about Arthur's marines file is that her personality was all but a wholesale description of Dorothy Zbornak, the character she would bring to life and infamy forty years after her time in the service.

"Described as having a poised and trim appearance (and exhibiting 'meticulous good taste'), Arthur was also considered to be ingratiating, frank, and open, though overly aggressive, and argumentative," said the National World War II Museum.[12] A special note on one assessment read: "Officious—but probably a good worker if she has her own way!"

A good worker, indeed: by the time she was honorably discharged from the marines in 1945, Arthur had achieved the rank of staff sergeant, and her discharge records revealed that she was on her way to "dramatics school," which would—as we all know—lead her to her true destiny.

After studying at the New School in New York City—under the famed German director Erwin Piscator[13]—Arthur turned her attention to the stage. She joined a theater troupe and auditioned for the lead role in the Broadway musical *Mame*. Though the role went to Angela Lansbury—who became a lifelong dear friend—Arthur successfully won the role of Vera Charles, a supporting role that won her both the rave reviews of Broadway and the coveted Tony Award for Best Featured Actress in a Musical in 1966.

Though Arthur didn't have many film roles—her most notable one, at least as far as *Star Wars* fans are concerned, was in the oft-controversial *Star Wars Holiday Special*, where she played Ackmena, a wise-cracking bartender in Tatooine's Mos Eisley cantina[14]—she would strike it big on television when the legendary producer Norman Lear invited her to audition for the role of Maude Findlay in 1971. Maude, a liberal feminist cousin of *All in the Family*'s Edith Bunker (and a perpetual thorn in the side of Edith's husband, Archie), was a hit almost instantly, and she received her own spin-off show of the same name just one year later.

Yet by the time *The Golden Girls* came calling a little more than a decade later, Arthur wasn't exactly keen on taking the role. As far as she was concerned, there was way too much overlap between Maude Findlay and Dorothy Zbornak. In fact, it took a call from McClanahan for the veteran actress to consider the thought of becoming Dorothy Zbornak.

"I called her and said, 'Why are you going to turn down the best script that's ever going to come across your desk as long as you live?'" McClanahan revealed.[15]

In true Arthur fashion, the elder stateswoman of the stage and small screen pushed back in her true sardonic fashion.

"Rue, I don't want to do 'Maude and Vivian Meet Sue Ann Nivens.' Booooorrrrring!" Arthur replied, according to McClanahan.[16] (In fairness to Arthur, her initial assessment wasn't that far off—especially given the original casting of the roles.)

It was only when Arthur realized that McClanahan and White switched roles—to the Blanche and Rose for whom they eventually would become world famous—that she became more interested in reading for the role.

And even though Arthur had turned down several television roles in the interim between *Maude* and *The Golden Girls*, it was Harris's whip-smart, witty writing for all four of the Girls that ultimately convinced her to bring Dorothy to life.

"It's funny, it's adult, and I will get off my ass again and go to work," she recalled.[17] "I didn't know it was going to turn into a cult [classic]. I just thought it was wonderful."

With the cast firmly in place, it was time for everyone to get off their asses again and go to work.

But no one could possibly expect what would happen next.

As an interesting and oft-forgotten sidenote, it's worth mentioning that shortly after *The Golden Girls* premiered, a woman by the name of Nancy Bretzfield filed a $5 million suit against NBC, the Walt Disney Company, and the creators of the show, claiming that they stole the idea for the show from her. Bretzfield claimed that she pitched a similar idea to NBC called "Getting Along" back in 1980, and her script was rejected for being inappropriate. Although it's not clear what the disposition of the lawsuit ultimately was, what's clear is that Bretzfield continues to profit from *The Golden Girls* name to this day. In 2019, Bretzfield opened an LLC in Florida (despite having a Beverly Hills, California, address) called Golden Girls Skincare; she dissolved the LLC one year later. Little else is known about Bretzfield today—though her LinkedIn page bills her as an "independent Internet professional."[18]

CHAPTER TWO

GRANDMAS GONE WILD

The Girls Subvert TV's Matriarchal Depictions

In 2010, Canadian communication theorist Marshall McLuhan infamously postulated that "the medium is the message." In other words, the form of the medium—in this case, television—embeds itself in whatever message it's trying to convey. In so doing, a symbiotic relationship is created between the viewer and the medium, thereby influencing both future messages and the way they are consumed by the viewer.

So, if today there is a pervasive—yet, interestingly, erroneous—belief that every woman in the 1950s was a "happy homemaker," it's because the medium of television made it so. So pervasive is this trope, in fact, that it's the basis of twenty-first-century conservatism and the oppressive "tradwife" movement.[1] And all it takes is a bit of the most tonsorial research to realize that this belief was nothing more than a television marketing campaign designed to get women out of the workforce so the men—who had just returned from World War II—could get their old jobs back.

Arguably, it was one of television's most successful campaigns—and one that *The Golden Girls* turned on its head in the 1980s. These weren't young ladies who had just graduated college—and neither were they mothers who had young children to raise and husbands to tend to. These were older women with grown children and dead or divorced husbands who were struggling to make it on their pensions and their (respectable, all things considered) jobs.

Let's remember that of all the Girls, octogenarian Sophia was the only one who was fully retired, though she certainly wasn't sitting home baking cakes all day. To the contrary, she volunteered at hospitals, enjoyed a very active social life, and even had a thriving sex life. Dorothy worked as a substitute teacher, Blanche worked in an art museum, and Rose worked at a grief counseling center until she was "downsized," after which she worked as a waitress and, finally, at a television station under consumer reporter Enrique Mas. Incidentally, Rose's "last" job on *The Golden Girls* may have been a nod and a wink to her role on *The Mary Tyler Moore Show*.

But even depicting these sixty-something women as having part-time jobs flew in the face of television convention.

Since the dawn of the television era, women have always been depicted in stereotypical roles. There's no shortage of scholarly research available about depictions of women on television from the 1950s and onward.[2] And as such a young medium—comparatively speaking, of course, especially when compared to other media like radio and motion pictures—it can be argued that the fast evolution of the depictions of women on television is nothing short of a miracle.

But it *is* worth noting how pervasive—and persistent—these stereotypes were, especially when it came to older women.

In the late 1940s and early 1950s, families on television looked very different—and variety (within the parameters of the separate-but-equal times, sadly—as no less of an authority than Betty White, who infamously refused to remove Black dancer Arthur Duncan from her eponymous television show despite pressure from both fans and censors,[3] can attest) was the spice of life.

I Remember Mama, which debuted in 1949, was a kindly (albeit a now long forgotten) show based on an immigrant Swedish family, while *The Goldbergs* (not to be confused with the show of the same name that premiered in 2013), which also first aired in 1949, was based on a Jewish family.

And then, of course, there was *The Honeymooners*, which debuted in 1952 and featured an unabashedly working-class family in a dilapidated Brooklyn apartment, making it a first of its kind, in that their lives were far from idealized (a precursor to the likes of *Roseanne* and *Malcolm in the Middle*, if you will).

And it went without saying that *I Love Lucy*—which debuted in 1951—featured a white woman married to her immigrant Latino/Cuban husband living in their (lavish, by every standard—and, by twenty-first century standards, one not affordable for a struggling musician and his stay-at-home wife) New York City apartment.

Betty White was considered a "godmother" of the television genre thanks to her groundbreaking eponymous show, which first aired in the 1950s.

But all the "first families" of television had one thing in common: the women in question either worked outside the home, or they worked over-time to change their domestic circumstances if they didn't bring home some bacon of their own.

The Honeymooners, for example, frequently featured Alice (Audrey Meadows) campaigning for women's rights, while *I Love Lucy*'s eponymous Lucy (Lucille Ball) was desperate to break into the entertainment industry alongside her husband, Ricky (Desi Arnaz).

Incidentally, Lucy's desperation to break into the entertainment industry had no basis in the reality of Hollywood: since the 1890s, women in the entertainment industry always were able to earn as much—and sometimes more—than their male counterparts. And wages aside, the entertainment industry was one of the few—if not the only—industry in which women had as much, if not more, ground for negotiation as their male counterparts. According to some scholars, women all but ran Hollywood in the silent film era—in fact, in the 1910s, Hollywood was described as a "manless Eden" because women were so prominent in the entertainment industry; the highest-paid director in 1916 was a woman by the name of Lois Weber,[4] who out-earned her contemporaries like Cecil B. DeMille and D. W. Griffith—and had to be pushed out forcefully to give their male counterparts some ground.[5] This was a pattern that would repeat itself in the late 1940s and early 1950s, though on a much larger scale, when "the boys" came back from war.

But by the mid- to late 1950s, increasing corporate pressure (read: threats of pulling much-coveted sponsor dollars[6]) forced television producers to make shows more homogenous. This meant that diversity—even if the "diversity" was just a Jewish family—was out, and the "all-American" white family was in, as seen on such shows as *The Adventures of Ozzie and Harriet*, *The Patty Duke Show*, and *The Donna Reed Show*. Gone were women pushing back against cultural and gender norms, fighting for the right to be seen as equal to the men they married and reading articles in *Ladies' Home Journal* that reinforced this belief that they, too, should make the same amount of money as their husbands for doing the same job (and sometimes doing it better than their husbands did).

In the place of these strong-willed, beautiful women were compliant Stepford wives, content with serving their husbands and children while maintaining perfectly coiffed hair, perfectly trim manicures, and perfectly stitched dresses and shoes . . . all while always maintaining a clean house and a home-cooked meal of meat and potatoes, with bonus points available if the meat and potatoes were homegrown, as well. Imagine telling your grandmothers and great-grandmothers from the 1950s about such concepts as Uber Eats, DoorDash, and Instacart—where would you even begin?

A modern reinterpretation of this trope suggests that it's actually a parody of itself—especially given how much money the female stars like Harriet Nelson, Patty Duke, and Donna Reed generated for themselves and for their networks—but that seems a bit of a stretch, to put it mildly, given that there's a certain subsect of modern American society that likes to cite these television shows as proof positive that things would be *so much better* in the United States if we all went back to this way of living, which never really existed in the first place.

In addition, both women *and* men were forced to conform to strict gender roles—and it perhaps went without saying that these gender roles were nothing if not stereotypical and heteronormative. Men were laborers and professionals who worked outside the home, while women were relegated to domestic roles (and maybe a secretarial or typing job or two, as the "little lady" may want to go shopping for a nice fur coat or a pair of shoes without dipping into her husband's wages), becoming little more than homemakers, wives, and mothers whose existence outside of their husband, their 2.3 children, and their dog was all but a tabula rasa. Who were they? What did they like to do? What were their hobbies? Who even were they before they became Mrs. Whomever? No one knew—and in a real way, no one even cared.

And if you were a woman who dared to buck this new social norm, lobotomies were often at the ready, and it took only a woman's well-connected husband to lock her away in a sanitarium—places that would later be revealed to be little better than hell on Earth, if your belief system provides for such a thing to exist. Any woman who dared to talk back to her husband qualified as "insane," and the only way out of these institutions—which were hubs of cruel and unusual punishment and not just for women—was for the woman to finally agree to submitting to her husband.[7]

Thus the stereotype of the 1950s housewife was born—at least on television.

But was this the reality of most women, at the time?

Not quite.

It's true that women often went to college to get what was derisively known as their "Mrs. Degree"—meaning that they went to college just to meet a man whom they eventually would marry and thus wouldn't need the degree for a notable career of any sort. "White collar" women were few and far between, and no one was campaigning for their improved visibility as they do today.

It's also true that marriage rates were at an all-time high in the 1950s (most likely due to nostalgia generated from World War II and the fear that "the boys" would be shipped off to God knows where to do who knows what with the blessing of the U.S. government) and that society shunned single, unwed mothers (a long way away from the "baby mama culture" that would later come to prominence in American pop culture). The birth control pill hadn't been invented yet, abortion was illegal,[8] and a teenage pregnancy often meant a "shotgun wedding" between the mother and the father of the prospective child.[9]

But it's also true that women were entering the workforce at higher rates than ever before. In 1950, 29 percent of the workforce was female—and that number began increasing steadily as the decade went on. Of the female workforce, half were over the age of thirty-five—and 40 percent of those women in the workforce had children at home.[10]

What's more, women who could afford it were encouraged to pursue higher education—against all odds, in some cases—and shatter the proverbial glass ceilings. Inspired by books like 1949's *The Second Sex*—written by the legendary Simone de Beauvoir—and articles in magazines like *Ladies' Home Journal* (whose slogan, in the 1950s, was "never underestimate the power of a woman") that called for political and economic equality between the sexes, women had enjoyed more than a little taste of freedom in the 1940s when "the boys" went off to war (just ask Private Bernice Frankel, aka Bea Arthur,who was one of more than three hundred thousand women who enlisted in the armed forces during World War II), and they weren't about to give it up so easily.

Women were also making gains in governmental positions, too. In the 1950s, General Eisenhower promised to "utilize the contributions of outstanding women to the greatest extent possible" were he elected president—and when he was elected to the highest office in the land, he fulfilled that promise. Among the women who were in his cabinet were Oveta Culp Hobby, secretary of health, education, and welfare; Bertha S. Adkins, undersecretary of health, education, and welfare; Clare Boothe Luce, U.S. ambassador to Italy; and Katherine Howard, deputy civil defense administrator.[11]

Despite their gains, however, women in the 1950s weren't climbing the corporate ladder like they would in the 1980s and beyond. They were still subject to a wage disparity that was both obvious and arbitrarily enforced—it would take until 1963 for the Equal Pay Act to be passed for it to come to an end, at least in theory—and society wasn't exactly encouraging women to pursue careers as doctors, lawyers, or engineers, let alone executive positions at Fortune 500 companies—and if you were a woman who wasn't white, your chances of upward economic mobility were all but nonexistent at this time, barring a miraculous financial windfall in the form of a dead relative or a lottery prize.

Often women—especially in small towns—were taught to keep their ambitions low and get a "little" job as a teacher or a secretary, with the proviso that work would stop altogether once she found a man to marry, who

President Dwight D. Eisenhower—seen here with his wife, Mamie, and actresses Irene Dunne and Rosalind Russell—made history when he appointed several women to his cabinet at a time when television shows depicted women as "happy homemakers."

would then support her and her resultant children. How romantic! How aspirational!

Sadly, too, not much has changed for women in the twenty-first century. Despite progressive strides, we are still light-years away from financial equity, let alone equality. Despite the Equal Pay Act, women still earn far less than men. In 2020, women earned only 83 percent of what their male counterparts earned. That pay disparity only increased depending on the woman's race: whereas white women earned about 79 cents for every dollar that white men earned, Black women earned only 64 cents for every dollar that white men earned and Latina women earned only 57 cents for every dollar that white men earned.[12]

But, also as can be expected, women who found themselves in a precarious financial position in the 1950s found themselves subject to the whims and mercies of a man who might prove to be tyrannical and oppressive in nature—if they were lucky. And if they weren't lucky, they might get a man who was physically and emotionally violent, with lethal results.

In the 1950s, there were no hashtags on Twitter to amplify the voices of women who were speaking about their experiences of domestic violence. There was no Time's Up, there was no #MeToo, and there was no collective groupthink to offer women advice, support, and resources to get them out of their precarious positions. Instead, in the 1950s, domestic violence was viewed as a "family" issue; law enforcement refused to get involved, and it wasn't even considered a crime.

It took until 1994—the same year that Nirvana released *Unplugged in New York*, that *Friends* debuted on television, and that the World Wide Web was invented—for the Violence against Women Act (VAWA) to be passed, thus making domestic violence a national crime. Prior to that, it was left up to the states . . . and to say that more than a few states left much to be desired as far as their laws were concerned would be the height of understatement. To put it in the context of this book: *The Golden Girls* was on the air at a time when domestic violence *still was not considered a crime* in some states.

What's more, in what only can be described as "blaming the victim" even by old-time standards, a study cited by *Time* in the 1960s claimed that women who were "bold" were, by default, "frigid," and all the man of the house needed to do to set things right in the household was to get a little alcohol in him.

"'The periods of violent behavior by the husband,' the doctors observed,[13] 'served to release him momentarily from his anxiety about his ineffectiveness as a man, while giving his wife apparent masochistic gratification and helping probably to deal with the guilt arising from the intense hostility expressed in her controlling, castrating behavior,'" reported the article, apparently not quite understanding that BDSM without consent is abuse, not kink, despite their fancy medical degrees.

This same study revealed that men who beat their wives were "in reality 'shy, sexually ineffectual mother's boys.'" But somehow, it was the "bold" women who dared to be treated with a modicum of respect—and not the flaccid wimps who still hadn't cut the proverbial apron strings and needed to beat up on women to feel better about themselves—who were the problem.

Safe to say, then, that things were more than a little bit of a mess in the 1950s—at least as far as women were concerned.

As the 1960s—and the social and societal upheavals that came with it—wore on, depictions of women on television began to change, as well. In the early 1960s, the same tired tropes of women were trotted out time and again—women who were married were preternaturally young, beautiful, and desirable, while women who remained single were depicted as ugly, angry spinsters who were undesirable by society—but by the middle of the decade, the first signs of feminism began to creep into popular television shows.

In 1961, Mary Tyler Moore's character Laura Petrie began questioning the roles of women in the home—and in the workplace—on *The Dick Van Dyke Show*. While Van Dyke's character of Rob Petrie—a comedy writer—was certainly genial enough, it wasn't enough to keep Laura satisfied with tottering around the house, catering to her family's every need. That same year, a newly divorced Lucille Ball debuted *The Lucy Show*, featuring a character that had no intention of following her husband—or any man, really—into show business or anywhere else. Then, in 1964, Elizabeth Montgomery portrayed a beautiful witch named Samantha on a show called *Bewitched*. During its eight-season run, it was clear that Samantha was the more powerful of the couple. Marrying a mere mortal man (portrayed by Dick York, then later Dick Sargent) and agreeing to become a housewife was met with strong disapproval from her witchy family (especially her mother Endora, played with acerbic aplomb by Agnes Moorehead). And finally, in 1966, Marlo Thomas's character Ann Marie was *That Girl* as she moved from the tiny hamlet of Brewster, New York, to the "big city" of Manhattan to make it big as an actress, taking odd jobs and getting into various hijinks along the way. Thomas's character was one of the first female characters to ever live on her own, without her parents or a domestic partner—a sign of things to come, when single women living on their own would become the norm and not the outlier—though she did have a boyfriend, Donald (played by Ted Bessell), a journalist who would eventually become her fiancé.

By 1970, a television show about a single, career-driven woman who lived alone and on her own terms hit the airwaves. Mary Tyler Moore's character Mary Richards was a television producer singularly focused on her career and bucking societal demands of settling down and having a family.[14]

Throughout the series (which, of course, gave a platform to future *Golden Girl* Betty White as Sue Ann Nivens), Mary dates several men but ultimately remains a single, unmarried woman throughout the series, which made her an anomaly for the time. Unlike Thomas's Ann Marie, whose "happily ever after" involved "settling down" and getting engaged, Mary's "happily ever after" involved climbing the corporate ladder and getting a nicer apartment, without a thought of getting married and having children.

Throughout the decades, women made advances on television—whether as mothers or women on their own—while *grandmothers* still were stuck in dismissive and reductive stereotypes. As a society, we were still decades away from seeing the likes of the brutal Lady Olenna Tyrell in *Game of Thrones* and the snippy Dowager Countess of Grantham in *Downton Abbey*

Marlo Thomas played Ann Marie in *That Girl*, and her depiction of a career-minded woman living on her own in "the big city" was considered groundbreaking for its time.

(arguably the British analogue of Sophia Petrillo, though she clearly came decades after the spicy Sicilian laid the groundwork). There was no vivacious Grandma Ruby on *Black-ish*, and the narcissistic Lucille Bluth—she with the persistent plastic surgery and hard liquor forever in a nearby flask—of

Arrested Development wouldn't even be a twinkle in a television censor's eye. A grandmother who *didn't* give a shit about her grandchildren? Perish the thought!

Rather, at this point in history, grandmas were little more than Irene Ryan's Granny Moses on *The Beverly Hillbillies*, a "frau in a frou," with her hair perpetually in a bun and hands perpetually baking an apple pie or two.

If the stereotypical maternal television character of the 1950s was a tabula rasa outside of the confines of her family, the grandmaternal character was even more so. She'd outlived her usefulness to society, after all, and she should be grateful that she'd had some sort of duty to do with her grandchildren . . . even if all she had to do was bake the kids apple pies while making her in-laws miserable in the process.

But that wasn't *The Golden Girls*.

That would never be *The Golden Girls*.

The grandmas of the *Girls* would fly in the face of conventional wisdom, whether we were ready for them or not (and, as it turned out, we were more than ready—we just didn't realize it until the show hit our airwaves).

And though they couldn't have been any more different, the *Girls* forever changed the way we, as a society, would view older women.

BACK IN ST. OLAF

The Folksy Wisdom of Rose Nylund

The first Girl we're going to look at—in honor of Betty White, whose death still seems all too recent in the twenty-first-century psyche—is Rose Nylund, the perpetually sunny and perpetually dim farm girl from St. Olaf.

Ultimately, she proved to be a lot more than that. More than just preternaturally sunny and stupid, Rose proved to be witty, acerbic when she needed to be, and knowledgeable about the things she *did* know about. She was sexually vibrant, a good friend to her housemates, and kind to children and animals (unless, of course, the children stole her teddy bear).

Throughout *The Golden Girls*'s history, Rose Nylund's backstory changed. In the beginning, fans knew that she was raised on a farm by the Lindstroms in a loving, happy family, filled with animals and children and lots of love (though, apparently, short on intellectual brains).

It wasn't until the show's sixth season—and, specifically, the show's second episode of the sixth season, titled "Once in St. Olaf"—that it was revealed that Rose was an adopted child. Though she allegedly always knew that she was adopted—and accepted the Lindstroms as her "real" Mom and Dad—her birth parents were a monk who took a vow of silence (named Brother Martin, played by Don Ameche on the show) and a young teenage farmhand named Ingrid Kerklavoner (whom we never see on the small screen).

Ingrid died in childbirth, and Rose was immediately placed for adoption. According to Brother Martin, he didn't know of Rose's existence until she had been adopted. Regardless, Rose languished in an orphanage for eight years until Gunter and Alma Lindstrom adopted her.

Betty White as Rose Nylund, the perpetually sunny—and perpetually stupid—Rose Nylund from St. Olaf, Minnesota.

A fun bit of trivia: in the season 4, episode 17 episode called "You Gotta Have Hope," Rose refers to her parents as "Gunter and Alma Nylund." However, as has been previously established, "Nylund" is her married name. It's not clear why the producers chose to leave this error in the show—but then again, the show is riddled with continuity errors, and no one enjoyed it any less.

By all accounts, Rose had a very happy childhood growing up in the town of St. Olaf, Minnesota.[1] But there's some disparity about her educational background: in the season 4, episode 8 show called "Yes, We Have No Havanas," it was revealed that Rose never graduated high school thanks to a particularly debilitating case of mononucleosis. But in the season 3, episode 5 show called "Nothing to Fear but Fear Itself," Rose revealed that she was her high school's valedictorian, graduating fourth out of a class of nineteen, and got the honor because "she drew the longest straw."

Regardless of her educational background—or lack thereof—there is one constant throughout Rose's life: her husband, Charlie Nylund. They originally met when they were children—Charlie sold Rose an insurance policy for her little red wagon—but Rose wasn't allowed to date until she was a senior in high school (though she went through "fifty-six boyfriends" before she finally got to him). Fifty-six boyfriends notwithstanding, they married, had five children, and remained loyal to one another until Charlie died.

There's also some disparity on the show regarding when Charlie died and how long Rose had been a widow. The 1985 pilot episode revealed that Charlie had been dead for fifteen years (meaning that he died in 1970). But in season 1, episode 22, "Job Hunting," Rose revealed that she'd been a homemaker when Charlie died in 1980 (a decade later than she'd previously stated). Regardless of this continuity goof, however, the point is that Rose and Charlie were the loves of one another's lives, and Rose didn't remarry after Charlie died. This is one of the many parallels that White shared with one of her most famous characters: after the death of her third husband, Allen Ludden, in 1981, White never remarried. She also referred to Ludden as "the love of her life."

But Rose didn't stay in mourning forever: although Rose had a series of boyfriends throughout the series, she eventually committed herself to one Miles Webber, a mild-mannered mustachioed professor with a particular love for poetry (especially that of Robert Frost), played with perfect aplomb by Harold Gould. He began dating Rose in season 5, episode 6 ("Dancing in the Dark").

But even that got put to the test when it was revealed that "Miles Webber" was his pseudonym. His real name was Nicholas Carbone, and he was an accountant for the mafia. Miles/Nicholas testified against his former employer—named "The Cheeseman," whom Rose inadvertently began dating in season 6, episode 21 ("Witness"), after Nicholas/Miles reentered the Witness Protection Program upon discovering that the Cheeseman was still alive and not unceremoniously gunned down as a news report had suggested—and they gave him a whole new identity as an Amish man.

Though Rose and Miles remain together for the remainder of *The Golden Girls*, their relationship ends during *The Golden Palace* spin-off. In season 1, episode 13, titled "Rose and Fern," Rose—who by now is running a hotel with Blanche and Sophia—and Miles are talking about getting back together, but Blanche tells Rose to date other people. Ultimately, Miles reveals that he's in love with another woman named Fern—and Rose not only ends up planning her wedding but attending the celebration so she can get on with her life.

If that seems like an "unhappily ever after" for one of the world's most beloved television characters, it may be a small comfort that there are some fans of *The Golden Girls* who don't acknowledge *The Golden Palace* as "canon"—that is, part of the official story—because it deviates so much from the original premise of *The Golden Girls*. These fans also do not hesitate to take to Reddit to voice their (very loud) displeasure about the spin-off.

———oɐɐo———

As a proud "St. Olafian," Rose is an amalgam of both small-town American values and Norwegian American traditions. Family and friends take center stage, and seemingly silly and topical traditions are honored. From abstaining from sex until the drought in St. Olaf is over (season 6, episode 10: "Girls Just Wanna Have Fun . . . before They Die"), to herring circuses (season 1, episode 25: "The Way We Met"), Rose honored what seemed to be the strangest—yet most earnest—traditions of her hometown. It gave her a sense of community and familiarity that was sorely missing from her life when Charlie died—and a connection to her hometown that the other Girls didn't have.

This led many to believe that she was an idiot.

But she was the furthest thing from it.

———oɐɐo———

There's a difference between naive and stupid—the former indicates an unawareness about the world, which is to be expected when one grows up in a town of fewer than five hundred people, whereas the latter indicates not knowing anything at all.

Although Rose wasn't as urbane as the Brooklyn-born Dorothy, as voracious in the bedroom as the man-eating Blanche, or even as Yoda-like in her wisdom as the snappy Sophia, she certainly knew a lot about the few things she did know. She knew how to plumb a toilet herself (season 1, episode 19, "Second Motherhood"—even though she didn't really know how to do plumbing until she turned eighteen, or so she claimed), just as an example. Like many "farm girls," she knew a lot about how to tend a garden, manage the house, and cook (except for the time she made "chipped beef" for the Girls—season 2, episode 17, "Bedtime Story"—which was sorely lacking in seasoning until Sophia stuffed it in her purse and topped it with some salt and pepper).

Rose Nylund wasn't one of the world's great thinkers, but she knew what she knew quite well—and that puts her ahead of the game in many ways.

Many die-hard fans on Reddit boards suggest that the Rose in seasons 6 and 7 was much more of a farcical character than the previous seasons—a failing that they credit to the transfer of writing from creator Susan Harris to future *Desperate Housewives* creator Marc Cherry. The consensus among

Redditors is that Cherry wrote the Girls in a more mean-spirited way, moving away from character-driven story lines and focusing instead on punchlines and one-liners. Many fans on the popular social site have commented that although Rose was never the sharpest knife in the drawer, she became almost "too stupid to live" under Cherry's tenure.

But there's also a modern phenomenon called "Flanderization"—named after Ned Flanders, Homer Simpson's next-door neighbor and archnemesis on *The Simpsons*—in which a minor characteristic of a character becomes a larger, more exaggerated characteristic as time goes on. In Ned's case, it was his devotion to evangelical Christianity; in Rose's, it was her "farm-girl naivete."

It stands to reason that Rose underwent a bit of "Flanderization" toward the end of *The Golden Girls'* run, and she was far from the first—or the last—character to get such a treatment on television.

But whether the character was indeed "Flanderized," Rose always retains her "heart and soul," for lack of a better word, and that's thanks to the comedic abilities of Betty White.

The character of Rose had many of the same characteristics that White had: she loved animals (every animal found a home with Rose, even though the Girls couldn't keep a pet themselves), she had a zest for life, and she was even harsh when she needed to be (such as in season 3, episode 1, titled "Old Friends," wherein she loses her beloved teddy bear, Fernando, after it was mistakenly given away in a charity haul and an enterprising young Girl Scout–like character, played by Jenny Lewis, holds Fernando hostage until Rose snatches him back, remarking, "sometimes, life just isn't fair kiddo").

But Rose also had many more characteristics that were nothing like White. Rose's naivete was a direct contrast to White's razor-sharp "old Hollywood" grit; she was, after all, a godmother of the television genre and knew her way around "the business" perhaps better than any of the other Girls did.

It's true, too, that White had a generally positive, happy disposition—much like Rose did. It's also true that this quality didn't sit well with some of her costars from time to time: although White generally got along well with Rue McClanahan and Estelle Getty, she had a notoriously thorny relationship with Arthur, who once allegedly called her a "fucking cunt" in frustration.

This story was recounted by Joel Thurm, the casting director for *The Golden Girls*, who also claimed that McClanahan also described White as a cunt, that White made fun of Getty as she began forgetting her lines—a symptom of the Lewy body dementia that would eventually claim her life—and that no one on *The Golden Girls* set liked White at all. It's worth noting that although White herself admitted that her relationship with Arthur was tense at best, she had a famously warm relationship with McClanahan—and Thurm is the only person to make these outrageous claims, which were made long after all the actresses were dead and couldn't respond to him.[2]

Dubious stories from casting directors aside, White was no Pollyanna—she certainly knew how to deliver a zinger with the best of them—and neither was Rose Nylund.

Despite Rose's "folksy wisdom"—plucked from a small town named after a Norwegian king later canonized a saint and unceremoniously dropped in the middle of Miami after her husband died—she was a lot smarter than she let on . . . an idiot savant, if you will.

Writing for *The Atlantic*,[3] Megan Garber points out that White continuously played her characters—both Sue Ann and Rose, in this case—with a dichotomy that many of her contemporaries failed to do. Aware, perhaps, of her role in society as a woman of a certain age who was coming of age at a certain time, White wasn't afraid to subvert traditional wisdom about women.

"White gave Rose some of the key elements of Sue Ann's public persona: Rose is optimistic and accommodating and always ready to flash that frank, blank grin," she wrote. "But, buoyed by the show's sharp writing, she is also much more than she seems. Rose is dim right up until she's brilliant (remember when she replumbed a bathroom, all on her own?). She is obliging until she's competitive. She's kind, unless you cross her."

In other words, Rose—like the actress who portrayed her—was far from a one-dimensional woman. It's easy to reduce people—especially women, especially at that time, and especially older women—to one defining characteristic. It's easy to view them through only one lens—a lens that often makes them identifiable to us as a society. In other words, it's *comfortable* for Americans to reduce sexagenarians to grandmotherly roles. Whether that lens is one in which a woman is merely viewed as a wife, a mother, a grandmother, or a spinster, it's one that's reductionist and—quite frankly—lazy.

Because women, in general, are complex creatures—and women were, and are, fully developed human beings when we finally encounter them.

White's Rose Nylund helped us see that even the "naive" ones have more than a little bit of wisdom to impart to us.

ROSE NYLUND:
THE TOP TEN BEST EPISODES

She was the sunny eternal optimist. She was the well-meaning but naive fool. And she had a wisdom that belied her surface-level stupidity.

Rose Nylund was a Golden Girl like no other.

So inextricable was Betty White from her signature character that the two became intertwined—you couldn't think of one without thinking of the other—and in her subsequent roles, until the day White died, we all—fans and colleagues alike—looked for elements of Rose in every character.

Somehow, too, we always found her.

Whether she was being naive or competitive—whether she was sharing her folksy St. Olafian wisdom or simply being a good friend—Rose Nylund was, in a word, funny. But in 180 episodes, there were some in which she was funnier than others. Indeed, then, these are the top ten episodes featuring Rose Nylund and the comedic genius of Betty White.

10. Henny Penny—Straight, No Chaser
Season 6, Episode 26

The Golden Girls did best when it was at its peak of camp and absurdity. Few episodes hit the peak of camp quite like season 6, episode 26, titled "Henny Penny—Straight, No Chaser."

As many may—or may not—be aware, the "Henny Penny"[4] fairytale is better known in the United States as "Chicken Little." And, of course, the Chicken Little fairy tale is a Brothers Grimm version of a folk tale with ancient—and unclear—roots, but it's meant to make light of people who engage in mass hysteria and paranoia (which means if the lesson applies today, it's a happy coincidence—mostly so the lawsuits don't start flying).

In a nutshell, "Chicken Little" is about a sweet-natured, albeit naive, chicken who believes the sky is falling after he's bonked on the head by an acorn. Throughout the course of the story, he meets other characters along the way, including Goosey Loosey and Turkey Lurkey. Depending on the version of the story being told, the friends either meet an unfortunate end as Foxy Loxy's main course for dinner, or they escape the evil fox's clutches and tell the king about the unfortunate situation with the sky.

In the hands of *The Golden Girls* writers, the Chicken Little fairy tale is retold by the Girls after the children who were cast in the play all come down with measles.

As hard as it is to believe, a measles outbreak wasn't an unusual occurrence around this time. In 1978, the Centers for Disease Control and Prevention (CDC) had a goal to eradicate measles by 1982. Unfortunately, it didn't reach its goal due to widespread vaccine misinformation. In 1989—two years before this episode aired—a horrific measles outbreak prompted the CDC to recommend a secondary measles, mumps, and rubella vaccine for school-age children. It took until 2000 for the disease to be declared eradicated by the CDC, but because of vaccine misinformation—further spread by the Internet and social media—the disease is making a comeback. In 2019, New York—and other states—tightened their vaccine exemption rules so that residents were required to get the measles vaccine regardless of their religious beliefs. Though this has done wonders for containing the disease, there is some concern that continued antivaccine propaganda will cause another outbreak, resulting in the World Health Organization rescinding the United States' measles eradication status.[5]

Regardless of the parlous state of medical affairs, Rose assumes the role of Henny Penny, Blanche takes the role of Goosey Loosey (who, in true Blanche fashion, is *the* most popular goose on the farm—prompting Sophia to quip, "and the eighth graders are seeing a play today about how to be that popular . . . safely"), and Dorothy plays the role of the lonely, dateless Turkey Lurkey, who always seems to have her beak in a book without a date to be found.

Sophia, for her part, dons thigh-high black boots and a tiny Peter Pan–style dress to play the role of the narrator of the story.

It's pure camp, it's pure absurdity, and it's purely perfect.

While Blanche and Dorothy certainly do a fine job in their respective roles, it's Rose who steals the show in a role that's unquestionably made just for her—a well-meaning but clearly not very bright chicken who thinks the sky is falling. And who knew that Betty White could sing? Whoever didn't know certainly found out after this episode.

But the best part of all is that White really seems to be enjoying herself as she sings along with the songs. "A piece of blue sky, just fell on my head / The wherefore and why, is best left unsaid," is nothing short of a classic line.

"Henny Penny—Straight, No Chaser" doesn't have an important moral message, it's not a commentary on the situation in Reagan's America, and it's not an exegesis on growing old as a woman in Miami—it's just plain campy fun, and it's certainly one of the best Rose Nylund episodes of *The Golden Girls*.

9. "High Anxiety"

Season 4, Episode 20

Though fans of the show could count on *The Golden Girls* to be campy when it wanted to be, the show was equally adept at dealing with serious social issues. One of the issues that the Girls tackled, and quite adeptly, was the issue of drug addiction—and much like in "72 Hours," Rose was the perfect character to have the affliction in the season 4, episode 20 show called "High Anxiety."

When it comes to addiction, far too many people—even in the twenty-first century—have the wrong idea about what an addict looks like. And in the 1980s, fewer folks understood the true nature of addiction—that is, that it is a disease—than they do today. The 1980s, too, had the added layer of Reagan's failed War on Drugs to battle, with the administration treating drug use and abuse as both a criminal offense and a moral failing instead of the disease that it is, and it goes without saying that the "war" targeted mostly poor—and Black—communities.[6] So if you were to ask the average person from the 1980s what a "typical" drug addict[7] looked like, it's all but guaranteed that the description didn't look a thing like Rose Nylund.

To White's interminable credit, she pulled off the nuances of addiction—in this case, to painkillers—with great aplomb. From the minute Sophia accidentally knocks the pills down the kitchen sink drain—thus sending Rose into her first tailspin—to the minute she comes home from rehab and makes it clear that she'll "never be cured,"[8] White's approach to the complexities of addiction goes above and beyond her comedic call. And the fact that we, the viewing audience, must accept Rose Nylund as an addict, yet love her anyway, is a testament to the power of television as a medium to change the narrative for the better, when it wants to.

Addicts—like everyone else—deserve love, too, even when it's far too easy to toss them aside. By putting a human face to addiction—and by further putting addiction on a face that looks like a beloved grandmother—"High Anxiety" became one of the best Rose Nylund episodes of *The Golden Girls*.

8. "A Piece of Cake"

Season 2, Episode 25

As the Girls gather in the kitchen to watch Sophia bake a birthday cake for her friend, Roberta, they reminisce about the various birthday cakes they'd had throughout their lives, making this a so-called flashback episode of the show. (Later, it's revealed that the cake was really for Blanche, for whom the Girls threw a surprise birthday party.)

While each of the Girls has her own story to tell about a birthday cake that was particularly special, the story that hits particularly close to the heart is the story that Rose tells about her last piece of cake in St. Olaf. As it turns out, it was for her last birthday in St. Olaf—which also happened to be her first birthday after the death of her husband, Charlie.

Rose's grief is still palpable as she sits alone, in an empty kitchen, talking to a chair where, presumably, Charlie once sat. When she blows out the candles, it's implied that she wishes for her husband to come back based on what she says afterward: "I know that's a silly wish," she said. "I know you really can't be here with me, Charlie."

One must wonder how much White drew from her own life—and her lifelong grief after the death of her beloved husband, Allen Ludden—to deliver this moving monologue.

Ultimately, Rose explains to Charlie's spirit that she can't stay in their home in St. Olaf anymore because it carries too many memories.

"I've decided to sell the house and leave St. Olaf, Charlie," she said to the empty chair. "The winters are rough here in Minnesota, and this place is too filled with memories to let me get on with my life. I need to start over without you, Charlie, and I think this is the best way."

Although there are certainly some funny quips throughout White's monologue, it's impossible not to tear up when she says, "I love you, Charlie—and I miss you," with obvious sadness in her voice.

There's also an argument to be made that Rose's personality shifted in Miami, helping her to move on from Charlie more easily. Logistically, there was no way that someone as naive as Rose could have survived life alone on a farm, which requires hard work, dedication, and well-rounded worldly wisdom. To get away from St. Olaf and leave all her memories behind, including the painful memories of losing Charlie, Rose adopted naivete as part of her personality.

This is an argument that Jim Colucci, author of *Golden Girls Forever: An Unauthorized Look behind the Lanai*, makes when discussing White's character. "Rose had to be the character who didn't know she was being funny," Colucci said to the *Today* show.[9] "The joke was kind of on her. She was just being naive. And if she did say something cutting, she didn't realize she was doing it. . . . And Betty did it with such aplomb. It was incredible. I just love to see different ways that she could be funny."

If this argument does, indeed, have some validity, it adds yet another layer of nuance to Rose as a character and is a further testament to the depth of White's acting ability. And though her segment on "A Piece of Cake" is brief, it's the one that packs the most emotional punch and makes it one of the best episodes of *The Golden Girls* to feature Rose Nylund.

7. "Mother's Day"
Season 3, Episode 25

Like "A Piece of Cake," "Mother's Day" is yet another flashback episode of *The Golden Girls*. It is, as its name implies, meant to celebrate Mother's Day—and the Girls are reminiscing about their most memorable days. Some of their memories involve other people's mothers (such as Dorothy's Mother's Day memories, which involve Stan's mother loaning them money to get through some tough times), whereas others involve their own mothers (such as Blanche's Mother's Day memories, when she recounts the last holiday she spent with her beloved mother in a nursing home).

But it's Rose's story about a very special Mother's Day in St. Olaf that steals the show.

While at the bus station, Rose befriends a lovely woman by the name of Anna, who is taking a bus to visit her daughter. Geraldine Fitzgerald—a veteran actress of both the big screen and the small screen, who starred opposite Bette Davis in *Dark Victory* and Rodney Dangerfield in *Easy Money*—played Anna in this episode. She would also later play Martha in season 5, episode 7, "Not Another Monday."

Because of inclement weather, the buses are taking longer than expected. Keeping her new friend company, Rose regales her with her typical "back in St. Olaf" stories. They're long and exhausting—because some things never change—but Anna is grateful for the company.

After Rose finishes telling her stories, Anna reveals that the daughter she's going to visit is dead—her Mother's Day involves spending time at her gravesite. Unfortunately, Anna fears that this will be the last Mother's Day that she'll be able to visit her daughter, as she'd escaped from her nursing home without permission.

Just then, a police officer pulls up to take Anna back to the home. Rose, in turn, stands up for Anna and informs the sheriff that there must be "some kind of mistake," because Anna is really *her* mother. The cop stands in the bus station bewildered, while Rose and Anna make their way to the buses, which just so happen to arrive at that very moment (though in actuality, it was an enterprising bus announcer named Jacob who recognized that the situation was escalating and quickly diffused it).

As an actress, White always aptly handled nuance with grace and humor—and it's evident in this episode of *The Golden Girls*. It's a brief segment, but like the segment in "A Piece of Cake," it's one that packs a powerful punch.

6. "The Heart Attack"
Season 1, Episode 10

During the first season of *The Golden Girls*, the episodes almost exclusively addressed issues of their own mortality—perhaps more than any other topic. And this, too, seemed to be the natural course of things. After all, the show was about women who were well into their sixties (and eighties) . . . even if Blanche fibbed about how old she really was on more than a few occasions. (But, after all, tall tales *are* part of the Southern tradition.)

Such was the case with the season 1, episode 10 show titled "The Heart Attack," in which Sophia thinks she's suffering a major coronary episode. (Fortunately, it turns out just to be a case of extreme upset stomach after she ate an almost Herculean meal.)

Although each of the Girls comforts their mother-like figure in her time of need, it's Rose's account of dressing Charlie in his final moments that really steals the show.

She tells Dorothy that she dressed him right before the paramedics arrived. As had been previously stated, Charlie died of a heart attack, which he suffered while making love with Rose. Naturally, he wasn't dressed and Rose managed to preserve his dignity by dressing him before the paramedics arrived.

Charlie told Rose that he loved her—"and then it was all over." Her voice catches a little when she says, with pride, that Charlie "was all dressed when the paramedics came."

Though she manages to inflect a little bit of humor in her delivery—such as when she explained that Charlie fought with her because she attempted to put a pair of white pants on him, and he didn't want to wear white after Labor Day—it's still a moving performance, one that again recalls White's devotion to her beloved Allen Ludden and how soon she'd begun working on *The Golden Girls* after he'd died.

In "The Heart Attack," Rose Nylund wasn't just a distant character—or a caricature—but someone very real to all of us. By making her into a real person—someone we can all relate to—White made "The Heart Attack" one of the best episodes of *The Golden Girls* that featured Rose Nylund.

5. "In a Bed of Rose's"

Season 1, Episode 15

Inasmuch as White could become emotional in scenes about death, she also could play to the gallows humor of it all. She did just that in season 1, episode 15 of *The Golden Girls* titled "In a Bed of Rose's."

As mentioned, Rose's beloved Charlie died of a heart attack while sharing their marital bed—one of the only parts of Rose's backstory about which the writers are consistent. As such, Rose is traumatized about ever sharing a bed with a man again, until she meets Al.

In this episode, Al and Rose are in the throes of passion when he, too, suffers a heart attack and dies. In addition to dealing with the reopened wound of losing yet another partner to yet another post-coital heart attack, Rose must deal with the one-two punch that no woman ever wants to experience when she calls the woman that Al claims is his sister only to discover that she was his wife.

Al's wife, Lucille, was played by Priscilla Morrill, best known for her role on *The Mary Tyler Moore Show* as Edie, Lou's ex-wife. Fans of the show were absolutely delighted to watch White and Morrill interact with each other on *The Golden Girls* given their history.

Later in the episode, Rose muses that she's now afraid to go away on vacation with another partner, Arnie, because she's worried that her time with him also will end with his heart giving out in the throes of passion.

Incidentally, *Golden Girls* fans first meet Arnie in the season 1, episode 3 show called "Rose the Prude." Arnie, who never appears on camera again (he doesn't appear on camera in "In a Bed of Rose's," either), is played by Harold Gould. But even though Arnie is never to be seen again, fans do see Gould again in the season 5, episode 6 show called "Dancing in the Dark," when he begins portraying Rose's new long-term boyfriend, Miles Webber.

But it's White's scenes with her former *Mary Tyler Moore* costar that steal the show. Their banter as "the wife" and "the other woman" are immediately reminiscent of the Sue Ann and Edie days, and it's clear in this episode that both White and Morrill are masters of the comedy craft.

At the time of "In a Bed of Rose's" first airing, it was easy to forget that White was such a master of comedy (remember, there was no Netflix or Hulu to watch classic episodes)—and wasn't afraid to get as bawdy as "the boys" did in the same arena—because she immersed herself so deeply in the character of Rose. But when paired with Morrill, White reminded everybody who they were really dealing with. It's no wonder, too, that this episode was the one that garnered White her sole Emmy win for *The Golden Girls*.

4. "A Visit from Little Sven"

Season 3, Episode 9

Speaking of "Bawdy Betty," fans who thought that Rose Nylund was little more than White's analogue were quickly disabused of the notion with the season 3, episode 9 show called "A Visit from Little Sven."

Rose's young cousin, Sven, comes to Miami to meet the woman to whom he's betrothed in marriage—a woman that he's never met, as it's an arranged marriage (which is, it's explained, a St. Olaf tradition[10]). But there's a monkey wrench thrown in the plan when Sven falls head over heels in love with Blanche.

So in love with Blanche is poor young Sven, in fact, that he's willing to call off his wedding to his betrothed just to be with her!

As can be expected, hilarity ensues. McClanahan takes center stage, alternating between playing the coquette and the vamp, joking throughout. She insists she doesn't want to break up with "Swen" (as she calls him), even though she began flirting with him only to make her inattentive boyfriend jealous. She feigns devastation when Sven ultimately leaves her for his bride-to-be, who turns out to be a thin, beautiful blonde that Sophia calls "the lean mean Swedish machine."

But this episode is one of Rose's best because of her shameless, brutal, and hilarious roasts of Blanche—all describing her sexual prowess in the bedroom and insulting her for daring to spirit Rose's baby cousin away from his one and only betrothed. Rose's roast of Blanche is just the first of many hurled at her roommate, all of which conclude with some form of the insult "slut," which makes it even more hilarious.

It's one of the first times that we see this side of Rose—but certainly not the last—and one that fans want to see more and more of as the series goes on. Although not often cited as a fan favorite show, "A Visit from Little Sven" is one of the best Rose Nylund episodes of *The Golden Girls*.

3. "Miles to Go"

Season 6, Episode 15

This episode, on the surface, initially seemed to spell the end of Rose's relationship with Miles, but it actually gave it an even more absurd twist. Fans of *The Golden Girls* frequently take the last two seasons of the show to task for not being as funny as previous seasons—and, indeed, for being more mean-spirited—and this episode certainly veered into the absurd more than other episodes about Miles Webber.

As previously mentioned, the credit—or blame, depending on your point of view—for this goes to Marc Cherry, who came on as a writer during the last two seasons of the show. As fans of Cherry's subsequent shows like *Desperate Housewives* are aware, Cherry likes snappy, bitchy one-liners rather than more nuanced jokes that, perhaps, the Girls deserved.

Still, fans who can look past the absurdity can appreciate the story at the heart of this episode. As it turns out, mild-mannered Miles—the college professor who loves poetry and Rose in equal measure—is really Nicholas Carbone, an accountant for organized crime, whose "Miles Webber" persona was provided by the U.S. government when he entered the Witness Protection Program.

One of Miles/Nicholas's clients happens to be a ferocious gangster by the name of "The Cheeseman," who Rose inadvertently dates in the season 6, episode 25 show "Witness."

"The Cheeseman" was played by Barney Martin, who later became known to *Seinfeld* fans as Morty Seinfeld, the title character's father. Though his first-ever role in show business was as Jackie Gleason's stand-in on *The Honeymooners*, Martin was a police officer with the New York Police Department for twenty years who worked his way up to the rank of detective before retiring from the force to pursue a show business career.

Sadly, however, Martin died in 2005.

But in this episode, Rose brings the laughs as she tries to reconcile the man she thought she knew with the man he really is (and, as it turns out, both Miles *and* "Nick" like their whiskey neat).

This is one of White's best episodes for the laughs—she certainly plays up Rose's naivete so well—but it's the ending of the episode that's truly moving. When Miles must take on a whole new identity because the Cheeseman discovered his whereabouts, he needs to go into hiding. He's not sure when he'll ever see Rose again . . . or *if* he'll ever see Rose again. Heartbroken, Rose tells Miles that he forgot his book of Robert Frost's poetry, and he tells her to keep it, "and when you read page 73, think of me."

Rose then opens the book and reads the passage out loud. "And when to the heart of man, was it ever less than a treason, to bow and accept the end of a love or of a season?"[11] she reads, tearfully, as the episode draws to a close.

White perfectly captures the heartbreak of a woman losing her beloved longtime partner at a time when she thought she'd never find love again after the death of her husband. It's a scene that White clearly seems to be drawing from her own life to perform, and she pulls it off beautifully.

"Miles to Go" combines all the elements of a great episode of *The Golden Girls*—laughter, tears, and even a few serious moments—but it's Rose Nylund's show, and she steals it with gusto, as well she deserves.

2. "It's a Miserable Life"
Season 2, Episode 4

By the second season of *The Golden Girls*, Rose had developed a reputation for being the sunniest member of the quartet. Always able to find the bright side of things, Rose was unfailingly nice to the point of naivete.

So when Rose has the opportunity to show her "dark side," it made for some very entertaining moments, especially when the audience wasn't used to seeing it. Nowhere is this more obvious than in the season 2, episode 4 show titled "It's a Miserable Life."

A play on the classic film, *It's a Wonderful Life*, this episode focuses on the fate of Freida Claxton, whose home is the site of a landmark tree in Miami.

Veteran actress Nan Martin brought Freida Claxton to life. A working actress for nearly her entire life, Martin had roles on such shows as *NYPD Blue*, *Nip/Tuck*, and *The Drew Carey Show* (where she played Mrs. Louder), in addition to starring in films like *Cast Away*, *A Nightmare on Elm Street 3*, and *The Other Side of the Mountain*.

Nan Martin, sadly, died in 2010.

Since the historic tree was scheduled to be cut down, the Girls (devout environmentalists, all—remember, these are the same ladies who campaigned to save the wetlands *and* against tuna fishing because dolphins became trapped in fishermen's nets) leap into action to try to save it. Claxton, however, has no intention of saving it—as far as she's concerned, the city can start pouring cement posthaste. No matter how much kindness Rose shows her neighbor (going so far as to procure pastries for her in an attempt to "sweeten her up"), she's still miserable.

In a nutshell, Claxton hates everything and everyone—hence the episode's name, "It's a Miserable Life"—and she tells Rose, "I hate you too!"

It's that final proclamation of hatred that sparks Rose to go into full attack mode. She delivers a scathing diatribe against Claxton, which she concludes with, "and if you don't like it, you can *drop dead*!"

To this, Claxton grasps her chest and falls to the floor. Sophia looks over and remarks, "remember when you told her to drop dead? Well, she did!"

The rest of the episode involves Rose wallowing in guilt, thinking that she killed Claxton (her friends, of course, reassure her that she didn't—and in fairness, she didn't). To make her feel better, the Girls decide to host a funeral for their neighbor, since she died without any family or friends (which should have been the biggest red flag for Rose, but that's naivete for you). As it turned out, the only women who attended Claxton's funeral were the Girls themselves (even though Sophia spent the first part of the funeral listening to a baseball game). Fittingly, too, Claxton's ashes were scattered around the tree that the Girls ultimately saved—only for a neighborhood dog to lift his leg on the ashes in memory of the most miserable Miami resident in the world.

Being that this is an episode from one of the earlier seasons of the show, the jokes trend toward camp more than shade or reading.[12]

However, what makes this a Rose Nylund spotlight show is how *un*-Rose-like White acts. It's spicy, it's sassy, and it features Rose telling someone to drop dead—what more could a fan ask for?

Besides, the episode teaches us all a very important lesson: live your life in such a way that you're not like Freida Claxton—alone, bitter, and miserable, with no one to attend your funeral—when you die.

1. "Ladies of the Evening"
Season 2, Episode 2

The word "slut" gets bandied about on *The Golden Girls*, but in "Ladies of the Evening" (season 2, episode 2), the Girls are sluts for real . . . in a manner of speaking.

At the beginning of the episode, the house in Miami is getting fumigated for termites—a normal, everyday occurrence for homes in South Florida, as failure to do so can attract all sorts of bacteria-loving, humidity-thriving vermin—so the Girls must go to a hotel while the house airs out. At the same time, Blanche wins tickets to see Burt Reynolds at a film premiere he's hosting, but she wins only three tickets. Inevitably, Sophia can't go, which doesn't sit well with the ornery octogenarian.

But, frankly, the other three Girls don't care, "because we're going to see Burt Reynolds!"

At the hotel, Dorothy, Blanche, and Rose decide to dress up extra fancy and enjoy a drink before heading off to see their favorite heartthrob—with Sophia left behind to stew in her own (very bitter, because she didn't get to go) juices. While at the bar, they're approached by a man who insinuates that he is willing to pay for their time and can't understand why they reject him, when he is a paying customer just like everyone else.

It's Dorothy who first realizes that the man is implying that they're prostitutes—and that they're in a bar, and hotel, that caters specifically to that type of crowd. Naturally, the next thing everyone knows, the police show up to execute a raid, and *everyone*—Dorothy, Blanche, and Rose included—are caught in the sweep.

Incidentally, contrary to what is commonly seen on police procedurals and espionage films, detaining someone simply for being in a place where a raid is being conducted is a violation of one's Fourth Amendment rights and grounds for a lawsuit. Put simply, arresting Dorothy, Rose, and Blanche simply because they were unwittingly in a hotel bar of ill repute—and especially since it was evident that they weren't conducting any shady business— falls under "unreasonable search and seizure," according to the 1979 *Ybarra v. Illinois* ruling. In other words, if they'd ended up with a rap sheet, they had the right to sue the state—and they would have won.[13]

It's up to Sophia to bail them out—and she does indeed go to the jail to get the other Girls. But she won't bail them out for free—in exchange for their freedom, one of the Girls must give up her ticket to see Burt Reynolds. When they refuse to do so,[14] Sophia snatches the tickets away, leaving the Girls in jail and heading off to see Burt Reynolds.

At the end of the episode, Sophia—who had bailed the Girls out shortly before she left to see Burt Reynolds, though she still made off with the purloined tickets—regales her housemates with tales about the evening, when none other than "Mr. Burt Reynolds" shows up to take Sophia to lunch.

"These are the roommates you were telling me about?" he asks Sophia, pointing to the Girls.

"Yeah!" she replies enthusiastically.

"Which one's the slut?" he stage-whispers to Sophia.

All three Girls raise their hands and chant, "I am!"

From its razor-sharp writing to Dorothy's tough talk in the jail cell, from Blanche's indignation at being lumped in with the professional prostitutes to Sophia's cackling when she bests them all, this episode is a true winner. But it's Rose's "Butter Queen" tale that seals it all with a kiss and makes it the best Rose Nylund episode in *The Golden Girls* pantheon.

CHAPTER FOUR

GYPSIES, TRAMPS, AND SLUTS

Blanche Devereaux, the Sex-Positive Sex Symbol

Being "sex positive" is a recent societal development—a product of the third wave of feminism, a social media sentiment shared by the average Generation Z semiprofessional who has nothing but time and the world at her feet—and something that seems nebulous to describe. What *does* "sex positive" mean, anyway? Does it mean sleeping with multiple men with aplomb? Does it refer to someone who doesn't measure a woman's worth by the number of proverbial notches on her belt? Or does it mean some combination of both—a woman who doesn't "slut-shame"[1] another woman who chooses to express her sexuality in a way that subverts conventional wisdom?

The answer, of course, is the latter.

But before being sex positive was truly a thing, the ever-endearing, ever-enduring character of Blanche Devereaux provided the baby boomer generation with a template. Given that "boomers" were notoriously sex negative (for lack of a better word)—given that they were the first to call a woman a slut, a whore, a gypsy, a tramp, and a thief if she didn't follow the strict conservative Christian values of the day—Blanche's importance on the small screen cannot be overstated.

Three of the four Girls portrayed vampy characters in their oeuvre. Arthur played the vampy Vera Charles in *Mame*, and White the vampy Sue Ann Nivens in *The Mary Tyler Moore Show*. But McClanahan's Blanche Devereaux is perhaps the vampiest of them all—a character that has not only endeared herself to many, many generations of women (something neither Arthur's Vera Charles nor White's Sue Ann Nivens was able to accomplish) but endured the test of time.

Rue McClanahan—seen here with Dustin Hoffman in the play *Jimmy Shine*—played vampy characters throughout the course of her career, but it was the character of Blanche Devereaux that redefined sex positivity for a whole generation of fans.

Like Rose, Blanche Devereaux's backstory changed throughout the history of *The Golden Girls* (though nowhere near as much as Rose's—it seems the writers were okay with forgoing a consistent backstory in the name of the punchline or of conveying an important message, which was completely fine for both fans and critics alike). Blanche Elizabeth Marie Hollingsworth was born in Georgia and raised on a fictional plantation called Twin Oaks.

Though there didn't seem to be any malice on the writers' part for making Blanche a product of the plantation-era south, there isn't a writer alive in the twenty-first century who would make this a part of a backstory for a comedic character of *any* age or color. However, it would be interesting to see what someone like Jordan Peele would do with this type of a backstory in the context of a horror film.

Raised as a southern debutante by her father, Curtis (affectionately referred to as "Big Daddy" throughout the series—though Dorothy once implied that he was a member of the Ku Klux Klan when she referred to him as "Grand Dragon" in the season 6, episode 4 show called "Snap Out of It"), and her mother, Elizabeth-Ann Bennett (though in the season 6, episode 21 show titled "Witness," she called her mother "Samantha Roquet" when she was trying to join the Daughters of the Old South[2]), Blanche also had two sisters named Virginia and Charmaine (neither of whom she had a great relationship with) and two brothers named Tad and Clayton. Though we never see Tad on the show, Clayton becomes an important character in both season 4 and season 6, as we will see shortly.

Blanche, throughout her childhood, was strongly desired by most of the boys in her neighborhood, although it's not clear whether this is true or—as she once explained to Dorothy—a tall tale, as is "tradition" in the Old South. Speaking of the Old South, Blanche was the picture of the stereotypical southern belle: she was a Republican, she hung a Confederate flag in honor of her southern heritage,[3] and she had a difficult time accepting her brother Clayton's homosexuality (though whether that was solely a product of the times, or of her identity as a southern belle, or even a bit of both is up for debate).

Despite her jokes about being nothing like Blanche, because Blanche was a man-hungry belle from Atlanta—"and I'm not from Atlanta!"—McClanahan's real life was probably the most disparate from her "reel life" of all of *The Golden Girls* cast members. She was a lifelong Democrat, a lifelong vegetarian and animal rights activist, and a staunch supporter of LGBTQIA rights who also regularly volunteered her time and donated money to various gay rights causes.[4]

Regardless of the truth about her promiscuous past, the love of Blanche's life was her husband, George Devereaux. Though it's unclear how they met, what's clear is that every decision that Blanche made after his death—due to either a car crash or the subsequent coma resulting from the crash, depending on which episode you watch—was in response to the grief of his loss. It can even be argued that her promiscuity—implied or actual—was part of her quest to find the next love of her life . . . or, at the very least, to carnally comfort herself since George can no longer do so.

The question of Blanche's children with George, too, has a bit of a backstory that changes. In the season 3, episode 3 show called "Bringing up Baby," Blanche comments that she's had four children but "I've never owned a Mercedes." But in various episodes, Blanche mentions the names of five different children: Rebecca, Janet, Matthew (aka Skippy, who doesn't appear onscreen until *The Golden Palace*, where he was played by then-unknown comedian Bill Engvall, of the Redneck Comedy Tour fame), Doug, and Biff. Regardless of whether Blanche had four children or five, George also is revealed to have a son named David (played by future *Desperate Housewives* and *Mad Men* star Mark Moses in the season 5, episode 18 show called "An Illegitimate Concern"), resulting from an affair he had while away on a business trip.

Nevertheless, now a widow, Blanche dates—and it's implied, sleeps with—a wide assortment of men throughout the show's run.

But it's important to note that Blanche avoided married men at all costs. And although some "gentleman callers" were worthy of her affections, others were not.

In the "worthy" category was the hunky caterer Jake, whom fans first saw in the season 2, episode 22 show called "Diamond in the Rough." Jake, who caters an event for the Girls, takes Blanche out on several dates and immediately falls in love with her. Although he proves himself to be kindhearted (such as when he stops to help someone who was broken down on the side of the road, thus making himself late for his date with Blanche) and gentle, Blanche ultimately dismisses him as a serious prospect because he's too "blue collar" for her. This earns the ire of many of the Girls, especially Dorothy, which makes Blanche realize—too late—that she's made a terrible mistake.

Other men in the "worthy" category included Mel Bushman (played by Alan King), who proves to be her longest-lasting "friend with benefits," with whom she enjoys many a laugh and an orgasm, and Jerry (played by Ken Howard, who appeared in the season 7, episode 15 show called "The Commitments"), who wanted to take things slow with Blanche and treat her like a lady.

Unfortunately, there were some men in the not-so-worthy category, too. In the pilot episode of *The Golden Girls*, Blanche almost married a bigamist named Richard, but the police caught him right before they were set to walk down the aisle. Then there was Ted, whom Blanche originally encountered in the library, but who ultimately proved to be dishonest when it was revealed that he was cheating on his wife ("Stand by Your Man," season 6, episode 11). Perhaps the worst was Rex Huntington, a man who Blanche thought had a temper but who ultimately proved to be physically abusive ("The Bloom Is off the Rose," season 6, episode 13).

Incidentally, Refinery29[5] counted the number of relationships Blanche had throughout the show's run—everything from one-night stands to references made about offscreen fiancés and her husband—coming up with a grand total of 164 men throughout the seven seasons of the show. Sophia had the fewest number of men, with a "body count" of twenty-four, but given her age, that number is quite impressive.

Whether the "many, many men" of Blanche's boudoir were good, bad, or indifferent, McClanahan's Blanche was a "lovable slut"—a sexually active woman who was depicted as enjoying the act in its sum totality, but also as a woman who was loved and accepted rather than reviled and judged. Throughout various episodes of *The Golden Girls*, Blanche and the Girls stripped the power that the word "slut" had over them and in so doing became sexually empowered themselves. Rather than be depicted as creepy old grandmas or as frigid, shriveled-up women waiting to die, Blanche and the Girls proved that you're never too old to enjoy a good night out.

Worthy of note, too, is that throughout various episodes of *The Golden Girls*, Blanche is called a "slut" by her roommates on more than one occasion, with Sophia's "slut-puppy" insult being the most famous, and hilarious, of all. That said, there wasn't malicious intent behind the name-calling—it's much like a pack of girlfriends calling each other "girl" or "bitch" today as a reclamation of the word from their would-be oppressors (be it in the form of men who couldn't have them or women who wanted to be them).

Writing for *Jezebel*,[6] Tracie Egan Morrissey hails Blanche as a sex-positive sex symbol for the ages. "Perhaps it was that choice of self-acceptance and confidence that made her character so lovable," she wrote. "In the stiflingly conservative sexual and political climate of the late '80s—during which some felt that the AIDS epidemic was a punishment for sexual promiscuity—a 52-year-old woman saying that she related to a fictional character who shamelessly and genuinely enjoyed her active sex life and spoke frankly about condoms was progressive to say the least."

Morrissey concluded her piece with the perfect summary—and tribute—to both the character and the woman who brought her to life. "As someone who made no bones about enjoying her life as a gay-friendly, animal-loving, sex-positive, imperfect woman, we can only hope we grow up to be half the Jezebel that Rue McClanahan was," she wrote.

BLANCHE DEVEREAUX: THE TOP TEN BEST EPISODES

She was sassy, she was whip-smart, and she was sexy. But, most of all, Blanche Devereaux was funny.

More than just playing her character as a southern belle stereotype, McClanahan infused her most famous character with grace, strength, and dignity that withstood the test of time. And though Blanche is today hailed as a modern-day sex symbol—a sex-positive role model for the ages—and a woman far ahead of her time, it was her more vulnerable moments—when she was sad and yearned for her husband, when she was loving and nurtured her children, and when she was scared of the inevitability of growing older—that made her a remarkable, multifaceted human.

But there are ten episodes of *The Golden Girls* in which Blanche Devereaux steals the show.

10. "Adult Education"
Season 1, Episode 20

Blanche Devereaux may have been sexually promiscuous and free spirited, but even she had limits about whom she would—and wouldn't—sleep with. She wouldn't sleep with married men—and if she found out they were married after she'd slept with them, she'd immediately send them away—and she wouldn't sleep with someone for whom she had to compromise her own morals.

The latter was the case in the season 1, episode 20 show titled "Adult Education"—a historic episode in its own right, because it was the first in which Rose mentioned "St. Olaf" by name. In this episode, Blanche takes college courses to get a promotion at work. Unfortunately for her, she's struggling in one of her classes—a psychology course—and she ends up doing poorly on the midterm.

After the test, Blanche approaches her professor and asks what she can do to improve her grade. The professor—perhaps unsurprisingly—doesn't offer her any extra credit assignments or tutoring, but he *does* suggest that she can improve her grade if she sleeps with him.

Blanche then tells the Girls about her professor's indecent proposal, and they immediately suggest that she report the professor's behavior to the dean. Blanche does so, but the well-meaning dean informs her that he can't do anything about it because there were no witnesses to the harassment.

Incidentally, this move would have been grounds for a lawsuit in real life. According to the U.S. Department of Education, Blanche's complaint immediately would have kicked off a Title IX investigation, regardless of whether witnesses were present at the time of the incident. "Schools must respond promptly to Title IX sexual harassment in a manner that is not deliberately indifferent, which means a response that is not clearly unreasonable in light of the known circumstances," according to the Department of Education. "Schools must offer supportive measures to the person alleged to be the victim."[7]

Regardless, a furious Blanche storms off when she realizes she's powerless to do anything about it—and more determined than ever to get a good grade in the class *without* compromising her values.

On the day of the final exam, the professor asks Blanche if she'd made her decision—and Blanche informs the professor that she won't be taking him up on his offer, because she knew she'd studied hard and passed the exam.

Ultimately, however, it's revealed that although Blanche successfully earns a higher grade, she doesn't get a promotion—because the woman who got the promotion had some plastic surgery, which impressed the decision maker (who is, it's implied, a lecherous man) more than Blanche's brains. But, Blanche says, she doesn't care—because although the woman's new and improved looks are temporary, Blanche's big brain is forever.

"Adult Education" tackles issues that are still quite salient today—though it's also certainly a product of its time, with its various jokes and its approach to a resolution. (Certainly, a university that responded this way in the twenty-first century would be talking about lawsuits and settlements. *The Golden Girls* writing room might have benefited from someone who could have looked up legal statutes here and there, because the writers certainly played fast and loose with the law.) But aside from addressing a salient issue—and calling, as they say today, a thing a thing—the episode shows that Blanche isn't just an indiscriminate courtesan, sleeping with any and every man who shows an interest in her. Rather, she's a woman who expresses her

sexuality on her own terms—a woman who believes in healthy and positive sexuality that isn't confined by archaic Judeo-Christian morality or the
judgment of others—and who refuses to compromise those values, no matter
what may be in it for her if she does so.

9. "The One That Got Away"

Season 4, Episode 3

As irresistible as Blanche was to the males of the species, there was only one
man who turned her down: Ham Lushbough, who embodied every bit of the
stereotypical high school heartthrob (which probably made the sting even
more palpable).

Blanche's efforts to woo him—thus giving her an "undefeated" record
with men—are explored in the season 4, episode 3 show called "The One
That Got Away."[8]

For years, Blanche has wondered why Ham Lushbough[9] refused to sleep
with her—every time the opportunity presented itself, he always responded
with "maybe some other time, Blanche." When he comes to Miami for a
visit, Blanche is bound and determined to get the former high school hunk to
add another notch on her bedpost.

As might be expected, Ham is light-years from his high school glory
days—which happens to the best of us but is a fact that doesn't go unnoticed
by the other Girls—but Blanche doesn't care, because she still wants to sleep
with him. Her pride won't allow this rejection to go unchecked, even if Ham
looks more like a ham than a prime cut these days.

In fact, it's Ham's refusal to sleep with Blanche even when he looks
less than becoming that drives Blanche into a full tantrum near the end of
the episode. It's only when she snaps at him that he reveals that he slept
with Virginia—Blanche's sister—who apparently looked so like Blanche
that Ham had mistaken the two sisters for decades. Worse yet, Virginia was
terrible in bed, which caused Ham to turn Blanche down each time thereafter.

But once Ham realized the error, he propositioned Blanche, whose response was, "maybe some other time," and nothing short of brilliant (and,
quite frankly, one of the sickest burns on the show).

"The One That Got Away" isn't one of the funniest episodes of *The
Golden Girls*—in fact, the premise of both the primary and the secondary
story (which involves Rose believing she spotted a UFO) are absurd. (Short
of Blanche and Virginia being identical twins—which they weren't—how
did Ham confuse the two sisters all those years ago?)

But the reason "The One That Got Away" was one of the best Blanche Devereaux episodes was because it demonstrated, yet again, that her sexuality was her own to give away—and keep for herself—when she so pleased. She made it clear that she always had the right to change her mind—and could make even the most handsome man feel two inches tall if he dared to reject her on baseless grounds.

That sort of stance, if nothing else, is empowering.

Perhaps that's the real message here to women of all ages: that they need to stop basing their desirability on the whims of men (who, as Ham Lushbaugh so aptly demonstrates, clearly aren't as intelligent—or as good-looking—as they think they are) and to look *inside themselves* for the validation that they so desperately seek.

8. "Strange Bedfellows"
Season 3, Episode 7

This is one of the most controversial episodes of *The Golden Girls* in the twenty-first century, mostly because of transphobic jokes that wouldn't dare be repeated in the twenty-first century. And though this is certainly not meant to be a "woke check" of *The Golden Girls*—remember that comedy is a product of its time, good comedy evolves with time, and when you know better, you do better—this is to suggest that we, as critics who examine how *The Golden Girls* shaped the cultural history of television, need to be mindful of how even the best shows can get it wrong.

Gil Kessler[10] is running to keep his role as a councilman in Miami, and the Girls host a fundraising party for him at the house. Sophia and Dorothy believe that Gil is too weak emotionally to run for office, but he proceeds anyway. After the party, the Girls are cleaning up when Blanche notices a file that Gil had left behind, so she runs to his house to return it to him.

Unfortunately, Blanche gets caught going into Gil's house by the paparazzi, which naturally leads the papers to speculate that Blanche is having an affair with Gil. Despite Blanche's protestations to the contrary, Gil insists that he is having an affair with Blanche, which leads to a falling-out between Blanche and her housemates after they confront her about her loose morals.

Ultimately, at another fundraiser, Gil comes clean to his supporters: not only did he *not* sleep with Blanche, but he reveals that the secret he'd been keeping is that he's a trans man who was born Anna Maria Bonaducci. (Sophia almost immediately deadpans, "I knew he was Italian!")

As can be expected, this announcement is shocking to everyone in attendance, and Gil/Anna Maria loses his bid for councilman.

Naturally, the Girls feel bad about treating Blanche so terribly, to which Blanche responds that she forgives them and then reveals another aspect of her personality: the secret about the charm of the "southern belle." Blanche admits that most of her stories have a "colorful" flair to them, and she's not surprised that one of them came back to bite her in the proverbial behind.

It's the revelation of these different layers of Blanche's personality—proving that she's not just a "dumb slut" who flutters about to and fro, like a poor put-upon wallflower for the 1980s—that makes this episode, flaws and all, one of the best Blanche Devereaux episodes in *Golden Girls* history.

7. "That Old Feeling"

Season 5, Episode 8

Grief is nothing if not an unusual beast—one that comes in crests and waves, especially when the death is that of a longtime spouse or partner. In Blanche Devereaux's case, she never truly got over the death of her beloved husband, George Devereaux. In fact, some have suggested that her promiscuity was nothing more than a feeble attempt to fill the George-sized hole that his death left in her heart—an admission she makes in another episode, which is explored in detail later in this book.

Research, however, suggests that most widows do the opposite of what Blanche had done. "Some widows totally lose interest in sex as one aspect of grief and are celibate for some time after their husbands' deaths, although with the passage of time, at least some report unsatisfied yearnings. Widowers' grieving appears less likely to involve loss of sexual yearning," reports one study.[11]

So when George's brother Jamie—who also happens to be his doppelgänger—comes to town, it makes sense that Blanche would fall in love with him. That's exactly what's explored in the season 5, episode 8 show called "That Old Feeling."

Incidentally, if Jamie was George's doppelgänger, it's because both characters were played by the same actor: George Grizzard. A Broadway veteran born in North Carolina, Grizzard typically portrayed southern characters. His dual character of George and Jamie Devereaux was just one example of that characterization; Grizzard also played southern lawyer Arthur Gold on *Law & Order* and southern gentleman Henry Hamilton in *Scarlett*, the television miniseries that was billed as the sequel to *Gone with the Wind*. Grizzard died in 2007.

The premise of Jamie's trip to town is the death of his mother—Blanche's mother-in-law—a woman known only as "Mama Devereaux" and who never really liked Blanche. So contentious was Mama Devereaux's relationship with Blanche, in fact, that Jamie tells Blanche and the Girls that Mama Devereaux's last words were, "I want her to have it, I want her to have it," and the "her" in this case was Blanche. Blanche is momentarily touched, thinking she is about to receive a beloved Devereaux family heirloom, until Jamie reveals that "it" was Mama Devereaux's terminal disease.

Jamie loves reconnecting with his sister-in-law and sharing memories about his late brother, but Blanche interprets these strolls down memory lane as romantic overtures.

Ultimately, while at dinner, Blanche reveals to Jamie that she's in love with him. Jamie responds by saying that although he loves her like a sister, he has no romantic feelings for her. He also tells her that the only thing they'd talked about since he touched down in Miami was George, and although he loved George too, shared grief is not the basis for a good relationship.

Flustered, Blanche goes into a mini-soliloquy before telling Jamie to "take that back, George."

Jamie corrects her and tells her that she called him George.

"You're just so much like him," Blanche responds.

"But I'm not him," Jamie replies.

Finally, Blanche breaks down in tears and tells Jamie that she felt like an old fool. Jamie comforts her and tells her that it's okay to feel what she's feeling and that he didn't hate her for feeling the way she did and she shouldn't feel foolish. They then share a tender moment when Blanche admits that she still misses George.

The final scene is an acting master class between McClanahan and Grizzard, who expertly portray both the bitter and the sweet simultaneously while talking about George. McClanahan was able to show Blanche's more vulnerable side—the side that misses her husband and who still mourns him all these years after his death. McClanahan's continued ability to portray Blanche as a multilayered character makes "That Old Feeling" one of the best Blanche Devereaux episodes of *The Golden Girls*.

6. "Stand by Your Man"

Season 6, Episode 11

As previously discussed, Blanche Devereaux may be the type of woman who is free with her sexuality—but she, too, has her limits. One of Blanche's limits, as previously mentioned, is married men: while Rose, Sophia, and Dorothy all get involved with married men at one point or another—and even justify staying with the men after they find out they're married—Blanche avoids married men like the plague.

Now, it can be argued—correctly—that sexuality and morality aren't necessarily intertwined, but in the context of the times—when women, especially older women, were shamed for freely flaunting their sexuality—seeing someone like Blanche Devereaux set boundaries for that sexuality is nothing if not remarkable to see. Rather than playing into the stereotype of "the wanton slut," who sleeps with anyone who gives her some type of attention, Blanche Devereaux is a slut with a moral backbone—and her enjoyment of sex isn't a moral failing, but a significant part of her unique humanity.

In fairness, however, the circumstances through which Sophia got involved with a married man are more bittersweet than the other examples. In the season 7, episode 14 show called "Old Boyfriends," Sophia finds an ad for "swinging seniors" in the personal columns, and she connects with a man named Marvin, who always seems to be accompanied by his sister, Sarah. But as Sophia and Marvin grow closer, Marvin reveals that Sarah is his wife, not his sister. As it turns out, Marvin and Sarah aren't swingers—Sarah is dying, and she wants to find a suitable wife for Marvin before she passes away. One can say, in fact, that Sophia's behavior was noble.

But Dorothy shamelessly hooks up with a married man in the season 1, episode 14 show called "That Was No Lady" (and with the same man, Glen O'Brien, in the season 5, episode 22 show called "Cheaters"), and Rose hooks up with a married man, Al, in the season 1, episode 15 show called "In a Bed of Rose's."

Regardless of the morality (or lack thereof) of shacking up with married men, the season 6, episode 11 show titled "Stand by Your Man" illustrates how far Blanche is willing to go to uphold her morals.

When Dorothy goes to the library to check out some books, Blanche decides to tag along. While there, she meets a man named Ted and agrees to a date with him. But right after she accepts his proposition for a date, Ted wheels away from the library desk, revealing to Blanche that he is wheelchair bound.

As might be expected, Blanche has her reservations about starting a relationship with a man in a wheelchair—but after chatting with her Girls and getting to know Ted better, she decides to continue the relationship and even thinks she's falling in love with him.

But in the end, Blanche discovers that she can't go to Philadelphia with Ted on a "couple's trip"—because he already has a wife. Immediately, Blanche becomes outraged (and rightly so) and throws Ted out of her house.

Ted naturally protests this decision and claims that his wife doesn't understand him.

"Well, I do—you're a cheat," she snaps as she holds open the door.

It's clear that not only is Blanche Devereaux unwilling to compromise her values to be with a man—no matter how much she cares about him—but she's confident enough not to fall for a cheating man's lies. Although some sexually promiscuous women behave that way because of their insecurities—using sex to fill what seems to be limitless void—other sexually promiscuous women behave that way because of confidence—they know that their sexual partners (or lack thereof) never directly affect their own self-esteem or self-worth.

Blanche Devereaux demonstrates that she is the latter in "Stand by Your Man," making it one of the greatest Blanche Devereaux episodes of *The Golden Girls*.

5. "Witness"

Season 6, Episode 21

Rose is the Golden Girl who gets the "A," or primary, story line in this episode, in which she begins inadvertently dating a gangster known as "The Cheeseman" after Miles reenters the Witness Protection Program. Miles returns, dressed as an Amish man, and they confront "The Cheeseman," who gets put back in jail. Miles then leaves the Witness Protection Program and lives his life as "Miles Webber" for the remainder of *The Golden Girls* run. He also returns in *The Golden Palace*, but he ultimately doesn't marry Rose.

But it's Blanche's "B" story line that steals the show and makes "Witness" one of the best Blanche Devereaux episodes of *The Golden Girls*.

Blanche is trying to join the Daughters of the Old South, an organization with Confederate ties. To become a member of the club, she must prove that she has true southern heritage, and to do that, she must trace her genealogy.

Blanche then works with Dorothy to trace her southern heritage. The pair spend hours reading documents like birth certificates, marriage certificates, and death certificates—before the advent of the Internet and Ancestry.com—until, ultimately, it's discovered that she has a grandmother who was born—as Dorothy put it—"*outside* of Georgia."

"How far outside of Georgia?" asks Blanche.

"*Buffalo*," emphasizes Dorothy, referring to the city in upstate New York.

Blanche panics and snatches the marriage certificate from Dorothy—and it's only after she reads it that she realizes she's in for another surprise.

"Oh," says Dorothy, nonchalantly. "Did I mention her last name was . . . *Feldman*?"

That sends Blanche into a complete tailspin—she screams and insists that "I can't be *Jewish*!" She then makes up her mind that she can't reveal her true heritage to the Daughters of the Old South, lest it refuse her membership in the club. Dorothy insists that Blanche is behaving badly and that she shouldn't have to hide her heritage to belong to the club, but Blanche will hear none of it. To her, being validated by a conservative organization with Confederate ties is the only way to validate her southern heritage. And this, unfortunately, is a belief that Blanche carries all the way through to *The Golden Palace*. It takes a chat with Roland (played by a then-unknown Don Cheadle), the manager of the hotel in the spin-off, for Blanche to finally realize that the Confederacy is steeped in racism and traitorous to the American cause ("Camp Town Races Aren't as Fun as They Used to Be"—*The Golden Palace*, season 1, episode 11).

Fast-forward to the meeting of the Daughters of the Old South, in which a woman named Louise Blakely also is applying for membership into the club. Louise is recounting her family tree when she briefly mentions an ancestor by marriage, Claude Livaudais.

This is enough to make one of the daughters stand up and question Louise's southern heritage, because as it turns out, Claude "once sold horseshoes to a Yankee soldier" during the Civil War. Naturally, this is the equivalent of treason to the daughters, who view even a tonsorial connection to the Union as tantamount to sympathizing with "Yankee" causes, and poor Mrs. Blakely is rejected by the club.

It's now Blanche's turn.

She gets up to the podium and first tries to avoid her genealogy situation by sweetly asking if she can give an exposition on what being a southerner means to her instead of recounting her family tree. When the daughters insist that she must recount her family tree, Blanche is visibly uncomfortable but proceeds.

She explains that she's Blanche Devereaux, née Hollingsworth, of Atlanta. She explains she's the daughter of Curtis Hollingsworth and Samantha Roquet,[12] of Augusta, Georgia, and Shreveport, Louisiana, respectively.

"Daughter of . . ." she begins, her voice trailing off as Dorothy gives her a knowing look.

Finally, Blanche can't hold it in anymore.

"*Feldman*," she spits. "I'm a *Feldman*, dammit."

Then she smiles sweetly and adopts her trademark coquettish voice. "Of *Buffalo*," she says in a singsong voice.

The members of the Daughters of the Old South try to usher Blanche off the stage, but not before she's able to deliver her soliloquy to the crowd.

"I am made up of many ingredients, but perhaps that is what gives me my uniquely American flavor. Yes, for I am an American, and I'm leaving. I don't need your lousy club to make me feel special," she concludes, before informing them that "you lost the war, get over it."[13]

Ultimately, it's Blanche's willingness to accept the truth about herself—and to tell others where they can go if they dare judge her—that makes "Witness" one of the best Blanche Devereaux episodes of *The Golden Girls*.

Also, one can't help but root for a southerner who tells the Confederacy-loving traitors to go to hell with gasoline panties on—in the most charming southern way, of course.

4. "End of the Curse"

Season 2, Episode 1

The Golden Girls, at its core, is a sitcom that deals with the concept of aging. "End of the Curse" deals with a bittersweet part of growing older, when women see themselves in a different way after a certain time in their lives. There's no better person to deliver that message than the vivacious, sex-positive Blanche Devereaux.

At the start of the episode, Blanche appears depressed, but she doesn't immediately say why. She then reveals to the Girls that she's pregnant, but she doesn't know if she can keep the baby or who the father is.

After the initial shock of the positive pregnancy test wears off, the Girls all pledge to help Blanche raise the baby, regardless of the circumstances. But when Blanche goes to the doctor, it turns out that her positive pregnancy test isn't because she's expecting a baby—it's because she's beginning menopause.

As absurd as this might sound, it's biologically possible. According to the University of Miami, a "false positive" pregnancy test can occur for women who are just entering menopause because there are still detectable levels of hCG (human chorionic gonadotropin, aka the pregnancy hormone) in the blood.[14]

But as can be expected, the menopause diagnosis sends Blanche into another tailspin, and she immediately enters a depressive state. She now thinks she's lost all her attractiveness, and to her, this means that her very essence is all but gone.

Later in the episode, it's revealed that Blanche is the last Girl to go through menopause. The Girls all recount their stories of going through "the change," and they all periodically refer to "the curse." The reference to "the curse," which is also in the title of this episode, is a euphemism for a menstrual period, and it comes from Biblical times. Specifically, "the curse" refers to Leviticus 15:19–22, in which a woman's monthly cycle is described as such: "When a woman has her regular flow of blood, the impurity of her monthly period will last seven days, and anyone who touches her will be unclean till evening. Anything she lies on during her period will be unclean, and anything she sits on will be unclean. Whoever touches her bed must wash his clothes and bathe with water, and he will be unclean till evening. Whoever touches anything she sits on must wash his clothes and bathe with water, and he will be unclean till evening." Biblical scholars also reiterate that a woman's menstrual cycle is a "divine curse" visited upon her thanks to Eve "falling" in the Garden of Eden. The euphemism, however, has fallen out of favor today, though it's (perhaps unsurprisingly) still used in England.[15]

After each of the Girls recounts her story, Blanche realizes that her menstrual cycle has no bearing on her feminine charms—in fact, she's just as sexy now as she was while she still had her period. She even accepts a date with the veterinarian who comes by the house to check on the mink farm.

It's worth noting, as a sidebar, that the "B" story in "End of the Curse" involves the Girls raising mink for profit. Reportedly, all four Girls—who were animal activists in real life and even recorded public service announcements for People for the Ethical Treatment of Animals—didn't like portraying mink farmers, as minks are harvested for their fur.

But the moral of the "A" story line is simple: "being sexy" isn't reserved for only young women. Women, in fact, can be sexy at any age—provided that they are of the age of consent or older. And "sexy" has nothing to do with your appearance—it's in how you carry yourself, in how you behave in the presence of the opposite sex, and in your natural essence.

Blanche Devereaux proved to a whole generation of women that life does not, in fact, end at forty—or even at fifty. In fact, it's only just begun. McClanahan pulled this episode off with gusto and set the tone for Blanche for the rest of the series. It's one of the best episodes of *The Golden Girls*, as well as one of the best Blanche Devereaux episodes.

3. "Journey to the Center of Attention"
Season 7, Episode 18

If there's one thing that Blanche Devereaux loves more than herself, it's being the center of attention. So much so, in fact, that she gets insanely jealous each time someone else gets the attention she feels she deserves. When Blanche finally comes to terms with this character trait in the season 7, episode 18 show called "Journey to the Center of Attention," she reveals a new depth that she never showed before. This makes "Journey to the Center of Attention" one of the best Blanche Devereaux episodes of *The Golden Girls*.

For what are perhaps obvious reasons—not the least of which being that she hasn't been on a date in a while—Dorothy finds herself depressed and whiling away her hours on the couch with a bowl of popcorn. To cheer her up, Blanche invites her to the Rusty Anchor, a local watering hole where Blanche is a popular attraction. Dorothy is concerned that no one will want to talk to her, but Blanche persuades her to go because "if there's somebody out there who is willing to dance with a corpse, there's somebody willing to dance with you."[16]

At the beginning of the party, no one is willing to dance, chat, or otherwise engage with Dorothy, so she begins singing with the piano player. The first song she sings is "What'll I Do," written by Irving Berlin in 1923 and later made famous by both Nat King Cole in 1952 and Frank Sinatra in 1962. The most recent version of the song was released in 2019, and it was recorded by *Family Guy* creator Seth MacFarlane, who released it on an album called *Once in a While*.

Dorothy's performance of the classic track immediately gets the attention of everyone in the bar—and it's obvious by the look on Blanche's face that she's none too pleased that Dorothy is now the center of attention.

The next time Dorothy goes to the Rusty Anchor, she takes sheet music for the song "Hard-Hearted Hannah,"[17] the vamp of Savannah. As can be expected, she gets raucous applause from the audience.

There's only one person who is unhappy about Dorothy's newfound musical freedom: Blanche, who is all but eaten with jealousy over her roommate's—and best friend's—newfound fame. It isn't because of any animus toward Dorothy—it's because she's not used to *not* being the center of attention. This, too, lends credence to the fans' belief that the last two seasons of the show featured an air of "cattiness" about them that didn't exist in the previous seasons. This behavior is incongruous with Blanche's behavior up until this point—prior to this, she relished the attention that she received from her "gentleman callers," but she was always ladylike enough to defer to the others when it was their time to shine.

Catty or not, Blanche decides to try to sing as well—and she chooses "I Wanna Be Loved by You," which is perhaps to be expected. Whereas Dorothy's singing delights the crowd in the Rusty Anchor, Blanche's singing is off-key, clumsy, and embarrassing. Flustered due to her inability to charm the crowd, Blanche begins sobbing and runs into the bathroom, with Dorothy hot on her heels.

Ultimately, the pair realize that they need to go to the Rusty Anchor on different days, so they can enjoy being the center of attention without competing with one another. But what's interesting—and beautiful—about this episode is that Blanche acknowledges Dorothy as "beautiful" for the first time in seven seasons. Her deference demonstrated maturity and grace—making this episode one of the best Blanche Devereaux episodes of *The Golden Girls*.

Besides, who wouldn't want to tune in to watch Rue McClanahan—and Bea Arthur—sing?

2. "Room Seven"
Season 7, Episode 10

The Golden Girls once again dealt with the subject of death in the season 7, episode 10 show called "Room Seven." But rather than dealing with mortality, "Room Seven" deals with the concept of the afterlife and those people the deceased leave behind. The "A" story line is where Blanche takes center stage, and it's where she learns the most important lesson of her life. And, of course, adding another dimension to the Blanche Devereaux character makes this the number two episode featuring the beloved beauty.

Blanche's grandmother's plantation[18] is under threat of demolition, and the news sends Blanche into a tailspin. She immediately hightails it to Atlanta—with the rest of the Girls in tow—to stop the demolition, even going so far as to handcuff herself to a radiator to prevent the demolition crane from leveling the plantation to the ground.

The sound of her grandmother's wind chimes reminds Blanche of what's important: that the memory of her grandmother and the important role she played in her life is worth more than a plantation—or anything else that's physical and tangible, really.

As she leaves the plantation for the final time, with the wind chimes in her hand, Blanche hears the laughter of a little girl—presumably Blanche as a child—and, misty-eyed, laughs despite herself. It's a moving scene, and one that continues to show Blanche as more than just a "wanton slut" who thinks of nothing but the next date—or the next morning.

The "B" story line is just as touching: it features Sophia having an out-of-body experience and ultimately meeting her beloved husband Sal in the

Hereafter. As a result, Sophia becomes more reckless with her behavior in the hopes of having another out-of-body experience. As can be expected, this perturbs Dorothy, who believes her mother is having suicidal ideations. But Sophia clarifies her behavior by saying that although she's no longer afraid of dying, it doesn't mean that she wants to die. The upshot of this story line, of course, is the same as that of the "A" story line: treasure your memories of your deceased loved ones but live in the present with those who are alive and well.

However flawed the final two seasons of *The Golden Girls* may be, the evolution of Blanche Devereaux is one thing that the powers that be definitely got right.

1. "Mrs. George Devereaux"
Season 6, Episode 9

Of all the episodes featuring Blanche Devereaux, the one in which she shines brighter than all the rest is the season 6, episode 9 show called "Mrs. George Devereaux."

Ultimately, the show's entire premise is nothing more than absurdity—both Blanche and Dorothy receive flowers from secret admirers, but whereas Dorothy's two bouquets of "lousy, stinkin' flowers" are from Lyle Waggoner[19] and Sonny Bono (half of the Sonny and Cher duo, and later a politician), Blanche's flowers (which fill up nearly the whole kitchen, causing Sophia to question whether someone had died) are from her presumably deceased husband, George.

As George would later reveal, he faked his own death[20]—his business partners were corrupt, they framed him as the culprit of their dirty deeds, and the proverbial walls were closing in on him—and stayed away from Blanche for her own protection. But now, enough time has passed, so he comes back for her—and he wants to marry her all over again.

As one can imagine, Blanche is more than a little torn about this revelation. Sure, she's happy that the love of her life has returned to her. But how could George lie to her this way?[21] All those years she'd spent with a broken heart, thinking that the love of her life was dead—but he was alive and in hiding—has Blanche flummoxed beyond belief. (In fairness to Blanche, *anyone* would be in the same situation.)

When both Sophia and Rose point out that Blanche is luckier than most—"my Charlie is dead, and nobody's giving *me* a second chance," snips Rose—Blanche decides to take George back. And they seal the deal with a hug in Blanche's room . . . where she suddenly wakes up.

As it turns out, Blanche was dreaming about George—a dream that she's had several times before, as evidenced by Dorothy's remark that Blanche "was having that dream again." But the difference this time is that Blanche "got to hug him"—the "him," of course, being George. Prior to this, Blanche always woke up before she got a chance to hug George—but because she got to hug him in the dream, she went back to sleep feeling happier than she'd ever felt since his death, as though the hug is what she needed to finally get a sense of closure about losing her husband.

She closes out the episode by looking at the ceiling and saying, "good night, George," wistfully and with more than a few happy tears in her eyes. Even the most stoic *Golden Girls* fan can't help but get misty-eyed seeing Blanche yearn for her beloved dead husband as she drifts off to sleep.

Because we've all been there—whether it be our husbands, parents, wives, partners, or even a platonic soulmate, we've all felt the pain of losing someone we love. Grief, loss, and pain is something we can all relate to, no matter our age, background, gender, or sexual orientation—and it's this universal emotion expressed almost poetically that makes "Mrs. George Devereaux" not only one of the best episodes of *The Golden Girls* to feature Blanche Devereaux, but one of the best episodes of the series of all time.

CHAPTER FIVE

SHADY PINES, MA

Adult Mother/Daughter Relationships Redefined through Dorothy Zbornak and Sophia Petrillo

All the Girls shared a special bond but none had quite the bond that Dorothy Zbornak and Sophia Petrillo shared.

It was more than the fact that they were mother and daughter—although, certainly, that went without saying. By the end of the show, Dorothy and Sophia were also the best of friends. That alone made their relationship more special than any like it before.

Born Sophia Grisanti in an unnamed town in Sicily, Sophia—like the other *Golden Girls* characters—had an ever-changing background story, though hers seems to change the least. Her year of birth isn't ever mentioned, but estimates place it somewhere between 1912 and 1922. Sophia's parents were named Angelo and Eleanor, and she had a brother named Angelo and a sister named Angela.

Sophia's life in Sicily, however, is nothing if not a colorful one. As a teenager, she had her fair share of suitors. She was briefly engaged to Augustine Bagatelli, a man from her village, and another paisano from her village named Giuseppe Mangiacavallo left her at the altar.

In the season 5, episode 23 show called "The Mangiacavallo Curse Makes a Lousy Wedding Present," it's revealed that Sophia put a "Sicilian curse" on Giuseppe when he left her at the altar all those years ago. As a result, his daughter begins fighting with her husband on their wedding day. It's only when Giuseppe stands up and claims that Sophia turned down his wedding proposal twice ("and so, from now on . . . I'm gay") that Sophia proclaims that "the curse is over." Or perhaps the curse ended because Dorothy and Blanche offered the distraught bride some much-needed advice when she was crying in the bathroom. Either way, it worked.

Sophia then was set up in an arranged marriage to Guido Spirelli, but she had the marriage annulled. Although not as common in the twenty-first century, it was very common for Sicilian marriages to be arranged by parents up until and throughout most of the twentieth century. In some smaller, more traditional, provincial towns—especially in the north of Sicily, where Arabic influence is most prevalent—the practice is still common today. Legally speaking, however, Italian law doesn't specifically address the subject of arranged marriages. If both parties consent to a marriage, there isn't really anything that anyone can do, regardless of whether the marriage was arranged. However, under Italian law, any marriage that occurs under duress, or if one or more of the parties is in a vulnerable state and cannot consent, is legally considered invalid.[1]

After her annulment, Sophia lit out to Brooklyn, New York, hoping to leave her Sicilian heritage and roots behind. (This was the writers' explanation for why Sophia had a Brooklyn accent, not a Sicilian one—which, in the end, was for the best, as Sicilian accents are notoriously difficult for even the most experienced actors.)

Sometime after she arrived in Brooklyn, she met and married Salvatore (sometimes spelled "Salvadore," although *Salvador* is the Spanish spelling and *Salvatore* is the Italian spelling, yet another error on the writers' part) Petrillo, and together, the pair had three children: two daughters and a son.

Sophia's daughters are named Dorothy (whom we discuss in greater detail here, obviously) and Gloria. Gloria, it's implied, was Sophia's favorite daughter growing up—and Sophia's preference for Gloria causes harm to Dorothy, such as it did in the season 7, episode 8 show called "The Monkey Show," in which Sophia encourages Gloria to sleep with Stan. Despite Sophia's preference for Gloria, however, it's evident that she's much more attached to Dorothy, who not only has taken responsibility for her mother's health but provides her with love and companionship in her later years.

When it comes to Sophia's son Phil, however, the story is a little different. Though it's evident that Sophia loves Phil—and does until the day he dies in the season 6, episode 12 show called "Ebbtide's Revenge"—their relationship is more complicated than Sophia's relationships with her daughters. Phil—a welder who was married to a woman named Angela, with whom he shared two children—was a cross-dresser,[2] which was very difficult for Sophia to accept.

"Ebbtide's Revenge" cracks plenty of jokes at the expense of cross-dressers, but it's interesting to note that Sophia makes none of them, despite being a character who wasn't afraid to make her fair share of blunt comments in other episodes. Reportedly—although this has never been confirmed—it's because Estelle Getty refused to say them and told the writers to take them out. Getty believed that a mother wouldn't be so heartless as to make jokes at her dead son's expense. Unfortunately, as various viral social media videos have since proven, she was wrong—but kudos to her for trying.

Complicated relationships with children aside, Sophia and "Sal" were married for more than thirty years, until he died of a heart attack. But there's some disparity as to what year he died—some episodes say he died thirty years prior to the pilot episode (which means he died sometime in the 1950s), whereas others say he died twenty-seven years prior to the episode (which means he died sometime in the late 1950s or early 1960s). Perhaps this was a function of Sophia's stroke or simply creative license on the writers' part. Regardless, Sophia suffers a stroke shortly after Sal dies and is put in the Shady Pines Retirement Home by her daughter, Dorothy. But when the home was damaged in a fire, she moves in with Dorothy and her two roommates.

And it's at this point that we introduce Dorothy into the frame.

Dorothy Petrillo was the first daughter of Sal and Sophia Petrillo, conceived after one of their first fights as newlyweds. Born in New York City and raised in Brooklyn, Dorothy was the stereotypical nerd: overachieving,

Estelle Getty, right, and Bea Arthur brought the characters of Sophia Petrillo and Dorothy Zbornak to life.

with her nose in a book, and "dabbling a bit in poetry" (as she mentioned in the season 2, episode 6 show called "Big Daddy's Little Lady").

As perhaps can be expected, being that person led to a series of unfortunate events for a teenage Dorothy: her first boyfriend was physically and emotionally abusive (as she mentioned in the season 6, episode 13 show called "The Bloom Is off the Rose"), which damages her self-esteem. Another high school boyfriend named John Noretti, who was supposed to take her to the prom, stood her up (or so she thought—it was later revealed that Sophia sent him away because of the way he dressed and his nasty attitude, as was revealed in season 6, episode 21, "What a Difference a Date Makes"), which further added to her self-esteem issues.

Eventually, Dorothy accepts a date with the "yutz"—as Sophia referred to him throughout the seven seasons of the show—Stan Zbornak, mostly because she felt she couldn't do any better.

Interestingly, the word *yutz* is a Yiddish word that means, essentially, "a foolish person." *Yutz* also implies a contemptible foolish person, rather than a likable one. It's not clear, however, why a Sicilian woman would use the word *yutz* in everyday conversation—this is either creative license on the writers' part or it's Getty's way of retaining an element of her "Jewish grandmother" persona in her characters. Perhaps it's a bit of both.

Perhaps as can be expected, Dorothy gets pregnant on one of her dates with Stan. In the pilot episode, Dorothy reveals that her father forced her to marry Stan when he found out she was pregnant. As a result, Dorothy and Stan dropped out of high school and had a shotgun wedding.

But all was not lost: during their honeymoon in Miami, Dorothy and Stan bought some property and eventually made it their home. Dorothy ultimately completes high school (and college!) and becomes a teacher—she begins teaching high school and eventually becomes a substitute teacher.

While Dorothy makes a success of herself—especially given the inauspicious circumstances under which the marriage began—Stan isn't so lucky. His various business ventures fail, and he takes several odd jobs—including as a novelty salesman—to make ends meet. Stan doesn't become successful until the season 6, episode 3 show called "If at Last You Do Succeed," when he patents a baked potato opener that he dubs "The Zbornie"—a name, Dorothy reveals, that Stan also gave his penis ("I put up with it for thirty-eight years, Rose, you don't want to know").

Though Dorothy and Stan remain married for many years and ultimately have two children—son Michael was the product of their teenage love affair and daughter Kate came a little bit later—it's revealed that Stan repeatedly cheated on Dorothy throughout their relationship.

Initially, Kate was the child who was the product of the teenage love affair. But in the season 7, episode 6 show titled "Mother Load," Stan convinces Sophia to attend therapy with him and Dorothy, during which Sophia launches into a tirade about all of Stan's failures as a father and a husband. When Stan asks Sophia if there was ever a time that she loved him, she thinks about it and mentions that she did in the moment when they "wheeled little Michael" out of the delivery room, which implies that Michael, not Kate, came first.

Regardless of which child came first, Stan lets his incessant infidelity slip in one episode, when he reveals that he took a date to Ebbets Field[3] while he was still married to Dorothy ("Bang the Drum Stanley"—season 4, episode 5). Ultimately, after thirty-eight years of marriage, Stan and Dorothy divorce after Stan has an affair with a flight attendant named Chrissy; worse yet, Stan informs Dorothy by sending an attorney to serve her with divorce papers, rather than directly addressing the matter.

Much to Sophia's chagrin, Dorothy and Stan periodically try to rekindle their relationship—and it's clear that Dorothy isn't fully over Stan, nor is Stan fully over Dorothy. In one episode, Dorothy forces Blanche to go on a date with Stan and then becomes visibly jealous when they have a good time ("Take Him, He's Mine"—season 2, episode 3). In another episode, Sophia offers to pay Stan to pretend to be married to Dorothy, but Stan refuses, claiming that it's "on the house," because he enjoyed the time he spent with his ex-wife ("My Brother, My Father"—season 3, episode 17).

At one point, Stan and Dorothy even plan to remarry—only for that wedding to get shot to hell when Stan presents a prenup to Dorothy to sign for "his protection" now that "The Zbornie" has provided a financial windfall. Dorothy calls off the wedding and tells the guests that she "decided not to make the same mistake twice" ("There Goes the Bride," part I and II—season 6, episodes 16 and 17).

Even though Stan and Dorothy don't ever work out again romantically—which is for the best—they do remain in each other's lives, because they share children and grandchildren . . . and after all their years together, Dorothy wouldn't want it any other way.

Though Dorothy doesn't have as many notches on her bedpost as Blanche, she does date her fair share of men (even though her lack of a sex life is a frequent punchline on the show). She openly and knowingly dates a married man named Glenn O'Brien, which started in the season 1, episode 14 show called "That Was No Lady," and they rekindled their relationship in the season 5, episode 22 show titled "Cheaters."

She rekindles an old high school flame with Barry Glick, but it doesn't go anywhere, because Barry reveals that he's gay ("Job Hunting"—season 1, episode 22). She almost has a relationship with a police officer named Al Mullins, but despite the passion the pair share, she ultimately decides against the relationship because she couldn't bear the thought of losing someone who willingly puts himself in harm's way ("To Catch a Neighbor"—season 2, episode 24).

"To Catch a Neighbor" also starred a then-unknown George Clooney playing a rookie cop named Bobby Hopkins. His young age and boyish good looks immediately endear him to the Girls, especially to Blanche, who likens Bobby to one of her sons. When Bobby is shot in the line of fire—he survives, as it turns out to be a flesh wound—Blanche is devastated.

Ultimately, Dorothy finds love again in the series finale of *The Golden Girls*. When Blanche's uncle, Lucas Hollingsworth—the younger brother of her beloved "Big Daddy"—comes to town for a visit, Blanche forces Dorothy to go on a date with him so that Blanche is free to go on a date herself. Though Dorothy and Lucas initially don't hit it off, they agree to pretend to be getting married to get even with Blanche.

The scheme works—just a little too well. The more time Dorothy and Lucas spend together, the more they genuinely enjoy one another's company. Eventually, they decide to get married for real—and Dorothy leaves Miami to live at the Hollingsworth estate in Atlanta. Sophia initially wants to go with Dorothy to Atlanta but ultimately decides to stay behind with Rose and Blanche, as she'd grown to view them as her surrogate daughters (she even lovingly cradles a photo of them and sighs, "goodbye, my girls" when she thinks she's leaving for Atlanta). This, of course, was the premise of the short-lived spin-off *The Golden Palace*.

It's interesting to watch the evolution of Dorothy and Sophia's relationship during the course of *The Golden Girls*—and it's even more interesting to watch Sophia—especially in action with Dorothy—and compare her with the stereotypical mother of the 1950s.

Although the writers chose to blame Sophia's stroke—and age—for her blunt, tactless comments, she was a more accurate depiction of the average 1950s mother than, say, the Donna Reeds and the Harriet Nelsons before her. Mothers of the 1950s weren't submissive and always smiling; rather, Wini Breines[4] reports that mothers were simultaneously coddling and permissive with their sons (vis-à-vis the *Time* article referenced in chapter 2 regarding the personality traits of men who were physically violent with their wives) and overbearing and domineering with their daughters.[5] This, too, coincides with how Sophia—however well-meaning—behaves

In *The Golden Girls* series finale, Dorothy (Bea Arthur) finds her happily ever after with Blanche's uncle, Lucas Hollingsworth (Leslie Nielsen).

toward Dorothy, especially once they start living together full time after the pilot episode.

As time goes on, Dorothy and Sophia's traditional mother-daughter relationship evolves. They treat one another as equals and, eventually, become the best of friends. Despite their differences—of which there are many—Dorothy and Sophia are fiercely protective of one another, refusing to allow anyone to harm the other, and they even share rare moments of tenderness that the other girls don't share.

For example, consider the season 1, episode 7 show called "The Competition," in which the Girls are pitted against each other in a bowling competition. Perhaps for obvious reasons, Sophia is good at the game (after all, it's quite like the Italian game of bocce). Earlier in the episode, Sophia wants to go to Sicily with Augustine Bagatelli (apparently, she didn't feel resentment about the short-lived engagement), but Dorothy refuses due to her mother's poor health. But when the bowling tournament comes up, Sophia decides to put the trip up as part of a wager—if she wins the tournament, she gets to go to Sicily, but if Dorothy wins the tournament, she gets a pair of heirloom earrings that she had wanted for the longest time.

The day of the tournament arrives, and Dorothy seems to be winning the tournament. But when she spots her mother with Augustine—and sees that she's incredibly happy with her old flame—Dorothy throws the game in Sophia's favor so that Sophia can go to Sicily.

As it turns out, Sophia knows her daughter quite well, and she knew that Dorothy deliberately threw the game, so she gifts her daughter the earrings, remarking that Dorothy had earned them fair and square.

Yet for all their tender moments, Dorothy and Sophia knew how to get under each other's skin when they wanted to. Sophia frequently insulted her daughter's love life—and lack thereof—and Dorothy threatened her mother with a return to Shady Pines (burnt down and all) if she got too far out of line. The ladies certainly knew how to draw their boundaries—and their battle lines—when necessary.

This changing relationship between mother and daughter also coincides with the natural evolution of the mother-daughter relationship, especially as the daughter grows from adolescence to adulthood. Writing for *Psychology Today*, Peg Streep[6] points out that a mother serves several roles for her adult daughter throughout her life, not the least of which includes being a "best girlfriend," her biggest critic, a police officer of sorts, always imparting her never-wrong opinions, and a wise woman who serves as the central role in her daughter's life no matter what happens.

Indeed, Dorothy and Sophia are more than just mother and daughter—they are best friends, they complete one another, and they have a relationship that far too many of us only dream of having with our own mothers. They defied both cultural expectations and society's definitions of what a mother *should* be, choosing instead to do what was right for them in the circumstance they created. Above all else, they loved each other beyond words—and worlds.

DOROTHY ZBORNAK: THE TOP TEN BEST EPISODES

Whether together or apart, Dorothy and Sophia went together like peanut butter and jelly. You couldn't have one without the other—and even when one wasn't in the physical presence of the other, the other's influence could still be felt.

As well it should have been—after all, they were mother and daughter.

Some critics argued that Dorothy Zbornak was little more than Maude Findlay in Miami. Certainly, fans of the latter show saw quite a few similarities between Maude and Dorothy, which makes sense, as they were played by the same actress. Even Bea Arthur herself gave pushback when initially approached about the role, claiming she didn't want to do a show about "Maude and Vivian meet Sue Ann Nivens." However, Dorothy is worlds away from Maude. She's sexy, she's confident, and she doesn't suffer fools.

Of course, there are some episodes of *The Golden Girls* in which Dorothy shines brighter than everyone else. Here, then, is the list of the top ten Dorothy Zbornak episodes, some of which include legendary interactions with her mother, Sophia.

10. "Big Daddy's Little Lady"
Season 2, Episode 6

Blanche gets the "A" story line in this episode, in which her beloved father, Curtis "Big Daddy" Hollingsworth, marries a woman several decades younger than he is, but it's Dorothy who steals the show, making "Big Daddy's Little Lady" one of the best Dorothy Zbornak episodes of *The Golden Girls*.

Dorothy and Rose decide to enter a songwriting contest, in which they must write a song that sings the praises about Miami for a chance to win a cash prize. In the beginning, Dorothy reveals that she'd be perfect to write the lyrics because she'd "dabbled a little bit in poetry in high school."

Rose's reply: "That's nothing to be ashamed of. A lot of tall girls who couldn't get dates wrote poetry in high school."

The songwriting process proves to be more arduous than initially thought. Rose argues that "thrice" is an acceptable word to use in a lyric (Dorothy: "Who in the hell says 'thrice'?" Rose: "It's a word!" Dorothy: "So is intrauterine. It does *not* belong in a song." Rose [*singing*]: "Miami—you're cuter than, an intrauterine . . . "). The Girls come up with a lyric that incorrectly suggests, "M-I-A, another M-I, M-I-A-M-I spells Miami Beach." (Blanche interrupts them—"Girls! [That] doesn't spell Miami Beach! It spells Miami!"—before they finally change the admittedly jaunty lyric, though Dorothy and Rose certainly bicker about it before they do.)

Ultimately, they get through the songwriting process, only to win second place in the contest. When asked what they received as a consolation prize, Dorothy responds, "treated badly."

But the Girls close out the episode with a rousing rendition of the song—"Miami, Miami, you've got style—blue skies, sunshine, white sand by the mile!"—which shows off Dorothy's (and, by extension, Bea Arthur's) musical chops. It's a delightful episode ending and proves to be one of the best Dorothy Zbornak episodes of *The Golden Girls*.

9. "My Brother, My Father"

Season 3, Episode 17

"My Brother, My Father" is a Dorothy and Sophia tag-team episode, one in which Arthur and Getty have the opportunity to play off one another and act out the mother-daughter roles in a family dynamic.

In this season 3 episode, Sophia tells Dorothy that Uncle Angelo[7]—Sophia's brother and Dorothy's uncle—is coming into town. Angelo, a Catholic priest, is unaware that Dorothy and Stan are divorced. Sophia insists that Stan and Dorothy pretend that they are married while Angelo is in town.

As previously mentioned, Dorothy and Stan divorced when Stan cheated on Dorothy with a flight attendant named Chrissy. They periodically tried to get back together before ultimately realizing that they were toxic for one another. But what's not discussed is that even during the 1980s—when the rate of divorce was still on the rise—there was a stigma attached to it, especially for women. In fact, in earlier episodes of *The Golden Girls*, Dorothy's marital status is used as a weapon against her and meant to convey that she's "undesirable" compared to the other Girls. It's unclear whether this is what motivated Dorothy to try to periodically reconcile with Stan or whether she was motivated by the familiarity he provided (better the devil you know than the devil you don't).[8]

What's more, until Pope Francis pushed for—and ultimately received—a revision of Catholic law regarding divorce in 2015, divorce was considered a sin that was grounds for excommunication from the Catholic Church, which is why Sophia pressured Dorothy and Stan to hide their divorce from Angelo. Today, divorce is no longer an excommunicable sin: Catholics who get divorced can receive sacraments in the church, but they cannot enter another Catholic covenant of marriage unless they successfully obtain an annulment. However, until divorced Catholics obtain an annulment, they are still considered married to their ex-spouse in the eyes of the Catholic Church, and any relationship they enter with anyone else is considered "adultery."[9]

In any event, Sophia, for her part, lures Stan into the agreement with the promise of cash and assures Dorothy that she'll have to pretend she's married to her ex-husband for only one day (which ultimately convinces her to do it—because she was adamantly against it prior to this).

As can be expected, there's a monkey wrench thrown into the plans when rain turns into a full-fledged hurricane, forcing the Girls[10]—and Stan and Uncle Angelo—to all shelter in place until the storm passes. This means that Dorothy and Stan must pretend to be married longer than originally planned. This results in brutal—yet hilarious—exchanges between the former Mr. and Mrs., with Dorothy capping it off with "my feet have *wiiiings*, barf bag!"

A few days later, Uncle Angelo wishes Dorothy and Stan a happy wedding anniversary (for obvious reasons, Dorothy and Stan no longer celebrate the occasion)—and Rose stupidly suggests that the divorced couple renew their wedding vows. ("It'll be perfect! It's sweet, it's romantic, it's spontaneous. . . . It's the dumbest idea I've ever had.")

Dorothy then drags Stan into the living room. As Dorothy rips into Stan (par for the course in their relationship), Stan confesses that the past two days with Dorothy have brought back a lot of good memories, and he'd hoped that Dorothy would consider marrying him again. When Dorothy hesitates, Stan replies, "If God didn't want us married, he wouldn't have sent a priest."

Just then, Uncle Angelo walks into the living room and ultimately reveals that he isn't a priest, presumably sending a message from the Most High that Dorothy and Stan are, in fact, better off divorced. As it turns out, Angelo promised his "dear, sainted mother"[11] that he'd join the priesthood on her deathbed. But on the way to the seminary, Angelo met a waitress named Filomena in a trattoria, and she had a "behind so round, so firm, you got to fall down on your knees and cry out at its magnificent regal beauty." The exaggerated nature of his comment gets stares of confusion from the rest of his family, to whom he confesses, "I'm a butt man."

Angelo and Filomena then spent the next seventy-two years in wedded bliss, living in Sicily, until Filomena (presumably) dies. Assuming Angelo was eighteen when he attempted to enter the seminary and married Filomena shortly thereafter, Angelo would have been ninety years old at the time of "My Brother, My Father." If he was twenty-one, he'd have been ninety-three—and if he was twenty-five he'd have been ninety-seven. So either Angelo exaggerates the length of his marriage to Filomena, or he looks really good for his age. For what it's worth, Dana was sixty-four at the time the episode aired.

At that point, everyone else comes clean, as well: Rose and Blanche aren't nuns, and Stan and Dorothy are divorced. (Uncle Angelo: "I'm thrilled. I never liked him. He's a *yutz*.") At that very moment, the hurricane lets up, and everyone goes on their merry way.

Before Stan leaves, Sophia hands him the $50 bill she promised him for services rendered. Stan hesitates, then hands the money back to his ex-mother-in-law. "That's okay, Sophia. This one's on the house."

The family dynamics, the love-hate relationship with Stan, and the bittersweet ending all make "My Brother, My Father" one of the best Dorothy Zbornak episodes of *The Golden Girls*.

8. "Dorothy's Prized Pupil"

Season 2, Episode 21

"Dorothy's Prized Pupil" is one of the episodes of *The Golden Girls* that is more salient now than it ever was before. In a post-Trump era and amid the rise of xenophobic violence—especially toward the Latino American community[12]—watching an episode about a Mexican American getting violently deported can prove to be a difficult watch, even though the arrest isn't one that would happen "in real life."

Though Immigration and Customs Enforcement certainly has extended its powers since the 1980s, it could not do what was depicted in this episode, either then or now. In other words, immigration officials would need to do a lot more than see an undocumented immigrant's name in the papers to execute an arrest—and they would need an arrest warrant to even think about entering the home without even knocking first, as they did in this episode.[13]

But if viewers can recognize this episode as a product of its time—without holding it to a standard set by more modern, violent times—it proves to be a remarkable watch. Certainly, it's one of the best Dorothy Zbornak episodes of *The Golden Girls*.

One of Dorothy's pupils, Mario (played by none other than Mario Lopez), writes an essay about what it means to be an American. Dorothy, impressed by the submission, enters the essay into a contest, which he ultimately wins.

Dorothy and the Girls throw a surprise party for Mario to celebrate his win, only for the party to be interrupted by immigration officials who saw the announcement of Mario's win in the local paper and realized that he was an undocumented immigrant. (The show, however, used the phrase "illegal alien," as was accepted parlance at the time.)

After the immigration police take Mario into custody, he runs away, and Mario's uncle calls Dorothy in a panic. Dorothy, remembering that Mario's essay was about feeling like he was most at home in America when he was with his friends at the movies, runs to the theater, where she finds Mario hiding out and watching a gory film. Dorothy convinces him to face the music and see what he can do to stay in the country. Dorothy also agrees to go with Mario to see the immigration judge, hoping to convince him to let Mario stay, as he can do a lot of good if he does.

Unfortunately, Dorothy's efforts are in vain, because the judge rules that Mario must return to his home country. Dorothy, however, promises to find legal ways to keep Mario in the country, and the two share a compassionate hug goodbye before Mario must leave.

Once upon a time, teachers were seen as guardians of children—those who cared for them, those who loved them in a special, innocent way—and Arthur captures that essence in delicate detail. This unique, nostalgic depiction of teachers makes this one of the best Dorothy Zbornak episodes of *The Golden Girls*.

7. "Old Boyfriends"

Season 7, Episode 13

"Old Boyfriends" is an episode of *The Golden Girls* in which Dorothy and Sophia's relationship takes center stage. Although Sophia takes the lead in the "A" story, watching Dorothy help her mother navigate the intricacies of an unconventional relationship is a joy to watch—and a testament to their burgeoning friendship as adults, above and beyond their relationship as mother and daughter.

Sophia finds an ad in the personals column, which she responds to in the hopes of getting a date. In the days before dating apps like Tinder, Hinge, and

PlentyofFish, folks who were looking to get "booed up" did so by looking in the "personals" sections of newspapers or magazines. The personal section featured a short description of the person, what he or she was seeking, and included a post office box where potential suitors could mail letters—with photographs—to entice the person into a date. Those with more money to spend and more discriminate tastes could hire a professional matchmaker to connect them with more refined ladies and gentlemen.

When Sophia's date, Marvin, arrives, he's accompanied by a woman named Sarah, who introduces herself as Marvin's sister and accompanies Sophia and Marvin on their date.

Dorothy finds this unusual but ultimately doesn't stop her mother—after all, everyone involved in this relationship, however unconventional, is well in their eighties, so they're legal adults by every definition of the word—and Sophia goes on the date.

Later, Sophia reveals that although she and Marvin have gone out on a few dates, they haven't been alone and intimate yet, because Sarah is always there. Dorothy then offers to pick up Marvin and bring him back to the house so he and Sophia can be alone.

Although this "house date" initially goes well, with Sophia making overt romantic gestures toward Marvin, it ultimately goes right to hell when Marvin reveals that Sarah is his wife, not his sister.

When Sophia reveals the truth to Dorothy (who quips, "you don't get any lemonade" to Marvin), Dorothy speculates about what could be going on with Marvin and Sarah, given that this sort of "arrangement" was unconventional, to say the least.

"Isn't it obvious? They put an ad in the magazine to lure an unsuspecting cutie like me into their web of sex games. They want me to be their love slave," Sophia replies.

When Sarah arrives, Dorothy immediately kicks into protective daughter mode and demands to know why Sarah and Marvin lied to her mother about their relationship. When Sarah replies that she wanted to make sure that Sophia was "the one they wanted," Dorothy immediately panics.

"Then it *is* true!" she shouts incredulously. "You wanted my mother for *sex games*! Oh my God, this is *so* unbelievable!" (Sophia's response: "it's not *that* unbelievable!")

That's when Sarah reveals that she has a terminal illness, with only a few months to live, and wants to ensure that her husband finds a suitable mate to take care of him when she passes away. She tells Sophia that she won't be able to rest in peace unless she knows that Marvin has a suitable companion to be by his side.

After talking it over with the other Girls, Sophia decides that she's going to continue the relationship and ultimately marry Marvin. Incredulous, Dorothy demands to know what her mother is thinking. Sophia replies that she really cares for Marvin, and if they can all be happy together and not be alone in their final years, what's the big deal?

In the final scene, Dorothy proposes a toast to the new couple, saying, "I predict nothing but disaster and tragedy for everyone connected with this travesty of an idea."

Initially, Sophia and Marvin seem to agree to go forward with the idea despite Dorothy's protestations. But when Sarah recounts the story of how she and Marvin met, Sophia recognizes the look in their eyes as they stare at each other lovingly, and she backs out of the deal.

"I was doing this because I wanted to help, because I know what it's like to lose the most important person in your life, but this isn't right. Look, Marvin, I like you, but I saw how you looked at Sarah a moment ago. I don't think you could ever look at me that way," replies Sophia.

When Sarah freaks out and claims that she "wasted so much time" on Sophia, Dorothy replies, "the only time you're wasting is the time that you and Marvin should be spending together."

The interplay between mother and daughter—especially as mother navigates an unconventional relationship—makes "Old Boyfriends" one of the best Dorothy Zbornak episodes of *The Golden Girls*.

But one can't fully appreciate the show without Sophia's final line of the episode: "You can never really replace someone you've lost. And the next time I answer an ad, it'll be from one of Blanche's magazines. Those people know what they want."

6. "Two Rode Together"

Season 4, Episode 16

When a parent grows older and enters his or her twilight years, it's a natural filial reaction to want to protect that parent at all costs—all with the (futile) hope of keeping him or her alive forever.

This is an unrealistic wish, of course, but you can't fault Dorothy for trying with Sophia. That's the basis of "Two Rode Together," one of the best Dorothy Zbornak episodes of *The Golden Girls*.

After another one of Sophia's friends dies, Dorothy feels that she and Sophia aren't making the most of the limited time they have left—so she decides to book a mother-daughter trip to Walt Disney World.

Although Sophia thinks she's getting ready to ride Space Mountain—one of the most popular rides at the park—Dorothy instead books a hotel where she and her mother can take a trip down memory lane as they watch slides, talk about old home movies, and look at family pictures.

As can be expected, this does not go over well with Sophia, who is desperate to ride Space Mountain. But even when she tries to escape and get on the ride, she's confronted with Florida rains, which naturally close the park.

Eventually, Sophia levels with Dorothy. "This weekend could have been a lot of fun, until you decided that we were going to spend some 'quality time,'" she says.

When Dorothy protests, Sophia reminds her what the *real* meaning of "quality time" is.

"Dorothy, this isn't *On Golden Pond*, and you're not Jane Fonda," she says. "Quality time has to come naturally; it happens when you're not thinking about it. Like when we're cutting vegetables. That's quality time."

Sophia uses an allegory to drive the point home: When she was a little girl living in Sicily, Sophia loved fireflies. She loved them so much, in fact, that she used to catch them in jars so she could watch them light up any time she wanted to—but every time she caught a firefly and put it in a jar, it ended up dying.

Aside from eventually learning to punch holes in the jar lids, Sophia hypothesized that those fireflies were like all of life's magical moments: "You can't capture them forever, no matter what Kodak tells you."

Ultimately, Dorothy takes Sophia for a ride on Space Mountain, which she calls "quality time."

What we learn here is not only how important it is to enjoy magic moments in the moment—rather than forcing them to happen—but to listen to our parents when they tell us what they want. After all, who knows better than they do? They lived in their bodies long before their children came along.

It's easy, then, to see why this is one of the best Dorothy Zbornak episodes of *The Golden Girls*.

5. "Questions and Answers"
Season 7, Episode 17

The beloved long-running game show *Jeopardy!* is used as a backdrop for the "A" story line of this episode, which happens to be one of the best Dorothy Zbornak episodes of *The Golden Girls*.

When the game show—hosted at that time by the late, great Alex Trebek—comes to Miami to hold auditions, Dorothy works overtime to try out for the show. She stays up late, studying like she's in school, and even has a dream about being featured on the show (where one of her opponents is Charley Dietz, played by David Leisure, who was a member of the main cast of *The Golden Girls* spin-off *Empty Nest*).

Incidentally, there's an interesting backstory behind *Empty Nest*. Originally, *Golden Girls* season 2, episode 26—which was titled "Empty Nests"—was supposed to be the pilot episode of the spin-off. The episode—starring Paul Dooley and the legendary Rita Moreno—had a completely different premise than what *Empty Nest* would become, and it didn't test well with audiences at all. In a 2012 interview with the Emmy Foundation, Moreno trashed the show, saying that the episode desperately needed a re-write from show creator Susan Harris, but she was sick that week, so the writing was left to the other writers (who clearly couldn't handle the task). They kept changing Moreno's character so many times that by the time she was ready to shoot in front of a live studio audience, she had to do "10, 15 takes," as she explained.

"Every day they kept changing my character, to the extent that by the time we got to do it in front of an audience I couldn't remember Line 1 because the attitudes had changed so many times. That was the most embarrassing experience," she said.[14]

One year later, the show was revamped with a whole new cast, and *Empty Nest* debuted after *The Golden Girls* in 1988.

Ultimately, when it's time to audition for *Jeopardy!* Dorothy nails all the questions that she's asked but isn't picked for the show. When she asks the producers why, they make it abundantly clear that although they appreciated her intelligence, they didn't appreciate her arrogance. Because she was so unlikable, she wasn't picked.

When Dorothy seeks comfort from Sophia, she reminds Dorothy that she was the same way in school, which is why nobody liked her.

Some fans of the show believe the writers depicted Dorothy harshly during the final two seasons as an act of "revenge" because Bea Arthur had made it clear that she wasn't interested in pursuing the show past the seventh season. Although there's no direct evidence of that, it's interesting to note that Dorothy seemed to be the target of more direct and overt criticism in the final two seasons than in prior seasons.

Regardless, the best type of love is, sometimes, tough love—and that's true at any age. Certainly we can all learn to be better people, even later in life. Dorothy is certainly one of the most beloved *Golden Girls* characters, which is why her evolution and growth—albeit done while kicking and screaming—is a wonder to watch. This certainly makes this episode of *The Golden Girls* one of the best featuring Dorothy Zbornak.

4. "The Actor"
Season 2, Episode 14

As a sort of meta nod and a wink to their careers, the Girls often found themselves participating in community theater productions. "The Actor," from the second season of the show, is an episode that features the Girls participating in one such performance. Although all the other Girls have star turns in the play (and the episode), it's Dorothy who steals the spotlight and makes this episode of *The Golden Girls* one of her best.

Dorothy, Rose, and Blanche all audition for the lead role in the local community theater's production of a play that's meant to be a spoof of *Picnic*, which stars a stunning actor named Patrick Vaughn[15] in the lead role.

As might be expected, Blanche goes out of her way to seduce Patrick— even going so far as to wear balloons in her bra to entice him (which ultimately pop, loudly, when he hugs her).

Unfortunately, Blanche's efforts are in vain, as are those of the other Girls, because none of them gets the lead part. The role, instead, goes to a woman named Phyllis, who immediately becomes public enemy number one in Blanche's eyes. But as some sort of consolation prize (if you can look at it that way), Patrick begins a clandestine affair with all three of the Girls—*and* the actual lead of the play, Phyllis.

On the day of the production, Dorothy must fill in as the sheriff. And it's Dorothy—dressed in her sheriff's outfit, no less—who first discovers the truth about Patrick's philandering ways and confronts him onstage during the play. Eventually, Rose, Blanche, and Phyllis all join in, and a flustered Patrick stomps off the stage in a huff.

That prompts a standing ovation from the audience, which thinks they're witnessing part of the play, and the actors take a bow to maintain the facade.

That level of chutzpah—that brazen willingness to confront someone obviously in the wrong, even in the middle of a live production—is one of Dorothy's hallmark traits. Because she was able to pull it off in front of a rapt audience—*and* receive a standing ovation for it—"The Actor" has become known as one of the best Dorothy Zbornak episodes of *The Golden Girls*.

3. "Snap Out of It"

Season 6, Episode 4

The Girls always behaved compassionately and were always the first to help the less fortunate, be it on the small screen or in real life. In "Snap Out of It," Dorothy and Sophia volunteer for Meals on Wheels, and the compassion they demonstrate in this episode makes this one of the best Dorothy Zbornak episodes of *The Golden Girls*.

Different states and cities have Meals on Wheels programs, but the goal of them all is the same: to deliver fresh, hot meals to the less fortunate. Volunteers provide these meals at no cost to the recipient, as well as wellness checks and light conversation. Donations to the organization are tax deductible, and some local programs—like the Meals on Wheels in Rockland County, New York—provide transportation to local senior centers, which also helps to reduce loneliness and isolation.

When Dorothy and Sophia are in a building handing out Meals on Wheels trays, Dorothy leaves a tray out for a man who is what the show description calls "an aging hippie."[16] Dorothy calls her mother's attention to the man, provoking a typical Sophia response: "Just be back before midnight, pussycat."

Dorothy takes it upon herself to slowly reintegrate the hippie, Jimmy, back into society, enticing him by naming all seven defendants in the Chicago Seven trial.

Incidentally, Dorothy's attempts to reintegrate Jimmy back into society are a *terrible* idea. According to the *Journal of the Royal Society of Medicine*,[17] extreme reclusiveness cannot be cured by merely taking the person into society, as Dorothy attempts to do. In fact, experts say that to successfully reintegrate, the recluse must undergo intensive therapy and should go out in public only with the aid of a professional until she or he is fully comfortable again.

Unfortunately, Dorothy doesn't have much luck—and in fact further drives him into a reclusive state—but she demonstrates a level of kindness, caring, and compassion—almost without a second thought—that shows that there's more to her than simply being the sarcastic Golden Girl. It also makes "Snap Out of It" one of the best episodes of *The Golden Girls* that features Dorothy Zbornak.

2. "The Case of the Libertine Belle"

Season 7, Episode 2

"The Case of the Libertine Belle"—which some fans speculate is a hat tip to Bea Arthur's good friend Angela Lansbury and her hit show *Murder, She*

Wrote—is a favorite of devoted fans of *The Golden Girls*. It's easy to see why: it's sharp, it's funny, and it has all the elements of a good television show, including murder, intrigue, and humor. Although all four of the Girls shine in their own way, it's Dorothy's one-woman show that makes this episode one of her best.

Blanche, who has been working in a museum for all seven seasons, now wants a promotion at the museum, which involves working as an assistant under the very handsome Kendall Nesbitt.[18] Angling for the promotion, Blanche decides to book a murder mystery weekend at a local hotel and invites everyone from the museum to participate in the festivities.

Unfortunately, the weekend doesn't last long—because Dorothy single-handedly solves the first murder mystery. Of course, things get hairy when a seemingly *real* murder takes place, and the presumed victim is none other than Kendall Nesbitt himself.

But it's Dorothy's interactions with Sophia that make this one of the best Dorothy Zbornak episodes of *The Golden Girls*.

When Dorothy, for example, demonstrates how a throat is cut for the first murder mystery, she grabs her mother's neck to demonstrate her theory.

"A throat is almost always cut from behind," she says. "Being right-handed, I would slash from left to right, but since the knife was found to the left of the victim, we can deduce that the murderer is left-handed. Notice that Gloria like most left-handed people wears her wristwatch on her right wrist!"

When Kendall Nesbitt becomes the next "murder victim"—though, at the end of the episode, it's revealed that he too was part of the murder mystery ruse—Sophia begs Dorothy to help with the investigation.

"Oh, Ma, that was a game—this is life!" Dorothy replies exasperatedly.

"Oh yeah, you were never really good at life," quips Sophia.

At the beginning of the episode, when Blanche reveals the plans for the murder mystery weekend to her housemates, Dorothy gushes in excitement.

"I have read every word Dashiell Hammett and Raymond Chandler ever wrote," she squeals. "Sam Spade and Philip Marlowe have become a part of me . . . 'She had more curves than the Monaco grand prix and was twice as dangerous. Her jewelry was mute testimony that Charlie Chaplin wasn't the only tramp who hit it big in this town.'"

Cue Sophia's interminable wit: "You do this on first dates, don't you, Dorothy?"

The exchanges between onscreen mother and daughter are nothing short of legendary, and that makes "The Case of the Libertine Belle" one of the best Dorothy Zbornak episodes of *The Golden Girls*.

1. "One Flew out the Cuckoo's Nest"

Series Finale

In terms of happy endings, few episodes—if any—are quite as satisfying as "One Flew out the Cuckoo's Nest." The two-part series finale of *The Golden Girls* finally gave Dorothy her much-needed happily ever after, following seven seasons spent chasing some of the best—and worst—men in Miami and ending up with her ex-husband, Stan, on more than a few occasions.

When Blanche's uncle, Lucas (portrayed by the legendary Leslie Nielsen), comes to town, Blanche tries to foist him on someone else so that she can go on a date. That someone turns out to be Dorothy, whom Blanche coaxes into a date with her uncle by telling her all sorts of tall tales—as is typical of Blanche to do—which she also does with Lucas to entice *him* to go on a date with Dorothy.

The beginning of Dorothy's date with Lucas doesn't go well, as they stare at one another in awkward silence. But once they begin talking, Dorothy and Lucas discover Blanche's scheming ways. They then plot revenge on Blanche, deciding to tell her that they'd fallen in love and decided to get married.

The next morning, Lucas and Dorothy put their plan into action and begin expressing their love for one another. When Lucas then proposes to Dorothy—and Dorothy accepts—Blanche goes into a tailspin, deciding to break up the engagement at any cost.

But to keep up the charade, Lucas and Dorothy must continue to spend time with one another. As they do, they fall in love. At the end of the first episode, Lucas proposes to Dorothy again, asking her to marry him "for real."

Dorothy naturally accepts—which leaves Rose, Blanche, and Sophia confused, since they thought Lucas and Dorothy were engaged already.

In the second episode, the wedding planning has been underway for more than two months, and Dorothy and Lucas apparently are having the best sex of their lives—so much so, in fact, that Dorothy says, "we named it!" (At the end of the series finale, it's revealed that their sex is named "Freddie Peterson.")

The day of the wedding finally arrives, and Dorothy hops in the limo to the church. Unfortunately for her, the limo's chauffeur is none other than her ex-husband, Stan, trying his best to halt his ex-wife's impending wedding. Ultimately, though, Dorothy persists, and Stan relents and drives her to the church to get married.

Incidentally, Dorothy's wedding dress, a frequent topic of discussion on fan message boards for the show, was designed by longtime show designer Judy Evans. Although Bea Arthur was quick to lavish praise on Evans, she disliked the wedding dress she wore on the series finale. "Don't get me started on the awful wedding dress Dorothy wore in the finale, as she married Lucas," author Jim Colucci said in an interview.[19] "You know the one—with the weird loops of white ribbon in a *V* on the neckline that look like used rolls of toilet paper. Bea wasn't one to criticize Judy's work, because she usually loved Dorothy's outfits, but even she said that was the one time she thought something Dorothy wore was ugly."

But it's the final scene that wrenches people's hearts even to this day.

Sure, it was the last-ever episode of *The Golden Girls*—and sure, it's what Arthur wanted above everything else—but that didn't make the breakaway any less emotional.

It starts with Sophia informing Dorothy that she's not going to Atlanta to live with her and Lucas—"frankly, I think I was in the way the first time"—before telling Dorothy that it's time to leave the nest.

"There's something I want to tell you. It's been my great privilege to be your friend as an adult. To spend these years with you," Sophia says.

"No, Ma. It was my privilege," Dorothy responds. "And that self-confidence is the greatest gift that you could have ever given me."

Then it's time to say goodbye to everyone else.

"Dorothy, you don't have to say anything," says Rose. "I mean, what can you say about seven years of fights and laughter. Secrets. Cheesecake."

"It's been an experience that I'll always keep very close to my heart," Dorothy replies, the tears openly flowing now. "And that these are memories that I'll wrap myself in when the world gets cold, and I forget that there are people who are warm and loving and . . ."

It continues in this vein, with laughter and tears in equal measure, until the final embrace of the three remaining Girls: Rose, Sophia, and Blanche.

According to the cast, the tears that Dorothy cried at the end of the scene were genuine. Although they tried not to be nostalgic about *The Golden Girls* ending, they all certainly had grown to like each other—and they very much thought of each other like a "family."[20]

From the genuine tears flowing from the whole cast to Dorothy and Sophia's delightful final exchange, to the "happily ever after" that Dorothy so richly deserved, "One Flew out the Cuckoo's Nest" is the best Dorothy Zbornak episode of *The Golden Girls* and the perfect send-off to a legendary show.

SOPHIA PETRILLO: THE TOP TEN BEST EPISODES

The sassy Sicilian—who had no less a fan than the Queen Mother of England—was the glue that held the other three Girls together. So big of a fan was Queen Elizabeth II's mother of the show that she invited the four Girls to perform live for her as part of the Royal Variety Performance at the London Palladium in 1988. Although many of the jokes were toned down for British sensibilities, the Queen Mother reportedly laughed the hardest at a Blanche joke. When Dorothy asked how long Blanche waited to have sex after her husband died, Sophia interjected, "Until the paramedics came." But that's nothing compared to Princess Diana's love of the show: reportedly, the late Lady Di, Queen front man Freddie Mercury, and actress Cleo Rocos used to turn on *The Golden Girls*, turn down the volume, and improvise lines from the show with "much naughtier storylines."[21]

The three younger Girls—in terms of the show's characters, of course, because in real life, Getty was younger than Arthur and White—looked to Sophia as a mother figure, someone to give them guidance and advice in place of their own mothers, who had died long before.

Even when she was being her usual caustic self—even when her filter was broken, and she said the first thing that came to mind—Sophia always did it with an undercurrent of love. There was no malice in Sophia's honesty, no need to harm people who were already vulnerable—just a straight-up need to tell the truth and shame the devil, as the old saying goes. Because, after all, only the people who truly love you will tell you the truth—no matter how ugly it is.

But there were some episodes in which Sophia's character shined brighter than the rest. Here are the top ten Sophia Petrillo episodes of *The Golden Girls*.

10. "Sisters and Other Strangers"
Season 5, Episode 21

In this episode, Blanche gets the "A" story, and Dorothy gets the "B" story, but it's Sophia who adds the seasoning to two stories that otherwise would not have stood the test of time. The "A" story is about Blanche and her sister Charmaine[22] fighting about speculation that the latter's best-selling novel *Vixen: Story of a Woman* is about Blanche. Charmaine ultimately reveals that *Vixen: Story of a Woman* is a roman à clef: "My book is based on my life!"

Blanche: "Oh please. That book just drips Blanche Devereaux. Only the names have been changed to protect the satisfied!"

The "B" story is about Stan's cousin Magda,[23] who stops by the house while visiting the United States from Czechoslovakia. Today, the country is divided into two sovereign countries—the Czech Republic and the Slovak Republic (also known as Slovakia)—but prior to that, Czechoslovakia was formed in 1918. After World War II, Czechoslovakia became part of the Soviet bloc, which was part of a group of countries that were under the influence of the then–Soviet Union. In 1989, the country peacefully deposed its government in what was known as the Velvet Revolution and split into two sovereign nation-states.

In fact, the Velvet Revolution is referenced in this episode of *The Golden Girls*, when Rose makes a cake depicting Magda's escape from the country, which she thought was violent and included barbed wire and barking dogs, but in reality was peaceful. Naturally, Sophia ate the candy dogs off the cake: "Well, they're good dogs, Rose."

Neither story makes much sense—and neither story seems to be connected to the other. That's where Sophia's quips come in, and she starts off with a bang, criticizing Dorothy's cooking ("Wouldn't it be easier to just put a pillow over my face while I sleep? Just set the table," Sophia snarls), and doesn't let up until the very end ("Dorothy, move the table—I wanna do a cartwheel," she mutters sarcastically).

And let's not forget the interlude story that Dorothy tells about Sophia letting Gloria get away with ruining her favorite doll (Dorothy: "She was *my* favorite!" Sophia: "*Gloria* was the one who had to get a rabies shot!").

Sophia is at her most fiery—and her most witty—in this episode, making it one of the best Sophia Petrillo episodes of *The Golden Girls*.

9. "Yes, We Have No Havanas"

Season 4, Episode 1

In the season 4 premiere, Sophia and Blanche violate the "girl code" when it comes to dating and end up spending the rest of the episode roasting each other. Although some modern commentators argue against the "girl code," claiming that it's nothing more than an anti-feminist attempt to "police" women's behavior, it's probably a good idea to avoid dating the men your best friend once dated. If nothing else, it's bad form.[24]

There were no limits to either Blanche or Sophia's insults, and to watch an octogenarian fight for—and ultimately win over—a man (who ended up dying—though, thankfully, not in either Blanche or Sophia's bed when he finally kicked off) makes "Yes, We Have No Havanas" one of the best Sophia Petrillo episodes of *The Golden Girls*.

As the name of the title indicates, Blanche entices a Cuban cigar mogul named Fidel Santiago.[25] Although things go relatively well, it wasn't the romance of the century. Nevertheless, Blanche is devastated when Fidel ghosts her after their date, so Dorothy, Rose, and Blanche decide to enjoy a "girls' night out" together to lift Blanche's spirits.

While the three Girls are walking on the boardwalk enjoying ice cream together after a very pleasant dinner, Blanche realizes that Fidel is on the arm of another woman, though initially no one sees who the other woman is.

As it turns out, it's Sophia.

"He's a man, I'm a woman, I've got what it takes, and he knows how to use it," Sophia says snappily, defending herself against Blanche's accusations. (This clearly doesn't go over well with Dorothy, who threatens to "lose her lunch" if Sophia gets any more graphic about her sex life.)

After some back-and-forth, Fidel proposes that he'd like to continue seeing both Blanche and Sophia—and, in his defense, he says that it's a decision that they will have to make among themselves.

Blanche, naturally, is horrified by the suggestion—"Blanche Devereaux has *never* shared a man!"

"Or a pizza," Sophia quips.

"And what is that supposed to mean, you wrinkled old crow?" Blanche snaps back.

With that, the rivalry is on. The back-and-forth between Blanche and Sophia includes some legendary burns ("Beat it, you fifty-year-old mattress!" "You're only going to sit in an inch of water?" "There's always room for Jell-O.") followed by shared mourning after Fidel ends up dying . . . and half of Miami's female senior citizen population is in attendance, because it turns out he was dating *all* of them.

Fidel's slutty ways aside, Sophia's legendary burns make "Yes, We Have No Havanas" one of the best Sophia Petrillo episodes of *The Golden Girls*.

8. "Girls Just Wanna Have Fun . . . before They Die"
Season 6, Episode 10

Though Sophia was nowhere near as promiscuous as Dorothy, Rose, and definitely not Blanche, she certainly got her fair share of notches on her bedpost. For an octogenarian, that's nothing if not impressive—and it proves that grandmothers don't just shrivel up and die when they turn fifty. In "Girls

Just Wanna Have Fun . . . before They Die," Sophia shows that even the oldest, most unlikely woman can be seen as a sex symbol and that makes this one of the best Sophia Petrillo episodes of *The Golden Girls*.

In this episode, Cesar Romero[26] plays Sophia's new boyfriend[27] Tony, who proves to be quite the lover—so much so, in fact, that Sophia finds herself falling in love with him. Flummoxed by this development, she asks Blanche for advice.

Blanche takes it upon herself to give Sophia a makeover—"I took an eighty-four-year-old woman and made her look like a sixty-five-year-old drag queen"—and even Dorothy remarks on her mother's newfound popularity ("Ma, don't do anything I wouldn't do!"—to which Sophia replies, "I think I crossed that line when I got a date").

Unfortunately—as might be expected—Blanche's advice doesn't work as well for Sophia. Sophia slips up and tells Tony that she loves him—and he doesn't respond in kind. This naturally devastates Sophia, and she tells Tony that she never wants to see him again.

Thankfully, it works out in the end: Blanche tells Sophia that the advice she gives works on "her type of men"—the type of men with which she has footloose and fancy-free relationships, not the type of men who want to settle down with women like Sophia. (Blanche also gives advice to Rose throughout the episode—which is the "B" story line—because Rose is required to stay celibate because of a drought in St. Olaf, and as one can imagine, Blanche's advice doesn't go well there either.)

Sophia finally agrees to meet with Tony again—and Tony reveals that he can't tell a woman he loves her, because he hasn't done so since he lost his wife. At that point, Sophia and Tony bond over shared losses—Sophia found it difficult to say "I love you" to a man after Sal died, too—and they work things out.

Seeing Sophia as a sexy, vibrant human being—even as an octogenarian—makes "Girls Just Wanna Have Fun . . . before They Die" one of the best Sophia Petrillo episodes of *The Golden Girls*.

7. "To Catch a Neighbor"

Season 2, Episode 24

"To Catch a Neighbor" is yet another episode of *The Golden Girls* that's steeped in absurdity. There is so much that is procedurally incorrect (at least as far as police tactics are concerned) with the entire premise of the episode—but then again, no one ever thought *The Golden Girls* was a police procedural. Still, this episode is a great chance to see a young George Clooney in one of his first major television appearances—and it is also one of the greatest Sophia Petrillo episodes of *The Golden Girls*.

The Girls invite their new neighbors, the McDowells, over for dinner. But shortly after they leave, two detectives from the Miami-Dade Police Department arrive and inform the Girls that the seemingly lovely McDowells are brokers of stolen jewels. The detectives—Clooney plays a junior detective and Italian Canadian actor Joseph Campanella plays a senior detective—then ask the ladies to stake out the couple at their homes, to which they agree to.[28]

The success of the stakeout is, in large part, due to Sophia's ability to think on her feet. When Mrs. McDowell makes an unannounced visit to the Girls, she catches the two detectives in the living room and demands to know who they are. It's Sophia to the rescue, explaining that Al is her son and Bobby is her grandson. But during Mrs. McDowell's unannounced visit, she invites the Girls to her home for a dinner party, which the detectives think is a perfect opportunity to use one of the Girls to plant a wiretap in their home.[29] Dorothy, who is quickly developing feelings for Al, volunteers to do it—and manages to pull it off.

As can be expected, the wiretap is successful—the detectives get the information they need, and they immediately make a move on the McDowells, but Bobby is shot (though not fatally) in the melee.

When Al finally asks Dorothy out on a date after the excitement winds down, Dorothy declines—she can't take a chance on a guy who runs *into* danger and not away from it—though she's sad that she must do so. Her mother's comfort gets her through the sadness—and it's comfort that's much needed.

Even though Sophia no longer had a filter thanks to the terrible stroke she suffered, she knew how to be a loving, gentle mother to her daughter when she needed it, and she could think on her feet, outsmarting even the toughest criminal. Watching her fire on all cylinders makes "To Catch a Neighbor" one of the best Sophia Petrillo episodes of *The Golden Girls*.

6. "Long Day's Journey into Marinara"
Season 2, Episode 19

There was much more to Sophia's family than just her children. In fact, Sophia was at her best with her siblings: in addition to her brother, Angelo,

Sophia had a sister named Angela,[30] with whom she had a difficult relationship. Their strained relationship takes center stage in "Long Day's Journey into Marinara," which also happens to be one of the best Sophia Petrillo episodes of *The Golden Girls*.

A send-up of *Long Day's Journey into Night*,[31] "Long Day's Journey into Marinara" highlights the age-old rivalry between Sophia and Angela. As Sicilians, who are notorious the world over for holding grudges that last generations, it's no surprise that Sophia and Angela's rancor began as teenagers. However, they resolved their feud in a previous episode (season 2, episode 12—"The Sisters") and have a good relationship.[32]

So good is their relationship now, in fact, that Dorothy suggests that her Aunt Angela move to Miami to be closer to Sophia—and even offers to let her stay with the Girls until she finds a place of her own.

This naturally sends Sophia over the edge, and she quickly reminds Dorothy that Angela has always wanted what Sophia has. And this prompts petty rivalries—including accusations of Angela stealing Sophia's face cream[33] and denture cream—until Angela finally finds a suitable apartment. As it turns out, Angela goes to the senior center to meet a few people. One of the men mentions that he's looking for a new roommate to share his beautiful beachside apartment, so Angela decides to take him up on the offer.

When Angela's new roommate arrives to help her move her stuff, none other than Tony DelVecchio—Sophia's boyfriend—shows up. Lo and behold, Angela is now Tony's new roommate, which opens the sisters' rivalry wounds and convinces Sophia that Angela is trying to steal her man.

After they hurl a series of Sicilian curses on one another, Sophia cools off, only to call Tony and hear "female noises" in the background, suggesting that Angela is in bed with Tony.[34]

Sophia stomps over to the apartment and finds both Angela and Tony in bathrobes, but they both explain that they're not sleeping with one another.

However, shortly after Tony professes his undying love to Sophia, another woman—also in a bathrobe—emerges from Tony's bedroom. As it turns out, Tony *was* two-timing Sophia but not with Angela. Nevertheless, when Angela discovers Tony's treachery, she teams up with Sophia, and the sisters take turns cracking him over the head with their purses ("you've insulted my sister's honor!").

Getty and Walker are brilliant together, and they play off one another just as well. "Long Day's Journey into Marinara" is one of the best Sophia Petrillo episodes of *The Golden Girls* for good reason.

5. "Grab That Dough"

Season 3, Episode 16

"Grab That Dough" is such a fan favorite—even today—that it was featured as one of the five episodes of *Forever Golden! A Celebration of The Golden Girls*, which aired in theaters for a limited time in 2021. But in addition to being a fan-favorite episode, it's also one of the best Sophia Petrillo episodes of *The Golden Girls*.

Sophia mails away for tickets to a game show[35]—titled, as the name of the episode implies, "Grab That Dough"—but she mistakenly gives the show her address in Sicily. By the time she gets the tickets for the show, the Girls have only twenty-four hours to get to Hollywood, California, to participate.

Somehow, they manage to book flights and hotel rooms in short order,[36] but nothing goes smoothly after that. The airline lost their luggage, which means they must go to the game show wearing the same clothes they'd been wearing for several hours.

Worse yet, the hotel concierge reveals that because the Girls arrived at the hotel too late, their rooms were given away, and there were no vacancies that night. However, as an act of "generosity," she allows the Girls to sleep in the hotel lobby. That only makes things worse, because their purses are stolen in the middle of the night.

But not even *that* stops the Girls' resolve—Sophia had the tickets hiding in her bra—so off they go to the show.

When they get there, they're greeted by the female cohost of the show—a young, pretty Vanna White–like analogue—and Blanche makes an uncharacteristic slut-shaming remark: "I just want you to know that the pictures of you in that sleazy, girlie magazine were so tastefully done. By the way, is that a real English bobby [cop] spanking you there in front of Big Ben?"[37] And, naturally, they all begin fawning over the host—Guy Corbin[38]—whom Blanche deems "such a hunk."

But before the Girls can compete on the show, Dorothy strategizes with Blanche to play with the Kaplan brothers, who had won several thousand dollars on game shows prior to this one. When Dorothy and Blanche break the news to Sophia and Rose, neither takes the news well.

"You're going to team up with these two *yutzes*?" demands Sophia.

"Cut the bull! You don't want us because you think we're too stupid!" shouts Rose.

"Get bent! We'll cream you!" shouts Sophia.

Guy Corbin then introduces all the contestants—calling Dorothy a woman who lives in Miami with her mother "who will pay anyone to take her out on a date," telling Blanche that "there must be a typo" when she claims to be forty, suggesting that Rose is the woman "most likely to get stuck in a tuba," and claiming Sophia is a "grandmother of six."[39]

When he gets to Sophia, she snaps in her usual fashion. "No, Guy, Rose is my daughter now," she spits, "and you, Dorothy, are the biggest disappointment to hit the streets since the AMC Pacer."[40]

As can be expected, the Kaplan brothers are a bust on the show—they don't answer any of the questions correctly—and it isn't long before Sophia and Rose are ahead in the game. Sophia brags about it during the commercial break—"So, Dorothy, how does it feel to have a big fat zero?"—but Dorothy ultimately pulls her team ahead in the lightning round, when she steps into the machine and grabs $900 from the Magic Money Machine.

There's some consolation for Rose and Sophia: each win $100.

Dorothy and Blanche then must decide whether they want to keep their winnings or trade it for a prize that's hidden behind a curtain. Stupidly, Blanche insists on choosing what's behind "the *win-duh*." When the "prize" is revealed, it's an electric skillet and a lifetime supply of soup.

Needless to say, the entire "Grab That Dough" trip was a bust. Fortunately, the Girls make up on the plane—it was either make up or watch *The Three Amigos* on the plane's big screen via headset[41]—but Sophia can't help but get off one last sarcastic remark.

"Dorothy, you let greed cloud your judgment. Money blinded you. You turned your back on people you love. You did a terrible, terrible thing. It's unforgivable," she remarks.

When Dorothy asks her mother how she can make it right, Sophia demands $100.

Dorothy negotiates the price down to $50.

"Done. I love you," replies Sophia.

It's Sophia's adventure—the other Girls are just along for the ride—and she ties it all together with a very neat bow at the end. It's no wonder that this fan-favorite episode is one of the best Sophia Petrillo episodes of *The Golden Girls*.

4. "Isn't It Romantic"

Season 2, Episode 5

Even though *The Golden Girls* scored several points for its portrayal of the more sensitive subjects of the time, it was still very much a product of its time. There were plenty of things that the show did that wouldn't be done today—some of which have been discussed in the context of other episodes—but there were also many more things that the show did that held up surprisingly well.

"Isn't It Romantic"—which was hailed as progressive for its time—is one such show. Hailed for its sensitive portrayal of lesbians, it's also one of the best Sophia Petrillo episodes of *The Golden Girls*, because we see firsthand how her love as a mother is unconditional.

The premise is simple: Dorothy's old school friend, Jean (played by former beauty queen Lois Nettleton), comes to town after she loses her longtime partner, Pat. Because of the gender ambiguity of the name "Pat," Blanche and Rose think that Jean lost a *husband*.

But Dorothy knows better—because she has known her friend for so long—and Sophia also claims that she knew because "a mother knows!" Dorothy, however, chooses not to "out" her friend,[42] mostly because she was afraid that Rose wouldn't understand the concept of homosexuality.[43]

Despite this secret, Rose and Jean hit it off quite nicely—to the point that Jean thinks she's falling in love with Rose. Rose, naturally, is clueless about what's going on and only catches on when Jean confesses her love to Rose when she thinks Rose is sound asleep.

To Rose's credit, she doesn't flip out or go into a "gay panic"[44]—rather, she says, "I have to admit I don't understand these kinds of feelings, but if I did understand, if I were, you know, like you, I think I'd be very flattered and proud that you thought of me that way."

Blanche, for her part, is *outraged* that Jean prefers Rose over her—once she figured out the difference between *Lebanese* and *lesbian*, of course.

But it's Sophia whose responses steal the show.

While lying in bed together, Dorothy asks Sophia what she would do if she found out that one of her children identified as gay.[45] After thinking a bit, Sophia responds, "If one of my kids was gay, I wouldn't love him one bit less. I would wish him all the happiness in the world."

This was after she gave some levity to the situation—which could be a bit uncomfortable for those in "middle America" who weren't familiar with homosexuality. "Jean is a nice person. She happens to like girls instead of guys. Some people like cats instead of dogs. Frankly I'd rather live with a lesbian than a cat. Unless a lesbian sheds. Then I don't know," she said.

All in all, Sophia proves to be the most understanding—and tolerant—of Jean's sexual orientation, which was nothing short of revolutionary for the time—and even more revolutionary when one considers that Sophia was a member of the Greatest Generation and not a baby boomer. Writing for *Logo*

TV, Louis Peitzman hails the episode as a watershed moment in LGBTQIA representation.

"Aside from a couple jokes about women turning gay because they're rejected by men—none of which are any worse than what you'd hear on many current sitcoms—the episode is really very progressive," he writes.[46] "Jean is treated with as much dignity as any other one-off *Golden Girls* guest, and no one seems to have any problem with her sexuality. Even the old Sicilian woman pledges her support for the gays."

How can anyone resist the charm of "the old Sicilian woman" in this episode? It's no wonder that "Isn't It Romantic" is one of the best Sophia Petrillo episodes of *The Golden Girls*.

3. "Valentine's Day"
Season 4, Episode 15

Like many other episodes of *The Golden Girls*, "Valentine's Day" is a flashback episode, which means there's no single cohesive story line that runs through the show, though there's a common theme (in this case, Valentine's Day).

Sophia, however, is still the standout character, which is why "Valentine's Day" is one of the best Sophia Petrillo episodes of *The Golden Girls*.

In this episode, the Girls—except for Sophia—have Valentine's Day dates and subsequently get stood up. So they sit around the table and reminisce about Valentine's Days gone by.

Sophia is first up, and she recounts that she and Sal were at a St. Valentine's Day Massacre.[47] Naturally, Dorothy calls shenanigans on the claim, to which Sophia replies, "I wasn't at *the* St. Valentine's Day Massacre. I said I was at *a* St. Valentine's Day Massacre."

Ultimately, the episode proves to be a classic in other ways—the Girls visit a nudist camp, Blanche helps a gay man propose to his partner by telling the story about how George proposed to her, and the Girls go shopping for condoms (which concludes with Dorothy screaming "condoms, Rose! Condoms! Condoms! *Condoms!*" in the middle of a drugstore)—but Sophia caps it off with a cherry when she leaves to spend a delightful evening with Julio Iglesias (Enrique's father, who was quite famous for a time).

Seeing Sophia land the heartthrob of the 1980s makes this one of the most satisfying episodes of *The Golden Girls*—and definitely one of Sophia Petrillo's best.

2. "The Days and Nights of Sophia Petrillo"
Season 4, Episode 2

"The Days and Nights of Sophia Petrillo" is an episode that proves that vitality comes at any age—and definitely one of the best featuring Sophia Petrillo.

The Girls promise to spend the day at home cleaning the house—meanwhile, Sophia informs them that she's off to the market to buy a nectarine. Dorothy, as any concerned daughter would do, tells Blanche and Rose that she's worried about her mother: she goes to the market every day for a nectarine and nothing else.

Somehow, though, the Girls never really get around to cleaning the house—they spend the day barely working on any projects of note but have plenty of time to sit around the table gossiping, telling old stories, and noshing on various treats (including the ubiquitous cheesecake).

Sophia, meanwhile, did much more than buy a nectarine.

She created a scene in the grocery store so the grocer could pick out the best nectarine for her.

She campaigned for her friend, Claire, to get a refund on a cut of meat that wasn't up to par (*and* got the friend to pay for her nectarine in the process).

At the boardwalk, she conducted a jazz band made up of fellow senior citizens—who played "When the Saints Go Marching In" to raise money for the senior center—and she made them work *hard* for their pay.

She volunteered at the hospital, where she ran into a young AIDS patient named Sam, and gave him her nectarine to "keep his strength up." She gave a lonely old lady a whole tray of flowers that were meant for an entire floor of patients.

Sophia was nothing if not a busy lady.

When she finally returns home, she tells Dorothy that she just went to buy a nectarine.

If there's one thing that's universal about good deeds, it's that they don't need announcements when they're taking place. People who do good deeds for all the right reasons don't engage in braggadocio or require fanfare to announce that they're doing good deeds. As far as Sophia is concerned, being a good person (advocating for her friends, raising money for the senior center, cheering up a lonely old lady, and showing compassion for a young AIDS patient) is something she does every day—no need for fanfare when she comes home.

Her natural effervescence—her natural love and affection for those less fortunate—and her desire not to court attention or the spotlight make "The Days and Nights of Sophia Petrillo" one of the best episodes of *The Golden Girls* to feature the character.

1. "Ebbtide's Revenge"
Season 6, Episode 12

The best-ever Sophia Petrillo episode of *The Golden Girls* is one that deserves its own chapter—which is coming up right now.

Interlude

AN ODE TO "EBBTIDE'S REVENGE"

Picture it: the United States in the late 1980s and early 1990s.

There you are—your beautiful, queer self—not accepted by society as a whole, but part of a "family" nonetheless. Although your parents, perhaps, may have kicked you out—leaving you to the elements and the streets, because their version of Christianity didn't preach accepting you—you still found a "home" where you had a "mother" and a "father," and you found several "children" like you.

You took on their names—names that were more in line with who you really were, names that honored your new "house," names like LaBeija[1] or Ninja[2] or Xtravaganza[3]—names that didn't make much sense to the outside world, but names that you kept anyway to identify both yourself and others like you.

Maybe you're Black, maybe you're white, maybe you're in the catchall category of Latino without concern as to whether that "Hispanic" blood was Mexican, Puerto Rican, Dominican, Salvadoran, or of some other origin in Central or South America.[4]

Whatever the case, you are invisible to everyone . . . except other people in your community.

You may be gay and butch. Or you may be gay and femme. You may even be a cross-dresser, a trans man or trans woman, or you may be what is today known as "gender nonconforming."

Back then, it was known as "genderqueer." It would take until 1995 for the term "gender nonconforming" to be used by activist Riki Anne Wilchins, who coined the term in a now-defunct magazine called *In Your Face*.[5]

Regardless, no matter what you called yourself, didn't they know you were born this way?

No.

That wouldn't come until many, many years later. If you were lucky, you would be alive to see a pop star set it to a catchy tune while telling everyone to "just dance!" and, little by little, to gain tiny—but still tremendous—victories for your equality and equity in both the courts of law and public opinion.

But thanks to this horrible mess of the current society, you were more likely to be a target than you were to be protected.

Let's not get into your legal rights—or more specifically, the lack thereof. Sodomy laws were still being enforced arbitrarily by your friendly neighborhood police departments, meaning that you could find yourself with a criminal record *even if you were having consensual sex with someone you loved*. Worse yet, you were forced to register as a sex offender for the rest of your life after completing your jail sentence.

Getting married, of course, was not an option—sure, some of you were lucky to have a "lavender marriage" here and there, in which you found a sympathetic woman to marry you, only on paper, to save face for your conservative, intolerant family back in the Midwest. Some of you even had a child, or children, with such a woman—though thank *God* for artificial insemination!

It would take many decades—and a reality show called *90 Day Fiancé*—to see that version of yourself on TV. Fans of the hit reality show are familiar with the breakout star Kenneth Niedermeier, who made history when he appeared on the show. Niedermeier, who appeared on the show with his now-husband Armando Rubio, was half of the first gay couple to ever appear in the franchise.

But prior to marrying Rubio, Niedermeier explained that he raised four children as a single father in the 1980s. At the time, gay men couldn't adopt children, and only heterosexual couples qualified for in-vitro fertilization and artificial insemination. To get around this loophole, Niedermeier pretended to be married to a woman who posed as his wife, which was a form of a "lavender marriage."

To this day, the identity of Neidermeier's dear friend has never been revealed, but as a man in his sixties, Niedermeier would have been one of those "elder gays" who saw the devastation of the 1980s up close and personal, which queer millennials and Gen Zers can hardly fathom. But the fact that he made it to his sixties made him one of the lucky ones.[6]

Nevertheless, you persisted—you may have had a "spiritual partnership," which didn't go very far in terms of protecting either of you legally. Because, as you would soon learn, you had *no* legal standing once your partner's very judgmental Midwestern family came flying into town in the event of illness or death. Suddenly, the parents who were "ashamed" became "family" again at your partner's deathbed. Suddenly, they could call all the shots—even if they were against both of your wishes—and neither of you had any say in *anything*. As for inheriting your partner's estate? In your dreams.

So by the time 1990 rolled around, you were bruised and battered in more ways than one, both literally and figuratively.

And you tuned into *The Golden Girls* on December 15, 1990 to watch "Ebbtide's Revenge."

And you get a case of déjà vu.

Because so much of what you're seeing looks *so* familiar.

The faceless Phil—Dorothy's brother—dies of a heart attack while trying on an evening gown at Big Gals Pay Less.

Cue the titters of laughter as his sister snarks on the circumstances while thinking about how she's going to eulogize her only brother.

Rose tries to lighten the mood as she tells the story of why she had to eulogize Lenny Linderflot, whom she didn't really know that well but who sat in front of her at school.

And then there was Blanche—dear, sweet, ever-slutty Blanche, who donned her reddest dress to wear to Phil's funeral. Was she running with the bulls in Pamplona, as Dorothy so infamously snarled?

Even Sophia—the mother of the deceased—gets off a few one-liners at Phil's expense.

Her son. Her only son. Who's dead. Even *she* can't keep it together to not make a joke at his expense. All because he's a little different, just like you.

But you *do* notice something different about Sophia.

She's not getting off her best one-liners. Her jokes are pallid and gray, much like her face. And she *does* seem more somber than usual—she is, after all, still his mother.

The jokes continue throughout the funeral.

"He looks so peaceful and natural," remarks one.

"As natural as a man can look wearing a black teddy," quips another.

And still someone else tries to normalize it all—to make them see that the person in the casket is a *human being*, just like them, and a member of their family above all else.

"It's a beautiful teddy," said Rose. "I think more men should wear teddies."

Bless her heart—Rose certainly tries to make the best of a terrible situation. And she *does* mean well—her heart is in the right place, even if her head isn't.

But despite everyone's best efforts, Dorothy—the sister of the deceased—can't help but scream in exasperation that Phil looks like he "died in a *Benny Hill* sketch."[7]

The priest—ready to deliver a prayer—can't help but wonder if he's at a "joke" funeral and asks out loud if he's on "one of those hidden video things."[8]

The only one who seems to be compassionate toward Phil—who seems to understand him like no one else could—is his partner, his wife Angela (whom Sophia calls "Big Sally" because she can't stand her), who remarks that the black teddy in which Phil is buried is a "beaut" and remembers their wedding fondly.

"We were married for twenty-six years, and my family still talks about that wedding dress," she recalls. "God, I wish I could wear a plunging neckline like that."

And then there are the guys from Phil's weekly poker game, who are all in black, who all wear veils to hide their faces, who all are dressed to the nines in fine dresses—and who, aside from Phil's wife, are the only ones truly mourning his death.

This seems all too familiar for gay and lesbian men and women, doesn't it?

And on it goes until everyone goes back to the house, after the funeral.

Phil's mother and widow continue going back and forth with one another, engaging in a decades-old tug of war, because Phil's mother cannot accept him for whom he really was.

That dress thing, Sophia spits over and over again. *Why didn't she stop the dress thing?*

Because, Angela says, *he's been doing that all his life*. It didn't start with her.

Again, Phil's mother's guilt and shame consume her. *Oh, it's* my *fault?*

Then she addresses the elephant in the room, prompted by Rose's comment.

"It was shame that kept Aunt Katrina from loving slow Ingmar—and it ruined her life," Rose says. "Oh, don't let that happen to you, Sophia. Let go of the shame. So what if he was different? It's okay that you loved him."

And that, somehow, gets through to Phil's mother, who finally admits that, yes, she did love him. He was her son. Her little boy.

"But every time I saw him, I always wondered what I did, what I said, when was the day that I did whatever I did to make him the way he was," she says, tearfully.

And Phil's wife—his dear, sweet Angela—reminds Sophia of what he really was.

"What he was, Sophia, was a good man," she says quite simply.

And the final line—the final words that break your heart, that finally acknowledge that Phil was more than just a corpse, a punchline, and a source of shame and guilt in his family—is uttered by his mother.

"My baby is gone," she says as she breaks down in heaving tears.

Looking at "Ebbtide's Revenge" through a modern lens, one realizes the layers of social commentary that are present in the episode and understands how truly brilliant the episode—and the writing—is.

In 1990, the AIDS epidemic had devastated the queer community for more than a decade. Of the more than one hundred thousand deaths that had occurred since 1980, more than thirty-three thousand of them—a full one-third—had been reported in 1990 *alone*.

Though things have gotten better since that time, the disease still is a very real threat. As of 2021, more than seven hundred thousand people have died of AIDS-related illness since the virus was first identified. Today, people can look forward to living long, full lives without fear of transmission—but the disease has not, by any means, been eradicated.[9]

But the devastation felt by the queer community did nothing to change the minds of the collective American mindset at the time, and compassion was in short supply. In 1990, more than 75 percent of all Americans believed that homosexual activity was "morally wrong," more than 54 percent of all Americans believed that homosexual activity should be illegal, and more than 60 percent of all Americans believed that homosexuals shouldn't be teachers in America's schools.[10]

In a nutshell, Americans thought queer men and women were "perverts"—and that sentiment was more common than not.

So when *The Golden Girls* got a series of jokes off at Phil's expense—delivered by Dorothy, Blanche, and to a much lesser extent Rose and Sophia—they were able to lower everyone's guard. In that moment, they connected with a wide swath of American society.

America could relax—after all, the Girls were taking aim at Phil just the way they, and everyone like them, had made fun of other queer men and women for *years* (and even patronized hateful comedians who told the most disgusting of jokes at the expense of said queer men and women).

Who cares that Phil is dead? He's wearing a black teddy. *He's so different*.

Isn't that the loud-and-clear message sent by American society? Who *cares* about all those corpses you're seeing around you, devastated by the ravages of AIDS—they're *queers*, they're not "real Americans," so what are you crying for? Let's instead poke fun at the way they walk, their mannerisms, the lisp in their speech, and the way they hold hands as they walk down the street.

The only people who mourned all those dead corpses were people like them, who were still alive and left behind and their loving partners, who were devoted to them in both life and death. God love them.

That's who we saw in Angela. That's who we saw in "the guys from Phil's poker game."

But then Sophia addresses the elephant in the room.

"The dress thing."

She turned away from her own son—ostracized him—because she felt guilt and shame that he wasn't like everyone else.

Imagine that you are now a part of that audience, at that time. Suddenly, you are forced to confront the truth of that statement—how, perhaps, you too have ostracized a family member because he or she was "different," because he or she was "queer," because he or she just didn't "do the right thing," in your eyes.

Then Rose delivers the home run—by avoiding an indictment of the very audience *The Golden Girls* were hoping to reach. Rose, in her kindness, forced the audience to face reality: it was okay that he (or she) was different. It's okay. You can love them.

With that line, she acknowledged both the shame and guilt that had riddled the audience's lives and allowed the audience to (finally) love the people who they previously thought they weren't allowed to love.

By the time Sophia begins bawling for her lost son—a callback to Getty's role in *Torch Song Trilogy*—we're all crying along with her. Suddenly, those corpses that the Reagan administration laughed about weren't just numbers in a "gay plague." They weren't "queers"—a term considered a slur at this point in history—or something worse. They weren't weird, or different, or perverted.

They were *our* babies. They were America's babies.

They were somebody's son, somebody's brother, somebody's uncle, some-body's cousin.

AIDS reached through time and changed the course of history and in its wake left a human-size hole in the hearts of the families—whether chosen or through blood—who were left behind.

But why call these people "America's babies"?

Well, it's simple: ask any parents—mother and father alike—and they'll tell you that there's nothing more devastating to them than the thought that their children—their babies—will die before they do.

Nobody in the world needs a mother and a father more than a baby.

Nobody in the world is more vulnerable, more in need of protection, more deserving of love and care than a baby—and ostracizing that baby, leaving that baby to its own devices to brave the elements of the harsh, cruel world we live in, and ultimately abandoning that baby to die, is a deliberate failure on the part of the parents.

The death of a baby is a universal human tragedy.

With "Ebbtide's Revenge," the audience was forced to face the universal human tragedy of their treatment of queer people: those corpses you, Middle America, belittled; those comedians that you, Middle America, patronized who spit on their graves; and those nameless, faceless bodies that you, Middle America, laughed at are the bodies of your dead babies.

It's the complexity of Sophia's emotions—guilt, for ostracizing her son while he was still alive; regret, because it's now too late to do anything about it; anger, be-cause no one understands the complexity of the emotions she's feeling; and most of all, grief, for the loss of her baby—displayed with such gusto and sensitivity by Getty that makes "Ebbtide's Revenge" not only one of the greatest Sophia Petrillo episodes of *The Golden Girls*, but one of the greatest indictments of the hypocrisy of a "Christian nation" that failed so many of its most vulnerable at a time that they needed support the most.

With the AIDS crisis, America failed its babies in all it had done and in all it had failed to do.

With "Ebbtide's Revenge," America saw the price of that failure brought to life on one of its most beloved comedy shows.

We know better, now, though.

And we need to not only *do* better, but *be* better, going forward.

CHAPTER SIX

THE TOUGH STUFF

How the Girls Tackled the Dark Side of Reagan-Era America

If one were to believe the modern-day depictions of Ronald Reagan—with members of America's Republican Party ready to all but carve his face into Mount Rushmore, a sacrilege unto itself considering the mountain's Native American history—one would think that he was nothing short of a quasi-messianic figure, the great salvation that a morally bankrupt America was lucky to have in power. But the reality is, despite the cult of personality that has sprung up around him in the wake of his death, Reagan's social and political policies were nothing short of nightmarish for many.

Fortunately, *The Golden Girls* wasn't afraid to stare those issues straight in the face. Although the show didn't wade too deeply into political waters or declare allegiance to one party or another, it certainly made it clear that it didn't buy into many of the Reagan administration's policies. In fact, on more than a few occasions, it took direct aim at the president's social and political policies.

The Reagan administration rightly received blowback—both then and now—for its handling of HIV, the virus that causes AIDS. Rather than tackle it as the epidemic that it would become, the administration called the virus a "gay plague" and found it to be a source of humor. This was best demonstrated by Reagan's press secretary, Larry Speakes, and his propensity to joke with members of the press about the disease.

The administration didn't take the HIV crisis seriously at all, and it was up to Reagan's successors to ultimately do something about HIV and AIDS before it finally became contained and, eventually, treated. By then, it was far too late for far too many people, gay *and* straight.

Incidentally, in the twenty-first century, when the media began raising concerns about the growing number of cases of monkeypox, the coverage in some mainstream outlets echoed the coverage of the AIDS epidemic nearly forty years prior. But unlike in the 1980s, folks in the twenty-first century were quick to call out the coverage for the problematic mess that it was. What's more, thanks to responsible reporting and contact tracing, the disease was eradicated quickly before it exploded into a full-blown epidemic.[1] One can't help but wonder how differently things might have been if the Reagan administration had taken the same tack when it came to HIV, its transmission, and AIDS.

Writing for *Vox*,[2] German Lopez reports that were it not for the actions of Reagan's successors, the life expectancy for those who had been infected with HIV, the virus that causes AIDS, would have been as low as it was in the early 1980s. "The exchanges also demonstrated that Reagan and his administration didn't take the epidemic very seriously, for which the Reagan administration is still heavily criticized," he reported. "His successors eventually acted, albeit often very slowly, on the crisis—leading to much more research, programs like the Ryan White CARE Act that connect people to care, and the development of antiretroviral medication that increases the life expectancy of a person living with HIV by decades."

But more than just taking the official tack that AIDS was a "gay plague," the Reagan administration was directly influenced by the Reverend Jerry Falwell and his noxious—albeit popular—brand of evangelical Christianity, whose teachings were starting to take root in the United States and would, eventually, become known as the "religious right."

The Reverend Jerry Falwell was so enmeshed with Ronald Reagan and his presidency that most people equated the Moral Majority with the Republican Party.

Falwell, as those who grew up in the 1980s are acutely aware, believed that AIDS was God's punishment for both those who practiced homosexuality and those who tolerated and accepted it.[3] This paralleled the Reagan administration's belief that AIDS was nothing more than a gay person's disease, thus forever equating the two in the public's mind.

In fact, so enmeshed was Falwell in the Reagan administration that Michael Sean Winters—author of the definitive biography of Falwell—told *NPR*[4] that the Republican Party was no longer the party of Reagan, but the party of Falwell and the so-called Moral Majority—a claim echoed by many political commentators today, though Falwell's name has been supplanted by Donald Trump in many political circles.

What's more, many people began equating Christianity, the Republican Party, Reagan, and Falwell to the point that one couldn't be said without the others in the same breath. So if someone didn't feel comfortable about something that Falwell said, that person often felt as if he or she was rejecting Christianity, the Republican Party, and Reagan by extension.

"The whole purpose of the Moral Majority was to conflate those in ways, and again, because of this fundamentalist mindset, often in very simplistic ways," Winters told NPR. "And so, when people said, you know, well, I just don't want to have anything to do with his politics, they almost felt they then had to abandon Christianity, because this is what Christianity had become in their mind. And I think he's very much responsible for that."

The Golden Girls mentioned HIV in a few episodes, but none was quite as definitive as the episode "72 Hours" (season 5, episode 17), in which Blanche takes direct aim at Falwell's claim of AIDS being a punishment for the world's sins ("AIDS is not a bad person's disease, Rose," she said. "It is not God punishing people for their sins."). Although this may seem hyperbolic, it was a pervasive thought at the time. A study conducted by Gallup in 1985[5] revealed that more than 20 percent of people felt "less comfortable" around those who were HIV positive. What's more, 80 percent of Americans felt that it was "probably true" that AIDS was almost exclusively a homosexual disease—and another 28 percent said they would avoid locations where homosexuals were present as a result.

Time and subsequent research did nothing to quell these misconceptions. In 1987, a follow-up Gallup poll revealed that more than half of all Americans (51 percent) believed that it was "people's own fault" if they contracted AIDS, and 46 percent of Americans believed that those who were so infected "only had themselves to blame."

Worst of all, the Gallup study revealed that in 1987 and 1988, between 43 and 44 percent of all Americans believed that AIDS was God's punishment for what they deemed to be "immoral sexual behavior."

So Blanche's on-screen declaration was more than just setting her naive, farm-girl friend straight: it was a battle cry against a worryingly increasing majority of American society. Although it seems almost stereotypical for a libertine belle like Blanche to take direct aim at the ultra-conservative Falwell, it almost wouldn't make sense coming from anyone else.

What's more, the fact that Rose herself was at risk of contracting the illness—a matronly heterosexual woman whose sexual practices were conservative at best—turned the stereotype of HIV and AIDS on its head, which, in a way, seemed to be the point.

Prior to scientists understanding the true nature of HIV—and, specifically, how it was transmitted (in other words, that it was a blood-borne illness and not an airborne one)—there was no shortage of misinformation about who could get the virus and how. Unfortunately, too, there was no shortage of "tainted" blood—blood infected with HIV prior to the advent of testing requirements—which is how Ryan White, a hemophiliac, became a poster boy for the burgeoning AIDS research movement after contracting the disease from one of those tainted transfusions.

It's also worth noting that Reagan was hesitant to write checks to scientists so they could do additional research on the nature of the disease, which, in turn, led to both the disease and misinformation about it spreading in equal measure. And thus, the vicious cycle continued.

These actions had consequences—deadly ones. By the end of 1984, more than ten thousand people were either infected with the virus or died from it. Even worse, identifying yourself as someone who was HIV positive put you at risk of being "outed" as gay by your community, which was far from sympathetic to you and your plight.

The social temperature was far from warm and welcoming to the gay community. Society's frigidness was not only exacerbated by the HIV virus, but further transmitted by a different type of virus: hate disguised as comedy.

The same year that "72 Hours" hit the airwaves, Andrew Dice Clay was one of the most popular comedians in the country, and he, along with preacher-turned-perpetually-screaming comedian Sam Kinison had an obsession with, and a hatred of, non-straight and non-white men that bordered on clinical obsession.[6] Critics of the time noted that Clay, Kinison, and their ilk were part of a growing trend of bigotry in comedy that existed solely for bigotry's sake. In other words, in 1990, "joking" was meant to be as cruel as possible, regardless of the consequences of those "jokes"—and the public ate up Clay's brand of cruelty-disguised-as-comedy.

And that seemed to be acceptable at the time, because AIDS was still such a taboo topic. Save for "very special episodes" of medical dramas like

St. Elsewhere and *Trapper John, M.D.*, television shows shied away from dealing with the crisis head-on. Despite the best efforts of television writers to normalize the disease by "giving" it to heterosexual characters, many in the queer community felt that these depictions weren't realistic because the disease was ravaging *their* community, with very little crossover to other communities.

Even as celebrities like Rock Hudson—the first high-profile actor to die of the disease—Arthur Ashe, and Elizabeth Glaser (wife of *Starsky & Hutch* actor Paul Michael Glaser) came down with the disease, Reagan and his administration still refused to acknowledge the severity of the disease—and when they did, it was often buttressed with the most offensive types of comments and jokes.

The fact that *The Golden Girls* tackled the AIDS issue with any level of humanity—and without making queer people the butt of the joke—was a feat in itself.

And *The Golden Girls* didn't just have a "special episode" of AIDS with "72 Hours." In the season 4, episode 2 show called "The Days and Nights of Sophia Petrillo," Sophia volunteers at a hospital, where she befriends a young AIDS patient named Sam and gives him a nectarine. Though this may seem like minutiae, it was actually a not-so-silent protest: the *Girls* not only gave a new, and different, face to AIDS, but made its audiences realize that the disease was ravaging humanity, and its victims deserved compassion and kindness, not scorn and marginalization.

That wasn't all the Reagan administration was responsible for in the 1980s.

Writing for *The Nation*,[7] Peter Dreier points out that Reagan's economic policies drove America head-first into a recession and that, to this day, the country is still feeling the fallout from his unsuccessful "trickle-down economics" policy, among others, which proved to enrich only the very rich while creating a widening economic gap between the working class and white-collar workers.

"During his two terms in the White House (1981–89), Reagan presided over a widening gap between the rich and everyone else, declining wages and living standards for working families, an assault on labor unions as a vehicle to lift Americans into the middle class, a dramatic increase in poverty and homelessness, and the consolidation and deregulation of the financial industry that led to the current mortgage meltdown, foreclosure epidemic and lingering recession," he wrote. "These trends were not caused by inevitable social and economic forces. They resulted from Reagan's policy and political choices based on an underlying 'you're on your own' ideology."

These issues—with perhaps the sole exception of "union busting," for which the Reagan administration was infamous[8]—were tackled in different *Golden Girls* episodes. Poverty and homelessness were addressed in several *Golden Girls* episodes, including "Brother, Can You Spare That Jacket?" (season 4, episode 8, in which Sophia and Dorothy encounter a friend of Sophia's in a homeless shelter because her family could no longer afford to keep her in the Shady Pines nursing home), "Sophia's Choice" (season 4, episode 22, in which Sophia breaks her friend, Lillian, out of "the worst nursing home in the city," only for Blanche to forfeit her breast enhancement surgery money to pay for a suitable one for Lillian), and "Triple Play" (season 5, episode 15, in which Sophia receives more than $100,000 in social security checks and is loath to return it to the government, because the meager funds she receives via the benefit aren't enough for her to sustain herself on her own).

References to the Girls' declining standard of living also were mentioned periodically throughout the 180 episodes of the show, with jokes about stretching a Social Security check to its limit, budgeting issues, and rent increases to offset surprise emergency costs like a new roof (the hilarious season 4, episode 11 show called "The Auction," which featured Tony Steedman—perhaps best known as Socrates in *Bill & Ted's Excellent Adventure*—in the role of the obnoxious Jasper DeKimmel, wherein the Girls bid on one of his art pieces under the presumption that he's dying— with the faulty intel provided by the ever-plucky, albeit forgetful, Sophia— to cover the cost of the new roof) made their way into everyday conversation on the show.

Perhaps another of Reagan's most infamous contributions to society was the myth of the so-called welfare queen, whose existence he started bemoaning in the 1970s. In a campaign speech in 1976, Reagan crafted a story about the average recipient of social help programs that continues to echo in the American consciousness to this very day.

"In Chicago, they found a woman who holds the record. She used 80 names, 30 addresses [and] 15 telephone numbers to collect food stamps, social security [and] veterans benefits for four nonexistent deceased veterans' husbands, as well as welfare. Her tax-free cash income alone has been running $150,000 a year," he said.[9]

This record breaker was a Black woman by the name of Linda Taylor, who is an outlier, not a norm, of the system. But Reagan's comments created a long-lasting—and insidious—legacy. Even though white people, to this day, receive the most social aid benefits[10]—in 2017, it was revealed that 6.2 million white Americans receive some form of governmental assistance compared to only 2.8 million Black Americans and 2.4 million Latino

Americans—the stereotype of social aid almost exclusively directed toward Black females persists.

With this belief firmly ensconced in the collective minds of Americans—whether they identify as racist or not (and most probably don't)—politicians on the more conservative end of the political spectrum have slashed available benefits, made them notoriously difficult to obtain and maintain, or both.

"Reagan is often lauded as 'the great communicator,' but what he often communicated were lies and distortions," reported Dreier.[11] "This phony imagery of 'welfare cheats' persisted and helped lay the groundwork for cuts to programs that help the poor, including children."

No episode of *The Golden Girls* turned this "welfare queen" stereotype on its head more than the season 5, episode 12 show called "Have Yourself a Very Little Christmas." In this Christmas-themed episode, the Girls volunteer at a homeless shelter for the holidays in the hopes that they can help alleviate the suffering of some of the city's less fortunate. Although the episode boasts its share of humor—with Stan, Dorothy's ex-husband, becoming the butt of jokes after his latest wife tosses him out on the street for (what else?) cheating on her—it also features a predominantly white supporting cast to portray the less fortunate. Even before it was fashionable to be "woke," *The Golden Girls* writers seemed to take extra-special care in not equating "less fortunate" with "non-white" in the viewers' minds.

In short, the 1980s—and the early part of the 1990s—was a socially, and politically, conservative time in the United States. This went beyond yearning for the stereotypical "family values" of the 1950s and became stifling and harmful to those who weren't rich, white, male, and Christian.

Amid this stifling, harmful environment, the Girls rode into the frame, answering each of these outrages with humor, sensitivity, and progressive aplomb.

It goes without saying, perhaps, that in the twenty-first century, the modern Republican Party and its devotees would lob the "woke" insult at Dorothy, Rose, Blanche, and Sophia for not falling in lockstep with its beliefs and heroes. (Incidentally, and contrary to popular belief, "woke" is not a neologism.[12] It first emerged as a word used in AAVE [African American Vernacular English, known derisively as "Ebonics," a term that has largely fallen out of favor] in the 1930s as a watchword used among Black people to, essentially, "guard your back.")

Although the Girls were more liberal than most, this isn't to suggest that the show was necessarily a fan of the Democratic Party, either. In the season 3, episode 8 show called "Brotherly Love"—in which Dorothy hooks up with Stan's brother, of all people—Rose appears in the living room in her nightgown. When Stan's brother, Ted, asks Rose what she does for a living, Dorothy quips, "She's Gary Hart's campaign manager. It doesn't pay much, but you don't have to get out of bed to do it."

Gary Hart was a senator who represented Colorado from 1975 until 1987. He declined to seek reelection to the Senate, choosing instead to run for president on the Democratic ticket. He was considered a front-runner for the candidacy, and came very close to obtaining it, until the *Miami Herald* reported his extramarital affair with Donna Rice shortly after his campaign began. The ensuing scandal forced Hart to drop out of the race, and Michael Dukakis ultimately earned the candidacy instead. Hart earned a political redemption of sorts when President Barack Obama made him the U.S. Special Envoy to Northern Ireland, a position he held from 2014 until 2017.

So it's not as if the Girls were campaigning for the Mondale-Ferraro ticket in their spare time.

In fact, it's safe to say that the Girls were more apolitical than most shows—choosing to stick to their moral code instead of pledging allegiance to one political party or another. And perhaps most surprising of all was the fact that the character who should have been the most liberal—Blanche, who freely strutted her sexuality more than her roommates—at times could be the most conservative. Meanwhile, Sophia, of the Greatest Generation, born and raised in a notoriously conservative country that's still "behind the times" in the twenty-first century, sometimes could be the most liberal.

The Golden Girls was not only able to tackle the worst parts of the Reagan era with humor, sensitivity, and aplomb, but the show revealed that life exists on a spectrum rather than merely in black and white.

In today's increasingly rancorous political environment—with politicians insisting that everything in life is a zero-sum game, where you're either with them or against them rather than compromising or agreeing to disagree—that sort of nuance is not only sorely missed, but something that we, as a society, need to return to sooner rather than later.

A COMEDIC MASTER CLASS

The Top Ten *Golden Girls* Story Lines

During the course of seven seasons—and 180 episodes—*The Golden Girls* taught a comedic master class to both their viewers and the comedic actors and actresses who followed in their wake. Although, certainly, some episodes are better than others, others stand out from all the rest in the pantheon.

These episodes not only stand the test of time, but they are also funny and feature the actresses at their all-time best. Women of a certain age can relate, and women *not* of a certain age can take comfort in knowing that life, indeed, does get better—and funnier—with age.

10. "Old Friends"

Season 3, Episode 1

In the first episode of season 3, *The Golden Girls* tackled the issue of aging and, more specifically, Alzheimer's disease. Perhaps unsurprisingly, it was also the episode that garnered Getty her Emmy win, though that win wasn't without its own cruel irony.

The first part of the episode features Sophia enjoying a leisurely day on the boardwalk, where she meets a genial man named Alvin (Joe Seneca), with whom she trades insults and shares a veal and pepper sandwich. Truly, then, this was a friendship made in hog heaven!

As time progresses, Sophia and Alvin's relationship deepens, but when Sophia attempts to engage Alvin about his deceased wife, Edna, he appears visibly upset. Sophia initially believes that it's because the memories of his wife are too painful to relive and comforts him when he openly weeps on her shoulder.

The next time they meet, Alvin is angry and snaps at Sophia, ultimately stomping away from their conversation. This behavior leaves Sophia feeling bewildered, angry, and confused, but that's nothing compared to what she feels when she learns the truth of Alvin's affliction.

During their next meeting, Alvin brings Sophia a soda, which she interprets as an olive branch of sorts. She responds by telling him she forgives him for the fight they had. But she's a bit perplexed when Alvin doesn't seem to remember the fight.

From a distance, Dorothy and a Black woman around her age—who later identifies herself as Alvin's daughter Sandra—observe their respective parents interacting with one another. The pair strike up a conversation, remarking that their parents have both good and bad days thanks to their advancing age, but Sandra confesses that her father "is only going to get worse."

As it turns out, Alvin's behavior—the weeping about his wife, the snappy attack, the forgetfulness about his fight with Sophia—stems from Alzheimer's disease. Sandra explains to Sophia that Alvin is getting progressively worse and that she cannot continue to care for him properly, even though she took a leave of absence from work to care for him. Soon, she said, she will send Alvin to his nephew in New York, because he's a doctor and can provide him specialized care.

Later that day, Dorothy reveals what Sandra told her about Alvin. Sophia's reaction, in turn, is remarkably human: "Life can turn right around and spit in your face," she said, musing that it's both a blessing and a curse to live to such an old age. She then engages in some gallows humor, noting that since she still has a few months before Alvin departs for New York, "that'll be enough time to finish the scarf."

In the final scene, Sophia once again sits on the park bench where she and Alvin had passed many a wonderful afternoon together. She's hoping for her friend to make an appearance, but he never does.

Fortunately, Dorothy waits for her mother close by.

When she fetches her mother to take her home, Dorothy suggests that Sophia can take the completed scarf to New York when she visits Alvin, but Sophia refuses, preferring to remember Alvin the way he was. Given the degenerative nature of Alzheimer's disease—a disease about which it's often remarked that the patient dies twice: once as the disease takes hold and once when the patient finally dies—Sophia's refusal to see Alvin in such a compromised state is as much a small mercy for her as it is for Alvin. It's also remarkable that Getty herself would be diagnosed with Lewy body dementia just a few years after this episode was taped.

But in true *Golden Girls* fashion, the episode closes with a sassy remark: when a man sits down on the bench as Sophia is leaving, she turns around and snaps back, "Hey! Someone's sitting there!"

This episode balances both humor and a serious topic in such a way that it's sensitive without being sappy and snappy without being sarcastic. "Old Friends" was also the first-ever sitcom episode that dealt with the reality of Alzheimer's disease,[1] making it a historic episode in yet another remarkable way.

Incidentally, there's a secondary story in the episode, in which Rose loses her childhood teddy bear, Fernando (another "old friend"), after Blanche accidentally gives it away in a charity haul for the fictional Sunshine Girls cadet troop. An enterprising cadet named Daisy, played by a young Jenny Lewis—a former child actress who would find fame as the front woman for Rilo Kiley and later as a solo act—held Fernando hostage until Rose ultimately snatches him back. At one point in the episode, Daisy offers one of Fernando's ears as ransom—an act that was based on the real-life kidnapping of Getty heir J. Paul Getty III, whose ear was sent to his family as ransom.

9. "Not Another Monday"
Season 5, Episode 7

The Golden Girls was never a show that was afraid of tackling difficult topics. But one of the most difficult topics the show ever addressed was assisted suicide (also referred to as "physician-assisted dying" or "aid in dying").[2] As controversial as the subject was—and is—"Not Another Monday" deserves credit for treating it with both the humor and the compassion it deserved.

The secondary story featured Rose, Blanche, and Dorothy preparing to care for the Lillestrand baby while the child's parents go on a weekend camping trip. Certainly, there were plenty of hijinks to be had when the baby develops a high fever. The Girls call Dr. Harry Weston,[3] whom Blanche relentlessly flirts with while he attempts to care for Baby Lillestrand. When Baby Lillestrand refuses to go to sleep, the Girls harmonize on a version of "Mr. Sandman," with Dorothy singing all the low notes.

The juxtaposition of the baby with the elderly not only provides humor in the episode but also a bittersweet melancholy as the main story progresses.

Shortly after Rose, Dorothy, and Blanche agree to watch Baby Lillestrand, Sophia enters the Girls' shared Miami home with her friend Martha, dressed in black, because they'd just returned home from a funeral. Although Sophia is clearly depressed about the death of yet another friend, Martha is particularly melancholy.

As it turns out, Martha is suffering from an unnamed terminal illness. This, combined with depression due to the passing of their dear friend, leads Martha to decide that she'd like to die by suicide. What's more, Martha informs Sophia that she'd like her to be in the room as she takes her final breath.

Upon learning of Martha's plans, Dorothy is—perhaps unsurprisingly—horrified. Rose attempts to weigh in on the morality—or lack thereof—of suicide, but Dorothy brushes her off, more concerned about what her mother's state of mind will be after watching one of her best friends end her own life.

Sophia, however, is undeterred, and informs the Girls that she plans to "do it."

On what would be the last day of Martha's life, Sophia manages to talk her out of it. She reminds Martha about how they first met: sharing a hospital room, where they bonded over how eager they were to get out of there because they "wanted to live." Sophia begs Martha to remember those times, and promises to be there for her in life, as Martha had wanted Sophia to be there for her in death.

"Like a friend?" asks Martha.

"Like a *best* friend," Sophia replies.

The episode closes with Sophia holding the Lillestrand baby and telling him that he's "got a lot of life to live," ending the episode on a bittersweet note.

Whatever one's opinion of assisted suicide—whether it's in line with one's moral compass or not (and far be it for anyone to dictate what someone else should or shouldn't believe—or whether one should or shouldn't accept a practice based on that belief system)—*The Golden Girls* tackled this unquestionably difficult problem with grace, sensitivity, and humor without passing moral judgments or proselytizing.

This loving approach to difficult problems went a long way in contributing to the Girls' incomparable legacy.

8. "Dorothy's New Friend"
Season 3, Episode 15

At the beginning of this episode, Dorothy is lamenting that her life has become particularly boring and monotonous. To add some spice and excitement into her life, she decides to attend a book reading by the author Barbara Thorndyke (played with pure WASP acidity by veteran actress Bonnie Bartlett), who uses her erudition as a basis for her self-aggrandizement.

The secondary story involves Sophia's efforts at flirting with a man at the senior rec center, which starts out with her crafting a homemade lasagna for him. While these two stories don't seem connected at the beginning of the episode, the writers tie it all together in a very neat bow by the end.

Dorothy is too cowed by Barbara's perceived celebrity to notice her bad behavior, which immediately is evident to Blanche and Rose, who are marginalized and dismissed by Barbara when Dorothy invites her to lunch.

For Dorothy's sake, Rose and Blanche give Barbara another chance and invite her to dinner. Again, Barbara is snobbish and aloof to Rose and Blanche, excluding them from her conversation with Dorothy and condescendingly explaining what a metaphor[4] is.

At a follow-up luncheon between Dorothy and Barbara, Dorothy shares her concerns about the strain on her relationship with Rose and Blanche. Barbara attempts to make amends by inviting them all, as a collective, to the Mortimer Club, which is presumably the most exclusive club in town.

On the night of the Mortimer Club event, Sophia's date from the senior center—who, it turns out, wasn't a fan of her lasagna, though she seems to have forgiven that transgression—arrives in a dated pale blue suit and introduces himself as "Murray Guttman." This prompts Barbara to demand to speak with Dorothy in the kitchen, which Dorothy obliges.

Barbara informs Dorothy that there's a problem. Believing that the issue stems from Murray's dated powder blue disco-era suit, Dorothy promises to tell Murray to turn his jacket inside out so that the blue doesn't prove offensive to a more fashionable audience.

Disturbingly, Barbara informs Dorothy that it's not Murray's jacket that's the issue—it's Murray's (presumed) religious beliefs.

"Guttman," she all but spits. "He's Jewish, isn't he?"

As it turns out, the Mortimer Club—the most exclusive club in Miami—is what Barbara euphemistically refers to as "restricted." The subtext, of course, is that no Jewish people are allowed[5]—and even a Jewish-sounding last name may prove to be a problem.

Dorothy, flummoxed by this news, is horrified. She demands to know why Barbara would belong to a club that has such "restrictions." Barbara tries to pass it off as the club's policy, not hers, but Dorothy isn't having it—after all, by patronizing the club in the first place, Barbara is condoning it.

When Barbara continues to dismiss Dorothy's concerns, Dorothy realizes that "Blanche and Rose are right—you are *not* someone I want as a friend." She then suggests that Barbara go to the Mortimer Club by herself. When Barbara asks for clarification, Dorothy delivers the zinger:

"Let me spell it out for you," she says. "Go to hell. Hmm?"

The anti-Semitism depicted in this episode is as subtle as a jackhammer, and it goes without saying that this sort of thing has no place in the modern world. But in a post-pandemic world where the Great Awakening prompted us as a collective to look critically at our history with everyone who wasn't white, male, rich, and some Christian denomination or other, much to Ron DeSantis's displeasure, it's even easier to argue that "Dorothy's New Friend" is more relevant now than ever before.

In 2019, 63 percent of all religion-based hate crimes targeted Jewish people, and "visible" Jews—such as Hassidim—were more likely to be targeted than "invisible" (read: secular) Jews.[6] Depictions of Jewish people in Hollywood often pander to specific stereotypes, even in the twenty-first century. No less an authority than Jewish comedian Sarah Silverman remarks on the disparity of the roles offered to people like her versus the roles offered to their goyim counterparts.

"Actors are actors, and they should play all different parts, 100 percent. Let me make that clear," Silverman said to veteran radio host Howard Stern.[7] "But . . . they finally make *RBG* the movie and it's a British woman, Felicity Jones. [*The Marvelous*] *Mrs. Maisel*—God bless her, she's brilliant—not Jewish. Even in *Jojo Rabbit*, which I loved, nobody was Jewish. *The Jew in the Wall* wasn't even Jewish. It was some actress named McKenzie! Is it the biggest injustice in the world? No, but I'm noticing it."

Pop culture commentators, too, have noticed that many Jewish actors are asked to "downplay" their Jewishness or conform to a premade stereotype about Jewishness when they take to the silver screen. In the context of *The Golden Girls*, it's worth noting that two of the show's biggest stars—Bea Arthur and Estelle Getty—are Jewish, yet they played Sicilian American women. One can't help but wonder if this stylistic change made Dorothy and Sophia more palatable to America at large than, say, if their names were Ethel and Miriam.

Incidentally, "Ethel and Miriam" wouldn't be too far out of reach for *The Golden Girls*. According to the show's mythology, Estelle Getty campaigned for Dorothy and Sophia to be Jewish. Reportedly, Getty thought it would be easier—for, perhaps, obvious reasons—to play an old Jewish woman than to play an old Sicilian woman. However, this tale is largely apocryphal, and no modern proof exists. For what it's worth, Susan Harris told the *New York Times* that the characters were based on people she knew in real life, so perhaps the conversation of their ethnicity—or religion—was a nonstarter in the first place.[8]

It's also worth noting that Jewish people make up less than 0.2 percent of the world's population. To be more specific, World Population Review reveals that only 0.19 percent of the world's population is Jewish. Christianity is the world's largest monotheistic religion, followed by Islam as a close second. More people, in fact, identify as members of a spiritism religion—such as neopaganism—than they do as members of the Jewish religion.

But in the twenty-first century, rising incidences of anti-Semitism suggest that it's more important than ever to dispel these dangerous myths on sight.

This doesn't take into account the myths and stereotypes that have taken a stronghold in Hollywood, to the point that some people believe that speaking out critically against Jewish people results in the immolation of one's career.

Put bluntly, many people—especially those who aren't successful in the entertainment industry, though Kanye West's recent comments suggest that some *in* the industry hold these misconceptions—believe that "Jews control Hollywood." This belief was galvanized in 2006 with Mel Gibson's infamous anti-Semitic rant, and it's one that 22 percent of the country currently believes (down from 64 percent in the 1960s). It's true that many prominent executive positions in the Hollywood industry are held by Jewish people, and it's also true that the Hollywood studio system, as we know it, was founded by Jewish men. But the Jewish men who founded the studio system were staring down the barrel of rising evil—an evil that would, eventually, culminate in Nazism and the rise of Hitler—and fled to the United States in the hopes of finding a more forgiving and tolerant life. To put it another way: though Jewish men and women have prominent jobs in Hollywood, they have them on the merits of their work, not due to their religion. Seth Rogen put it best when he said that if indeed Jews did run Hollywood, there would be a lot less anti-Semitism—and Jewish stereotypes—than there are today.[9]

We've seen what happens when we don't nip the stereotypes in the bud—and, certainly, no one wants a repeat performance of Germany in the 1930s and 1940s.

7. "Sophia's Wedding"
Season 4, Episodes 5 and 6

In this two-part story, Sophia settles a grudge with an old friend . . . whom she ends up marrying.

Here's the backstory: the Petrillos (Sophia and her late husband, Sal, who is also Dorothy's father) and the Weinstocks (Esther and Max) were close friends in Brooklyn, New York. So close, in fact, that Sal and Max were in business together (true to stereotype, they opened a pizza/knish stand). However, at some point, Max gambled away all the money they made from the business, which ended up causing friction between the Weinstocks and the Petrillos forever more.

That is, of course, until Esther Weinstock dies. Sophia gets a call in Miami from an unnamed source who informs her of the death, but when Dorothy offers to go to the funeral with Sophia, she refuses, "and you know why!" (It's here that Dorothy recounts the story to Blanche and Rose.)

Ultimately, Dorothy ends up convincing Sophia to go to Brooklyn for Esther's funeral. In the next scene, they are at the post-funeral reception for Sophia's former dearly departed friend. Upon encountering Max, Sophia begins snapping at him. In his grief, Max finally reveals the truth about the lost money from the pizza/knish stand all those years ago.

As it turns out, it wasn't Max who lost the money—it was Sal, who took their earnings to a horse track and lost it all. To prevent Sal and Sophia from falling out, Max took the blame for the loss, which caused the rift in their friendship. To Max, it was worth it, because he was able to save the marriage of two people he loved.

Later, after they return to Miami, Dorothy remarks to Blanche and Sophia that she's proud of her mother for getting past this petty argument, "even though she knows she'll never see him again."

But no sooner does Dorothy make this proclamation that she walks in on her mother and Max Weinstock in bed together, clearly in a state of postcoital bliss. (This is also confirmed by Sophia's response—"Afterglow!"—when Dorothy demands to know what is going on.) Sophia then reveals that not only are she and Max getting married, but they're reopening their beloved pizza/knish stand to make things right after all these years.

Incidentally, eagle-eyed fans of *The Golden Girls* will note that one of the Elvis impersonators who turn up at Sophia and Max's wedding is none other than a young Quentin Tarantino, who would go on to direct films like *Pulp Fiction* and *Once upon a Time in Hollywood*.

In the second half of the story, Sophia and Max run the stand on Miami Beach, and it turns out to be successful, but they don't have a place to live, so they move back in with Dorothy, Rose, and Blanche. Naturally, hijinks ensue, especially when Max takes his glasses off and accidentally gets in the shower with Dorothy.

Ultimately, Sophia and Max decide to separate—divorce, after all, goes against Sophia's Catholic beliefs, and she's "in spitting distance of Saint Peter!"—because they realize that they got married for the wrong reasons (nostalgia, as it turns out, is not a good basis for a relationship).

In "Sophia's Wedding," Sophia marries her former enemy, Max Weinstock, and opens a pizza/knish stand on Miami Beach.

This story line makes the top ten list not because of the story itself—it's pure campy kitsch, after all, and not profound by definition—but because it makes us look at Sophia in a whole new way: as a wholly sexual being—even as an octogenarian—who enjoys the act with a boyfriend (who eventually becomes her husband).

Considering the Girls started out in the business at a time when censors didn't want young *married* television couples sharing a bed on the small screen, watching two unmarried octogenarians in postcoital bliss was nothing if not revolutionary.

Contrary to popular belief, *I Love Lucy* was not the first show to depict a married couple in bed together. That honor went to a long-forgotten show called *Mary Kay & Johnny*, which went on the air in 1947. But at that time, only 250,000 homes in the United States had televisions, and the show aired only in the greater New York area. Additionally, couples who were married "in real life"—such as Mary Kay and Johnny, Lucy and Desi, and Ozzie and Harriet—were "allowed" by the censors to share a bed on the small screen. Apparently "middle America" automatically would think that two actors who weren't married to each other were engaging in a hot, steamy affair if they shared a bed on a set (despite countless actors who will tell you that there's nothing less sexy than being on a bed in the middle of a studio with hot lights beating down and countless members of the crew staring you down as you shift your "modesty sock" to hide the family jewels).

The first couple to share a bed on-screen who wasn't married in real life was Darrin and Samantha (played by Dick York and Elizabeth Montgomery, respectively) on *Bewitched*, which happened in 1964 (although one might argue that the animated *Flintstones* cartoon from 1960 came first).

Once again, this episode—like many others—was proof positive that the Girls weren't just muffin-baking crones, ready to shrivel up and die when not in service to their children or grandchildren. They were active and vital, they had full lives that were well lived, and they continued to enjoy the company of each other . . . and men.

6. "Brother, Can You Spare That Jacket?"
Season 4, Episode 8

Many a *Golden Girls* episode kicks off with some sort of absurdity—and the more absurd the scenario, the deeper the lesson, and the more satisfying the payoff.

Nowhere is this winning formula more evident than in the season 4, episode 8 show called "Brother, Can You Spare That Jacket?" (a hat tip to the 1932 song, "Brother, Can You Spare a Dime?" which addressed the various struggles many Americans faced during the Great Depression, and was first featured in the Broadway musical *Americana*[10]).

In this episode, the absurdity in question was that Dorothy won $10,000 on a scratch-off lottery ticket—the equivalent of $25,000 in twenty-first-century money. Although it's not statistically hard to win a scratch-off ticket—approximately one in five scratch-off tickets produces a win of some kind—it *is* statistically difficult to win a scratch-off prize of that magnitude.

Nevertheless, Dorothy beats the odds, and the Girls put the winning ticket in Blanche's new leather jacket for safekeeping. They then get ready for a celebratory dinner.

Sophia, however, is unaware that Dorothy put the winning ticket in Blanche's jacket—she was in the other room during the commotion. Having learned nothing from the season 3, episode 1 show "Old Friends," in which a prized possession is mistakenly donated—Sophia sends Blanche's jacket (with the winning ticket in the pocket) off with a young postulant nun.

When the ladies return from dinner, they frantically look for the jacket. That's when Sophia reluctantly reveals that she accidentally put the jacket—which she thought looked old and tattered—into a charity haul. The Girls, desperate to track down the jacket, eventually find themselves at a homeless shelter (which is where the jacket ended up after being worn by Michael Jackson, auctioned for charity, and eventually donated to the homeless).

Ten thousand dollars is a lot of money—so all four Girls decide to pose as homeless people and spend the night in the shelter, hoping to track the jacket down.

But while there, they end up learning a more profound lesson than they'd imagined.

Blanche encounters a young man who reminds her of one of her sons, who ended up homeless because he couldn't find a job and eventually descended into alcoholism. However, he points out that there's more to his story than meets the eye, because "I've already got my doctorate."

Rose, meanwhile, encounters a Black man from a town not far from St. Olaf, and they strike up a friendly, animated conversation. He reveals that he ended up homeless after a series of layoffs shook his financial stability.

And Dorothy and Sophia—who share a bunk—encounter a woman named Ida Perkins, who was in the Shady Pines nursing home with Sophia. When the nursing home burned down, Ida ran out of money. Failing to find family to help her, Ida ended up on the streets.

Eventually, the Girls start looking for the jacket. While they're looking, they encounter other faces that look all too familiar to them, including a mother with her young child. Despite their desperation to find the winning lottery ticket, they suddenly realize that there's more to life than winning money for them to spend frivolously.

When Blanche reveals that she found the lottery ticket, the Girls silently debate whether they should keep the ticket. Ultimately, nodding their approval, they hand the ticket to Sophia, who promptly gives it to the Catholic priest who runs the shelter.

"Here you go, Padre," she says in her trademark Brooklyn accent. "Thanks for everything."

In addition to tackling the issue of homelessness with an empathy and kindness that was sorely lacking in many depictions of the situation at the time (and, unquestionably, even more sorely lacking today), "Brother, Can You Spare That Jacket?" showed how the unhoused aren't just the stereotype of wayward addicts with moral failings. Rather, they're everyone from the elderly who ran out of money to the average working man who is down on his luck thanks to a series of unfortunate events. They're even mothers and their young children.

But most of all, they're veterans. According to the National Coalition for Homeless Veterans, approximately 13 percent of the homeless population are veterans of the armed forces. Black and Latino veterans are more likely to be homeless than their white counterparts, and male veterans are more likely to be homeless than their female counterparts.[11]

No one *asks* to be homeless. No one *hopes* that it happens to them. And certainly, no one *wants* the judgment and prejudice that come with the homeless experience.

In short, there's a human component behind the crisis of the unhoused—and no matter who they are or how they got there, they deserve to be treated with the dignity and respect that is naturally afforded other humans. What's more, the Girls proved that a little bit of empathy goes a long way . . . and, in the end, it's up to us to be the change we want to see in the world.

5. "Sister of the Bride"
Season 6, Episode 14

This episode is the upshot to the season 4, episode 9 show called "Scared Straight." In the season 4 episode, Blanche's brother Clayton comes out as a homosexual after a painful divorce (but not before falsely accusing Rose of sleeping with him, which creates a series of unfortunate events that strains Blanche and Rose's friendship). Although Blanche eventually accepts Clayton's truth, this hard-won acceptance is put to the test when Clayton wants to take his latest relationship to the next level.

Since this episode aired in the days before emails and text messages, the main story starts with Blanche receiving a letter from Clayton announcing that he's coming to town and bringing a "big surprise" with him. Blanche hopes that Clayton will be bringing his latest female suitor, but Dorothy is quick to remind her that her brother is gay. Blanche, however, believes that "that gay thing" was "just a phase he was going through," much like his penchant for gladiator movies in high school.

Dorothy's sardonic response to this revelation: "Almost the same thing." The joke, of course, implies that the writing was on the wall all along, but everyone around Clayton, including Blanche, refused to see it.

It also sent a clear message, long before science proved it as a fact, that being gay was inherently ingrained, not a choice one makes—that gay men and women were, as Lady Gaga put it, "born this way."

Naturally, when Clayton arrives, his surprise is Doug, a calm and quiet man whom Clayton introduces as his "very special friend" (after Blanche mistakes him for the taxi driver—remember, this was in the days before Uber and Lyft). Doug ultimately reveals that he's a police officer, which prompts Rose—who is still convinced that Doug is a cab driver—to ask if Doug is doing undercover work. As can be expected, Sophia cracks an innuendo-laden joke at both Rose and Doug's expense, and Rose's remark that Blanche just "loves policemen" merits another blunt comment from Sophia about the penchant being a "hereditary trait."

Predictably, Blanche's acceptance of her brother's new relationship falls more than a little short: upon realizing the nature of Doug's relationship with her brother, she's immediately uncomfortable and less than welcoming to her brother's new partner.

Later, Blanche, Sophia, and Dorothy are in the kitchen, where both Dorothy and Sophia are generous with their compliments about both Clayton and Doug. Blanche reveals that she's very upset, though she feels she hid it well from her brother and his partner. Dorothy, naturally, disagrees with this assessment, and points out that Blanche began sobbing when Clayton asked his sister for more fruit cocktail.

"I don't mind Clayton being homosexual—I just have a problem with him dating men," Blanche remarks. She then asks if there are homosexuals who date women, to which Sophia replies that those homosexuals are called "lesbians."

Her discomfort with Clayton's sexuality increases as the show goes on. When Clayton asks about the sleeping arrangements, Blanche panics again, demanding to know what she should do since Doug and Clayton want to sleep in the same room. When Dorothy suggests that Doug and Clayton sleep in Blanche's room while Blanche sleeps on the couch, Blanche refuses, rhetorically asking what the neighbors will think if they see two men in her bedroom. Sophia's reply: "They'll think it's Tuesday."

Dorothy and Rose call out Blanche on her hypocrisy, pointing out that she can't say she's accepted her brother's sexuality if she can't accept what it entails in its totality. Although Blanche acknowledges that she needs to stop overreacting—especially since both Clayton and Doug are consenting adults—she immediately shrieks in horror when the pair go for a walk and Sophia snarks that they're "skipping while holding hands." (It was a joke, one designed to elicit an extreme response from Blanche—and it works.)

It gets worse: when Rose invites Clayton and Doug to attend the charity banquet where she believes she's going to win an award (ultimately, she doesn't—and therein is the secondary story line of the episode), Blanche rants to the Girls that she didn't want her brother and his boyfriend out together in public, because she was concerned about the judgment of the attendees.

Unfortunately for Blanche, Clayton overhears her conversation and jumps into the fray, revealing that he and Doug are getting married and they're registered at Neiman Marcus.

The "wedding," of course, isn't a big wedding—and, at this point in history, it's not legally binding, either. It's a "commitment ceremony," but Blanche is still none too pleased with the prospect. She immediately starts snapping at Clayton and declaring the wedding a "stunt" before stomping off into her room and slamming the door.

At the charity event, Blanche decides to stay home in protest of Clayton and Doug's attendance but ultimately decides to come through to support Rose. That "support," however, is short-lived, because it isn't long before Blanche is causing a scene when someone asks Clayton and Doug to introduce themselves (she begins yelling "Fire!" to get people to leave the table).

At this point Clayton finally loses his patience with Blanche. "Blanche, how could you do that? What did you mean when you said you accepted my being gay? That it was fine so long as I was celibate? So long as I didn't fall in love? Doug is a member of the family now. My family! And if you don't like it, you don't have to be a part of my family," he snaps.

In the final—and perhaps most definitive—scene, Blanche is musing to Sophia that Clayton was making much ado about nothing. She also couldn't understand why Clayton was so insistent on marrying Doug.

Amazingly, it's Sophia who imparts some wisdom instead of sarcasm.

"Why did you marry George?" she asked Blanche.

Without missing a beat, Blanche responds that she married George because they loved one another, and they wanted the world to know.

"That's what Doug and Clayton want, too. Everyone wants someone to grow old with. And shouldn't everyone have that chance?" responds Sophia.

Ultimately, Blanche realizes there's only one question that needs to be asked of her future brother-in-law: "do you love him?" When Doug responds in the affirmative, Blanche gives her blessing and accepts the relationship.

Now, to be clear, there are plenty of jokes and innuendos in this episode that wouldn't be made in the twenty-first century. And far be it from me to "woke-check" *The Golden Girls*. It's completely unfair to hold a twentieth-century show to twenty-first-century standards. Comedy changes over time, and our understanding of different communities evolves in kind.

But for its time, *The Golden Girls* was extremely progressive. What's more, despite its shortcomings, there was never any malice—implicit or intended—in any of the jokes. And despite this episode's shortcomings and borderline inappropriate jokes, "Sister of the Bride" not only tackles important social issues of the day, but also conveys the eternal message of the importance of love and family . . . no matter what that looks like.

4. "The Accurate Conception"

Season 5, Episode 3

For someone who revels in her sexual freedom and promiscuity—for someone who behaved outside the social norms of a woman her age in the late 1980s and early 1990s—Blanche Devereaux has elements of her personality that are more than a little bit conservative. When fans least expected it, the "traditional" side of Blanche Devereaux reared its head, which made for some interesting and hilarious moments.

Nowhere is this more obvious than in the season 5, episode 3 show called "The Accurate Conception."

Now, in fairness to everyone involved, it was very rare for sex to be spoken about openly and frankly on primetime television shows at the time. It was even *more* rare for "nontraditional" sexual topics—non-hetero sex, in vitro fertilization (IVF), fetishes, and artificial insemination—to be discussed so frankly.

One year after this episode aired, journalist Connie Chung made headlines when she shared intimate details about her IVF treatments, which she was undergoing with her husband, talk show host Maury Povich.[12] Chung's efforts, however, were unsuccessful, and the couple ultimately adopted a son they named Matthew. Whereas twenty-first-century celebrities often take to social media to share intimate (and sometimes uncomfortable) details about their "fertility journeys," this practice was unheard of in the 1980s and 1990s.

So an episode of *The Golden Girls* that addressed artificial insemination and single motherhood was nothing if not groundbreaking.

At the beginning of the episode, Blanche and her long-estranged daughter Rebecca—whom fans last saw in the season 3, episode 14 show called "Blanche's Little Girl," in which she escaped a relationship with an abusive man—are finally reconnecting. But during their mother-daughter bonding time, "Becky's" trauma from her past relationship rears its head when she informs her mother that she'd like to get pregnant by artificial insemination and raise the baby as a single mother.

Blanche is horrified by the revelation and immediately tells the Girls about what her daughter plans to do. As might be expected, they're all horrified by the prospect—but, ultimately, Dorothy brings everyone back to reality, reminding them that they all conceived their children in different ways.

Dorothy's story was the most memorable, in which she claimed that she was "totally unconscious." When Sophia expresses doubts about the story, Dorothy insists that Stan "must've slipped her something." Sophia's response: "Apparently!"

"The Accurate Conception" dealt with the uncomfortable topics of artificial insemination and single motherhood in trademark *Golden Girls* fashion.

The rest of the episode involves Blanche coming to terms with the process by which her latest granddaughter—who is named Aurora—is conceived. After all, her daughter is an adult, and adults can—and should—do what's right for them.

Certainly, much has changed since "The Accurate Conception" aired. Television shows like *This Is Us*, *The Mindy Project*, and *Parenthood* have tackled parenthood issues involving infertility, adoption, egg freezing, and surrogacy, with varying degrees of success. And rather than feeling ashamed about their struggles with fertility, many celebrities—including Priyanka Chopra, Tyra Banks, and Ellen Pompeo—have opened up about their "journeys." However, this episode of *The Golden Girls* was one of the first to tackle artificial insemination in a realistic—and humorous—way.

3. "Mixed Blessing"
Season 3, Episode 23

In the late 1980s and early 1990s, interracial relationships were still a minefield to navigate. A 2010 report revealed that one in seven marriages in the United States were either interracial or interethnic—more than double what it was in the 1980s. What's more, most Americans in the twenty-first century approved of interracial marriage—a huge, positive change from the 1980s.

This change and acceptance, however, was largely generational. The study revealed that although 90 percent of people aged thirty and younger approved of interracial or interethnic marriage, only 30 percent of people aged sixty-five and older approved of interracial or interethnic marriage. The study also revealed that this generational gap was indicative of how such practices were not only unacceptable during the "boomer" era, but illegal until *Loving v. Virginia* in 1967 rendered bans on interracial and interethnic relationships as unconstitutional.[13]

But at this point in history, interracial and interethnic relationships were still an anomaly, or at least not as mainstream and common as they are today. Even so, they're still not without controversy, as anyone who has ever been on any type of social media platform can attest.

Regardless, "Mixed Blessing" tackles the subject of interracial relationships with both sensitivity and humor, without veering into stereotypes and microaggressions.

Dorothy's son Michael—one of two children she shares with her ex-husband, Stan—stops by for a visit and tells his mother that he's marrying his bandmate, a lovely woman named Lorraine.

Later in the episode, Michael stops by with Lorraine—who turns out to be a Black woman who is decades older than Michael. It's not the "Black" part that bothers Dorothy—it's the "much older" part. Ironically, though, when Lorraine's family stops by to meet the Girls, it's not the "much younger" part that bothers them—it's the "white" part.

As can be expected, foibles and follies ensue—Rose and Blanche barge in wearing mud masks, which looks like blackface on first glance;[14] Sophia asks Lorraine's mother about the stereotype of Black men in bed—but, ultimately, both sides of the family begin to bond.

Unfortunately, Sophia shakes things up when she reveals that Lorraine and Michael decided to elope because their families didn't approve of their relationship. Everyone—Lorraine's family and the Girls—rush to the chapel to try to stop the nuptials. It's only then that Michael reveals that Lorraine is expecting a child.

Although neither Dorothy nor Trudy (Lorraine's mother) is thrilled about the prospect of their children marrying, they decide to accept the union for the sake of the grandchild who is on the way. Both women resolve to do what mothers have done since the dawn of time: accept the marriage for the sake of their children "and complain about it to anyone who will listen."

As with other episodes of *The Golden Girls*, there are many jokes that couldn't be made today (with the one about Black men in bed near the top of the list). And, as with other episodes, *The Golden Girls* didn't tackle the subject of interracial relationships perfectly—especially by modern standards. However, all things considered, "Mixed Blessing" is one of the finest episodes in the show's history.

2. "Sick and Tired"

Season 5, Episode 1 and 2

This two-part episode was the season premiere of the fifth season of *The Golden Girls*, and it drew more than thirty-four million viewers in its first airing. Based on Harris's own experience with chronic fatigue syndrome,[15] "Sick and Tired" illustrates the reality of how the medical establishment dismisses women's pain—and little has changed after all these years.

If white women feel "unseen" by the medical establishment thanks to implicit bias, nonwhite women—especially Black women—feel especially invisible. A 2016 study revealed that medical students still believe that Black men and women have thicker skin than their non-Black counterparts, and they also believe that Black men and women feel less pain than their white counterparts. Their beliefs were based on historical misconceptions, which may have originated from a nineteenth-century study conducted by a man named Thomas Hamilton, whose "research" involved torturing his Black slave to "prove" his false hypotheses about Black women and pain. Unfortunately, such beliefs are still held by many doctors in the twenty-first century. So although Dorothy's predicament in this episode is certainly terrible, it could have been even worse if she were a Black woman.[16]

The humor in this story is in short supply, and it only comes from the secondary story, which involves Blanche trying to write the Great American Romance Novel and failing, miserably.

A storyline involves Dorothy's quest to find out what's wrong with her. As of late, she's been more tired than usual—so tired, in fact, that she can barely come to dinner or enjoy time with her friends. She sees a battery of doctors, all of whom are dismissive of her complaints. One particularly noxious doctor, Dr. Budd,[17] suggests that Dorothy simply should dye her hair blonde and that Dorothy may be mentally compromised—despite Dorothy producing letters confirming that she's mentally stable.

Dr. Budd's dismissive diagnosis leaves Dorothy feeling particularly defeated, and she breaks down in tears. Rose, being a good friend, comforts her and reminds her that she does, in fact, believe Dorothy's claims of being sick.

"I know," replies Dorothy. "But nobody believes me."

Finally, a friend of Dr. Harry Weston successfully diagnoses her with chronic fatigue syndrome. The doctor in question—Dr. Chang—naturally was the butt of many Asian-based jokes from Sophia. Although they weren't malicious per se, they certainly aren't politically correct by twenty-first-century standards.

Even though there's no cure for the disease, Dorothy is relieved to finally have a name for her illness.

The dismissive nature of Dorothy's doctors in the episode was far from an anomaly at the time. First, chronic fatigue syndrome—as it was then known—was often dismissively referred to as the "yuppie flu."[18] The implication of the name was that it was nothing more than a by-product of life in the 1980s, an affliction solely of the Me Generation, which indicated that theirs was a life lived far too quickly—the result of wanting to die young, stay pretty, and leave a beautiful corpse.

It took until 2009—twenty years after this episode aired—for the medical community to take chronic fatigue syndrome seriously and isolate the virus that caused the disease, ultimately proving that the disease wasn't all in patients' heads.

"Researchers report that 68 of 101 patients with the syndrome, or 67 percent, were infected with an infectious virus, xenotropic murine leukemia virus-related virus, or XMRV," revealed a 2009 report in *Discover Magazine*.[19] "By contrast, only 3.7 percent of 218 healthy people were infected. Continuing work after the paper was published has found the virus in nearly 98 percent of about 300 patients with the syndrome."

For her part, Harris told *Vulture*[20] in 2017 that the entire episode was based on her own experiences with the disease, and the doctors who dismissed her symptoms.

"I had all the symptoms, but had very bad experiences with doctors, some of whom told me to dye my hair a different color and asked whether Paul and I were getting along in our marriage," she said to the outlet, all but signaling the Dr. Budd character. "The episode was my way at getting back at all the doctors who didn't believe me; my revenge script for all the people out there who had a disease like that. In the end, it turned out I did not have chronic fatigue syndrome—it was an adrenal issue—but the fact that the episode inspired so many people to go to the doctor was incredible."

Despite the number of years that have passed since this episode first premiered on NBC, women are no better off now than they were when the episode first aired. A recent study by Duke University[21] revealed that one in five women felt that their healthcare providers either dismissed or ignored their claims, and 17 percent said that they felt they were treated differently by their healthcare providers due to their gender (compared to only 14 percent of men who feel their healthcare providers dismissed or ignored their claims and only 6 percent of men who feel they were treated differently by their healthcare providers due to their gender).

What's more, the twenty-first century is much more open and inclusive, even when it comes to dealing with mental health. The implication that Dorothy is somehow more "worthy" of treatment simply because she's mentally sound or that her pain should be taken seriously *because* she's mentally sound—as if those who suffer with mental illness cannot feel pain or that their pain is somehow less than that of others—doesn't sit well by modern standards.

That said, "Sick and Tired" is a crowning achievement for *The Golden Girls*. Writing for *Bitch*,[22] Diane Shipley—who herself suffers from chronic fatigue syndrome—explains that this episode not only inspired her to take control of her own health, but made her feel seen on television for the first time in her life. What's more, Shipley feels that the episode had that effect on everyone who suffers from some sort of debilitating illness, especially those that aren't visible to the public.

"Three decades later, 'Sick and Tired' remains a cultural touchstone for people with chronic illnesses because—even though "tired" doesn't come close to capturing the bone-deep exhaustion sufferers feel—it's one of the most sympathetic and informative onscreen portrayals of ME/CFS, as well as a memorable reference point," she writes. "Not only was it ahead of its time in taking ME/CFS seriously, but it remains one of the few truthful representations of chronic illness to appear on television. Sadly, pop culture representations of ME/CFS are still rare and, where they do appear, typically reinforce negative stereotypes about the condition."

1. "72 Hours"

Season 5, Episode 15

Of all *The Golden Girls* episodes—the 180 episodes featuring Dorothy, Rose, Blanche, and Sophia—"72 Hours," the fifteenth episode from the fifth season of the show, is the crown jewel of the series. No other episode has been able to encapsulate both serious issues and humor while providing teachable moments for both the characters and the viewing audience.

In this episode, the Girls are getting ready for a charity event when Rose receives a letter from the hospital where she got her gall bladder removed three years ago. This, clearly, was during the age prior to electronic communication, and the chances are high that in the twenty-first century, Rose immediately would have received multiple calls on her cell phone or a strongly worded email telling her to come in for a test.

As it turns out, Rose received a blood transfusion while getting her gall bladder removed, and that blood transfusion may have been tainted with HIV, the virus that causes AIDS. To find out whether Rose is indeed HIV positive, she has to have a blood test—and the results aren't available for seventy-two hours. During the early days of HIV, the fastest test that was available took at least three days to provide accurate results. Today, however, at-home HIV tests can provide results in as little as thirty minutes—which, if nothing else, saves a lot of heartache and worry for those who may have been exposed to the virus.[23]

When Rose goes to the hospital for a blood test, all of the Girls are in tow, mostly to provide the emotional support she clearly needs. The receptionist informs Rose that she can give a fake name to maintain her anonymity. (She chooses "Dorothy Zbornak," much to Dorothy's chagrin.) Nowadays, Rose would be protected by the Health Insurance Portability and Accountability Act (commonly known by its acronym, HIPAA), which was passed in 1996 and added to the Social Security Act, but in these times, the best she can do is give a false name.

Blanche tries to comfort Rose with her own story about her experience with HIV—after she had a scare, she was tested for the virus. Once she found out she was negative, she decided to be more cautious and less indiscriminate with her sexual practices. Blanche also tells Rose that she makes sure she knows her partner's sexual history and HIV status before agreeing to going to bed with them.

Upon returning to the house, Rose remains worried about the possibility that she may be HIV positive. Blanche tries to comfort her, but Rose snaps, demanding to know why she—who is, comparatively speaking, a "good girl" when it comes to the number of sexual partners she's had—must face this potential illness, while Blanche seems to be unscathed by the disease.

"AIDS is not a bad person's disease, Rose," Blanche growls. "It is not God punishing people for their sins."

Blanche's admonishment was a direct response to Reverend Jerry Falwell's quote about people with AIDS. According to the "pastor"—a man of God in name only—God sent AIDS to punish American society for daring to be tolerant. "AIDS is not just God's punishment for homosexuals; it is God's punishment for the society that tolerates homosexuals," he said. Then again, Falwell also blamed "abortionists" for 9/11 and claimed that the Antichrist was male and Jewish, so perhaps the phony pastor isn't exactly a fount of Christian wisdom and tolerance. That, however, didn't stop millions of people from believing his nonsense.[24]

Rose humbly admits that Blanche is right, to which Blanche snaps that she's "damn straight." When Rose apologizes, and Blanche does the same, Rose asks Blanche how she managed to deal with the waiting after her HIV test.

"I just kept it to myself and acted like a bitch to everyone else," she replies matter-of-factly.

"Well, no wonder we never knew!" replies Rose.

Later, Sophia reveals that she's been using Dorothy's bathroom instead of the other ones in the house—out of fear that she might contract HIV if Rose is, indeed, positive. Dorothy sharply admonishes her mother and reminds her that HIV cannot be transmitted via toilet seats. As the Girls sit down for tea, they notice that large *R*s label some of the cups. That's when Sophia reveals that she marked the mugs that Rose used so that she wouldn't use them. This, too, angers Dorothy, and she snatches the mug away from her mother.

Sophia's response: "I know, intellectually, I can't catch it—but now that it's so close to home, it's scary."

Eventually, the Girls talk about what they'll do if Rose is HIV positive—and they all decide that they'll support her, no matter what. In an act of solidarity, Sophia reneges on her earlier stance and asks Dorothy for the labeled mug.

When the Girls finally return to the hospital, Rose is—of course—HIV negative, which means that she can now focus her efforts on the charity event coming up.

In addition to being one of the first shows to ever approach AIDS—a very touchy subject in the 1980s and 1990s—with sensitivity and humanity that was sorely missing at the time, "72 Hours" tackles the subject with acerbic but loving humor that dispels the preconceived notions of the disease, while giving a nod and a wink to the community that was most afflicted by it.

Betty White herself said that "72 Hours" was one of her favorite episodes of *The Golden Girls*. She also commended the writers for choosing to make Rose—instead of Blanche—the one who had to endure the wait.

"Not only were people understandably afraid of AIDS, but a lot of people wouldn't even admit it existed," she said.[25] "So, this was a daring episode to do, and the writers went straight for it. It's interesting that they picked Rose for that situation. Blanche was such a busy lady, but if it had been her story, it would have taken on a whole other color. But with Rose being Miss Not-Always-with-It, it came as a real surprise."

Writing for NPR,[26] Barbara Fletcher points out that "72 Hours" was the episode that turned all the AIDS misconceptions on their head. As hard as it is to fathom, AIDS was a "new" disease in the 1980s and 1990s—"72 Hours" aired in 1990, and the CDC had only developed the first commercial blood test just five years prior to the air date—and misconceptions about the disease were rampant. That's in no small part due to the sheer number of deaths caused by HIV. Since 1981, more than one hundred thousand people have died of complications due to the virus, and one-third of those deaths were in 1990 alone.

This may seem like small potatoes given the number of deaths from COVID—and there was no shortage of misinformation there, either—but losing that many people from one disease is nothing if not frightening, especially when it hits so close to home for so many people.

"Rose's dialogue embodies several misconceptions about HIV infection, pervasive at the time: that 'people like her'—an older, middle-class, heterosexual, 'innocent' woman—shouldn't get such a disease, that none of her friends will want to associate with her now, and that she is being punished for some kind of bad behavior," she wrote. "This is what *The Golden Girls* was so good at: bringing home those topics that, often, made people uncomfortable—racism, homosexuality, older female sexuality, sexual harassment, the homeless, addiction, marriage equality and more—and showing us how interconnected and utterly human we all are at any age."

No episode of *The Golden Girls* encapsulates what they were so "good at" better than "72 Hours." With the perfect mix of humor and sensitivity—all while tackling a topic that was nothing if not difficult to broach at the time—it is, quite frankly, the best episode of *The Golden Girls* ever committed to celluloid.

CHAPTER EIGHT

THE END OF AN ERA

All good things must come to an end, and *The Golden Girls* was no exception.

By the end of the fifth season of the show, Bea Arthur began to get upset with what she viewed as "Dorothy bashing" by the writers' room. Jim Colucci, who wrote a book about the behind-the-scenes goings-on of the show, told *Fox News*[1] that Arthur—who was the most like her on-screen character in real life—began taking the scripted slights personally.

"Bea was offended," he told the outlet. "When the writers called Rose [Betty White] dumb or Blanche [Rue McClanahan] a slut or Sophia [Estelle Getty] old, it could roll off those women's backs because they were not like their characters. Unfortunately, the things that were said about Dorothy were that she was big and ugly. And that wears on an actress after a while."

Arthur, too, made it clear that she was a stage actress, first and foremost—and she had every intention of returning to the stage. She had no intention of making the character of Dorothy Zbornak the center of her acting legacy—though, really, that wasn't ever up to her to decide—and she felt that the quality of the writing was slipping with each passing season.

But most of all, Arthur wanted to get out while the show was still on top—*The Golden Girls* was still beloved by its viewing audience when it went off the air in 1992.

Despite growing animosity between Arthur and the rest of the Girls, the writers knew that they wanted to give her—and her character—a proper send-off. There would be no brutal murder here, no going upstairs and never coming down again, no jumping the shark. Rather, writer Mitchell Hurwitz told *The Today Show*[2] that it was all but imperative to do the right thing by his longtime coworker.

"We knew we wanted to kind of give her a fitting tribute and a fitting departure from the show," he said. "She was very moved by the last episode. And she wrote me this lovely note about it. And that was really a privilege. I always felt lucky to be there at all. And to be given a chance to write something that was meaningful for her was really special."

Nevertheless, it wasn't easy for Arthur to say goodbye to her longtime friends—and vice versa.

"I remember there were a lot of goodbyes said that week. And she didn't want to leave. I think Dorothy didn't want to leave and I think Bea Arthur didn't really want to leave," Hurwitz recalled. "It was kind of amazing to be part of something where so much emotion came out of her. . . . As you can see, when you watch it, Bea is really moved trying to say goodbye to these people. And I think they were surprised that she was as moved as she was. I don't think she was surprised, because you know, she was a very deep person. But she didn't show it often. And so, the ending, I think, ended up being very affecting, because we really saw, you know, not only the character leaving, but Bea Arthur dealing with the fact that she was leaving."

The final show of the series was a literal event, drawing numbers that are almost unheard of in the twenty-first century. More than twenty-seven million people tuned in to "One Flew out the Cuckoo's Nest." Although other shows enjoyed staggering numbers—*Friends*, for example, had more than sixty-five million people tune in to its series finale in 2004—such viewership numbers are all but impossible to achieve in an era of streaming. Consider, for example, the series finale of *Black-ish*, which ended in May 2022—and drew only about two million people for its series finale.[3]

When *The Golden Girls* came to an end, its spin-off, *The Golden Palace*, was launched in its place.

By all accounts, *The Golden Palace* had all the right ingredients and should have been as big a hit as its predecessor. Though Arthur was no longer in the picture, *The Golden Palace* featured an all-star cast that included future Oscar nominee Don Cheadle as the hotel manager, Roland, and Cheech Marin as Chuy Castillos, the hotel's chef.

The premise of the show was simple: having sold the Miami home that was the site of *The Golden Girls*'s various hijinks for seven years, the remaining Girls invest in a stripped-down hotel with only two employees, Roland and Chuy.

Like its predecessor, *The Golden Palace* featured several special guest stars that looked more than a little bit familiar. Bobcat Goldthwait starred as a recently released murderer (season 1, episode 2—"Promotional Considerations"), Margaret Cho starred as a doctor and proprietor of a

The Golden Palace—which featured an all-star cast—should have been just as big as its predecessor, but it wasn't.

Chinese restaurant that was *also* named the Golden Palace (season 1, episode 4—"One Old Lady to Go"), Jack Black starred as a cab driver (season 1, episode 8—"Seems Like Old Times, Part 2"), Barry Bostwick starred as one of Blanche's potential suitors (season 1, episode 9—"Just a Gigolo"), and Joely Fisher, Ricardo Montalban, Stephen Root, and George Burns all stopped by. Even Bill Engvall—future star of the Redneck Comedy Tour—made an appearance as Blanche's son, Matthew, and Ned Beatty gave an awesome performance as Blanche's disabled brother, Tad.

Although Arthur stopped by as Dorothy to check on her mother for a two-episode story arc,[4] it wasn't enough to save the show from its inevitable cancellation after only one season. Simply put, the original chemistry just wasn't there. As far as the fans were concerned, there was no point in continuing with a show that didn't have the same color and flavor as the original.

After *The Golden Palace* was canceled, Getty joined the cast of *Empty Nest* as Sophia Petrillo. Ultimately, Getty would play Sophia until 1995 in various shows, retiring the character ten years after she originated it.

So *The Golden Palace* was cancelled. The last time McClanahan appeared as Blanche Devereaux was on May 14, 1993, in *The Golden Palace* episode called "The Chicken and the Egg"; ditto for White's Rose Nylund. But Getty continued playing Sophia Petrillo through episodes of *Empty Nest, Nurses*, and even an episode of *Blossom*, starring future *Jeopardy!* host Mayim Bialik. All told, Getty finally retired the character of Sophia Petrillo in 1995, ten years after she originated the character in the pilot episode of *The Golden Girls*.

But that was far from the end for *The Golden Girls*.

The show was first syndicated in 1989, moving *Wheel of Fortune* from NBC to CBS in so doing. Ever since that time, *The Golden Girls* has been in continuous syndication in the United States, with networks ranging from Lifetime TV to CMT purchasing the rights to air the show. The advent of streaming brought the show to Hulu in 2017, where it is still available as of this writing in 2022.

The Golden Girls is also available in other countries, as well. It aired in Italy on RAI Uno, and currently airs on various networks in the United Kingdom, Canada, Australia, Germany, New Zealand, and Southeast Asia.

Fathom Events[5] also celebrated *The Golden Girls* in movie theaters. In 2021, *Forever Golden! A Celebration of the Golden Girls* was released in theaters. The special showing featured the top five fan favorite episodes of the show: "The Pilot" (season 1, episode 1), "The Flu" (season 1, episode 21), "The Way We Met" (season 1, episode 25), "Ladies of the Evening" (season 2, episode 2), and "Grab That Dough" (season 3, episode 15).

Film and television weren't the only medium in which fans of the show could enjoy the series. *The Golden Girls: Live!* debuted off Broadway in 2003, and although it was a big hit among the New York City crowd, it shut down quickly after receiving a cease-and-desist letter from the original creators of the show. The show, however, wasn't without its gay fans, as Dorothy, Rose, Blanche, and Sophia were all played by men in drag.

Although the off-Broadway show didn't last long for legal reasons, two puppet shows—*Thank You for Being a Friend* and *That Golden Girls Show: A Puppet Parody*—have been approved by the creators and continue to spark interest to this day.

Even a tonsorial glance at Etsy—an online swap meet of sorts where creatives of all stripes sell their wares—features a wide variety of *Golden Girls*-themed *everything*, from soaps to underwear.

It seems like the Girls are, indeed, icons—even in the twenty-first century.

But their true iconic status can be found in the queer community.

CHAPTER NINE

FRIENDS OF DOROTHY

The Girls Become Gay Icons

For most of the nineteenth and twentieth centuries, sodomy laws in the United States were enforced to regulate all forms of non-procreative sex.

Sodomy charges were often tacked on to existing sexually based offenses. These were used predominantly against homosexuals and were based on British colonial laws that were designed to subjugate the empire's colonized peoples, who—perhaps obviously—didn't subscribe to the puritanical Judeo-Christian beliefs espoused by their conquerors.

The goal of these laws—also perhaps obviously—was to subjugate, denigrate, and marginalize already vulnerable populations even further.

"These laws invade privacy and create inequality," reports the Human Rights Watch.[1] "They relegate people to inferior status because of how they look or who they love. They degrade people's dignity by declaring their most intimate feelings 'unnatural' or illegal. They can be used to discredit enemies and destroy careers and lives. They promote violence and give it impunity. They hand police and others the power to arrest, blackmail, and abuse. They drive people underground to live in invisibility and fear."

That's exactly what happened to the queer community in the nineteenth and twentieth centuries. They were further driven into the underground, forced to be clandestine even when they didn't want to be, and denied the right to peacefully exist by those who had no business worrying about such things anyway.

In the late 1960s,[2] sodomy laws were used in a new—and brutal—way against the gay and lesbian population in the United States, which was quickly becoming an increasingly loud voice in the ongoing fight for civil rights. And believe it or not, there was actually quite a bit of intersectionality between the civil rights movement of the 1960s and the rise of queer acceptance around the same time.

That's thanks to a man named Bayard Rustin.

Though the increase of sodomy prosecution of the LGBTQIA community began in the 1960s, there was an infamous arrest that dominated the headlines back in the 1950s. In January 1953, a decade before he would make headlines for spearheading the 1963 March on Washington, Bayard Rustin was arrested in Pasadena, California, on the grounds of "lewd vagrancy," which was the charge used against gay men at the time to criminalize their sexual acts—even if the acts were consensual, as they were in Rustin's case. He was convicted of the charge, spent sixty days in jail, and was forced to register as a sex offender—a stigma he carried for the rest of his life, until he died in 1987. He was posthumously pardoned by California governor Gavin Newsom in February 2020. It's interesting to note that Rustin's arrest took place in a district of Los Angeles, which is allegedly more "liberal" than most of the country. One can only imagine what went on in more conservative cities and states. Incidentally, in 2022, it was announced that a movie was going to be made based on Rustin's life, with Colman Domingo in the titular role.

Unfortunately, in a move that can only be described as the conservative empire striking back against a rising, more liberal voice in favor of more progressive views of queer men and women, several states—including Kansas, Arkansas, Kentucky, Missouri, Montana, Nevada, Tennessee, and Texas—rewrote sodomy laws so that they could be used specifically to target and ultimately prosecute queer people. Two more states—Maryland and Oklahoma—ruled that sodomy laws did not apply to heterosexual couples, meaning that a sodomy charge was a scarlet letter of sorts. And several other states—including Alabama, Florida, Georgia, Mississippi, North Carolina, North Dakota, Pennsylvania, South Dakota, Utah, Virginia, and Washington—informally rewrote their sodomy laws specifically so that they could target gay people—and, more specifically, gay men. Society had certainly leaped ahead socially, in the 1960s, but the laws certainly didn't reflect that change.

Despite the increasing acceptance of the LGBTQIA community in the mainstream zeitgeist, the law was slow to catch up with the changing social tide. Just one year after *The Golden Girls* went on the air, the Supreme Court ruled that sodomy didn't have constitutional protections, which meant that it was perfectly legal for states to make laws against it.[3]

The Supreme Court case in question was the 1986 case of *Bowers v. Hardwick*, which gave Georgia permission to criminalize oral and anal sex.

Hardwick, a homosexual man, was arrested after the police caught him having consensual sex with another man in the privacy of his own home. With the ruling, Hardwick—and other gay men—ran the risk of being arrested, prosecuted, and convicted for the felony crime of sodomy, even in the privacy of their own homes and even in the case of consensual relationships with other adults.

Although 1996's *Romer v. Evans* held that states could not discriminate against gay people simply because they "didn't approve" of their behavior, states often got around this by enforcing sodomy laws against gay men and conveniently looking the other way when it came to straight men.

It took until the 2003 *Lawrence v. Texas* case, which ruled that criminal punishment for sodomy was unconstitutional, for this legal terror to finally come to an end.

So queer people—and, specifically, gay men—were under constant threat of arrest and prosecution simply for living their lives. As such, they had to devise slang terms to both describe—and identify—one another in "polite company."

One such common popular phrase comes from the early twentieth century.

The first recorded use of the phrase was in the 1909 book *The Road to Oz*,[4] written by L. Frank Baum, which featured the beloved characters from the *The Wizard of Oz*.

During one of her subsequent visits to Oz, Dorothy befriends a character named Polychrome (known as "Polly" throughout the book), who can't seem to make heads or tails of Dorothy's motley crew of misfits, weirdos, and freaks. "You have some queer[5] friends, Dorothy," she said.

"The queerness doesn't matter, so long as they're friends," was the answer.

This, combined with Judy Garland's status as a gay icon,[6] cemented the phrase "friend of Dorothy"[7] into the American lexicon. It was a term that both identified gay men to one another and endeared them to like-minded individuals who served as both cover and community when necessary.

By some estimates, "friend of Dorothy" was first used during World War II, though the term "Mrs. King" was also common parlance. It's not clear what "Mrs. King" referenced—the origins seem lost to the annals of time—but some linguistic experts believe that "friend of Dorothy" doesn't refer to *The Wizard of Oz* character, but to the writer and socialite Dorothy Parker, a popular figure of the time who was also married to an openly bisexual man.[8]

Regardless of the true origins of "friend of Dorothy," it's no longer as commonly used as it once was, especially among the millennial and Gen Z queer community. Thanks to the prevalence of social media—and with the greater acceptance of the community by the populace at large—the phrase "friend of Dorothy" has fallen largely out of favor. Perhaps millennial and Gen Z queer people feel "safer" in their own skin—or at least freer to express themselves, with more outlets at their disposal thanks to the Internet, social media, and cell phones—and thus don't need such terms to provide cover and community as their boomer and Gen X counterparts did.[9]

But in the context of *The Golden Girls* and given the increasing assault on the hard-won gains by an increasingly right-wing Supreme Court and a so-called Moral Majority, perhaps the phrase might come back into common parlance. This is not to suggest the need to shove queer people "back in the closet," but rather to suggest that using the term could provide a sense of safety during such volatile times.

It's worth noting, too, that "Moral Majority" is more than a bit of a misnomer.

Contrary to its name—and to paraphrase the grunge group L7's biggest hit "Pretend We're Dead"—the Moral Majority is neither. When the Moral Majority was first formed by the Reverend Jerry Falwell in 1979, only 25 percent of the United States identified as evangelical Christian, which means that three-quarters of the United States was not evangelical. What's more, evangelical Christians are not a monolith—writing for the *New York Times*, Gabriel Salguero pointed out that Latino evangelicals voted for Barack Obama, who didn't receive the backing of other evangelical voting blocs—and in 2021, only 14.5 percent of the American population identified as evangelical.[10]

"The story [*The Golden Girls*] was about these women who were a little bit older," said NPR's Linda Holmes.[11] "So, they had an opportunity to say, hey, you know, you might not be used to gay couples or interracial couples or whatever. If you have this discomfort, here are these women kind of running up against whatever discomfort they may have or not have."

For many queer kids—and for kids who didn't feel like they quite "fit in," whether queer or not—seeing women who could have been their mothers, their grandmothers, their aunts, or their cousins approach topics that were new to them, foreign to them, and that clearly caused them some level of discomfort—topics that were taboo "in their day"—with a level of love, empathy, and understanding that may have been bereft in their own lives was nothing if not a comfort to them.

As one of the few mainstream shows to tackle these topics with such sensitivity—and humor—*The Golden Girls* did its part to normalize these types of conversations. It integrated queer people into society as a whole, ensuring that they were more than just a punchline for a sophomoric joke on *Saturday Night Live*—or, worse yet, the target of Andrew Dice Clay's hate-filled, rage-fueled missives that bordered on psychotic and obsessed—and helping its audience see that queer people were *human*, first and foremost, and deserving of just as much love as their straight counterparts.

Indeed, no matter how dated some episodes of the show—especially the earlier ones—may be, love, empathy, and understanding are universal, and seeing it on television is a welcome respite from an otherwise cold, cruel, and calculating world.

"The main takeaway after each episode, regardless of its story, must be the underlying theme of the show: Everyone deserves support, friends, and love," wrote Logan Raschke for the *Daily Eastern News*.[12] "That's what Blanche, Rose, Dorothy, and Sophia mean to each other. The show is so touching, impactful, and prominent on top of being hilarious and entertaining."

The added bonus was that reel life and real life overlapped. More than just being welcoming and accepting on *The Golden Girls*—even in the face of discomfort—the actresses who brought the Girls to life were just as involved in LGBTQIA activism when the cameras stopped rolling.

Since the 1970s—when it wasn't nearly as fashionable to do so and, in fact, risky on many levels—Bea Arthur embraced and campaigned on behalf of the gay community. In private, she hosted dinner parties at her sprawling Los Angeles home, where gay men—who were very closeted at the time, as they were targets of arbitrarily enforced sodomy laws if they weren't—were free to be their fully authentic selves without fear of reprisal. "They were always excited to come to her house," said Matthew Saks, the elder of Arthur's sons, to *The Hollywood Reporter*.[13] "I remember Rock Hudson was over once and him clearing the table. He was balancing five dishes on one hand. I was like, 'How can you do that?' He said, 'Before I was in the Navy, I was a waiter.'"

Arthur continued her activism into the 2000s, when a one-woman show raised $40,000 for the Ali Forney Center in New York City. The center, which was in financial peril, was saved from closure thanks to Arthur's generosity.

"These kids at the Ali Forney Center are literally dumped by their families because of the fact that they are lesbian, gay or transgender—this organization really is saving lives," Arthur said to *Next Magazine* in 2005.[14]

When she died in 2009, Arthur bequeathed a $300,000 check to the Ali Forney Center, which ultimately carried the organization through the country's recession at the time. In response, Carl Siciliano—the executive director of the Ali Forney Center—promised to name the first building the organization ever owned in Arthur's honor. In 2017, that promise was ful-filled when the Bea Arthur Residence, in New York City's East Village, opened its doors to house eighteen homeless LGBTQIA youth.

"For Bea and her golden girls, all troubles could be resolved with cheesecake and friendship," Siciliano wrote for the *Huffington Post*.[15] "The Bea Arthur Residence will also be a place where LGBT youths will find friendship, support and love."

Arthur's on-screen mother, Estelle Getty, was also an outspoken activist for the LGBTQIA community. Harvey Fierstein, who costarred with Getty in *Torch Song Trilogy*, told the *New York Times*[16] that Getty not only cam-paigned for HIV/AIDS activism at a time when it wasn't fashionable to do so, but cared for victims of the virus including her nephew, Stephen Scher, and her *Torch Song Trilogy* costar Court Miller.

In several interviews, too, Getty made clear that she refused to engage in homophobic behavior despite its acceptability at the time. "I will not do gay bashing jokes," she said in 1987 at the AIDS Project Los Angeles White Party.[17] "I've been in show business all my life, and the majority of my friends are gay. I don't deny that. A lot of my friends have died from AIDS."

In 1996, Getty was involved in the capital campaign for Beacon Place, a shelter for HIV-positive patients that also provides palliative care to its patients. Located in her nephew Stephen's hometown of Greensboro, North Carolina, Beacon Place is still open as of 2022.

"Stephen needed something like Beacon Place in 1991, but this wasn't available," she said to the *Greensboro News and Record*[18] when the shelter opened.

In addition to being a vegetarian and an outspoken animal rights activist, Rue McClanahan was an outspoken gay rights activist, as well. Since her little-known stint in the 1971 indie film *Some of My Best Friends Are*—which was set in a gay bar and featured the legendary Fannie Flagg and Warhol girl (and transgender icon) Candy Darling—McClanahan was an "out" and proud advocate of the queer community. She frequently appeared at pride events and fundraisers for LGBTQIA causes and advocated for same-sex marriage in the United States.

Most notably, McClanahan participated in the 2009 Broadway benefit, *Defying Inequality*, which featured a star-studded cast[19] and raised money in the hopes of defeating the controversial Prop 8 bill[20] in California.

Betty White—the Golden Girl who lived the longest of the four—had a long-standing history of standing up for the LGBTQIA community, even in the face of direct threats to her standing in Hollywood circles.

In addition to recording AIDS awareness public service announcements, White took every opportunity to speak up on behalf of the community.

"I don't care who anybody sleeps with," she said to *Parade*[21] in 2010. "If a couple has been together all that time—and there are gay relationships that are more solid than some heterosexual ones—I think it's fine if they want to get married. I don't know how people can get so anti-something. Mind your own business, take care of your affairs, and don't worry about other people so much."

She reiterated this sentiment on a 2014 episode of *Larry King Live*.[22] "Oh, I don't care who you sleep with, whom you sleep with, it's what kind of a human being are you," she said to the veteran talk show host.

Bear in mind that gay marriage wasn't legalized, at the federal level, until 2015. White began advocating for the legalization of gay marriage five years before the Supreme Court struck down all bans on the practice.

The year before, she donned purple—while joking that she'd changed her name to "Betty Purple" for one day—to stand in solidarity with bullied LGBTQIA youth.[23]

For decades, we have thanked Rose, Blanche, Sophia, and—yes— Dorothy for "being a friend." Sometimes, they might have been the only friends we had.

And over the years, the Girls demonstrated that they were more than just friends—they were family, *chosen* family, family that was loving and supportive when time, distance, or even familial rejection left viewers' "real" families at a distance. One can see, then, why the queer community—especially in the 1980s, when they were subject to more judgment, discrimination, and ostracization—gravitated toward these women.

To say we are "friends of Dorothy," then, is to say we are part of a collective that eschews judgments, proselytizing, and hatred in favor of support, friendship, and love.

And that's not such a bad thing after all.

CONCLUSION

An Incomparable Pop Culture Legacy

What started as a sitcom born out of a sketch that seemed—at least on the surface—rather stupid, tired, and banal turned out to be an iconic sitcom that has withstood the test of time and turned its stars into icons that have transcended generations.

But what is it, really, that makes *The Golden Girls* so iconic? What makes the show so important, so unique, and so timely in the twenty-first century?

There are a number of factors, of course—and they all have to do with the women at the core of the show: Beatrice Arthur, Rue McClanahan, Betty White, and Estelle Getty.

Much like Arthur's prior show, *Maude*, before it, nothing was off-limits for the Girls. Whether they were addressing homosexuality, artificial insemination, or AIDS, the tough topics were fair game. But they didn't beat us over the head with proselytizing or morality—rather, they addressed even the toughest topics with equal amounts of humor and love, proving to all of us that we, too, could handle them in the same way.

Indeed, the show created a "safe space" before it was popular to do so—and that made it easier for every other show in its wake to address the toughest of topics with humor and love.

Prior to the debut of *The Golden Girls*, women older than fifty were depicted as dowdy, matronly, and all but nonexistent outside the core of their nuclear family. They were blank slates—they were asexual—they were little more than an extension of their families.

But thanks to *The Golden Girls*, older women were seen in a whole new way: as career professionals, as warm and understanding friends, and as fully realized sexual beings. Though all the Girls were vivacious—they had hobbies, they had jobs, and they did volunteer work—Blanche Devereaux took it up a notch. She was sexy and she knew it—and she made sure everyone else did, too.

The Golden Girls also was one of the first shows—if not *the* first show—to tackle queer issues in a respectful, insightful way. Queer people weren't just the punchlines of a hateful joke, and neither were they ridiculous stereotypes. Rather, they were multilayered, nuanced people who needed love—and were worthy of it, regardless of what certain politicians suggested to the contrary.

The way the Girls tackled queer issues was so groundbreaking, in fact, that they are *all* considered gay icons to this very day. And it wasn't just the fictional characters that were iconic—the actresses were "about that life" in both their reel lives *and* their real lives, adding to their iconic status. They walked the walk and talked the talk—and a whole generation of queer people who may have felt that they didn't have anyone to look to for the love and affection that they so desperately craved suddenly had four mothers, four aunts, four elder sisters, four cousins that they didn't have before.

Most of all, the *Girls* was proudly progressive in an era that was very conservative—and its brand of social progressivism was so forward thinking that the issues it raised over the course of 180 episodes are still relevant to this day.

Writing for *Scary Mommy*,[1] journalist Sa'iyda Shabazz encapsulates why we love our Girls decades after the show went off the air. "Television and the world have come a long way in 35 years, but *The Golden Girls* still feels as relevant as ever," she wrote. "Perhaps that's why it's never gone out of syndication. The four women on the show taught an entire generation what growing older can look like. It taught us how to be the friends who turn into family. Now it's teaching a new generation the same thing. I'm grateful to live in a world where Dorothy, Blanche, Rose and Sophia exist."

And though none of the Girls are with us today, their legacy will live on forever.

All that's left to say to our beloved Dorothy, Rose, Blanche, and Sophia, then, is thank you.

Thank you, ladies, for being a friend to *all* of us.

Thank you all for being our friends.

ACKNOWLEDGMENTS

The act of writing a book is a solitary act, to be sure, but I am by no means without a system of support and love that leaves me humbled and grateful. This space, then, is dedicated to these people.

First and foremost, I need to thank the Universe—for lack of a better way of putting the energy that binds us all—and my two greatest teachers, Rev. Dr. Lady Auset (and her husband, Lord Ra) and Sorceress Cagliastro of the Iron Ring. I also need to thank Rih and Jordan of All about Intentions for all they've done in helping me manifest the life I want and Harold Sconiers, the greatest life coach a girl could ask for.

Next, I need to thank the five greatest human beings on Earth: my nephews Tony, JuJu, Nijah Bear, and my baby King Bing Stinkie, and my niece Jahni Girl. *Titzie loves you!*

To the rest of my family: my mom Anna, my sister Marissa, my brother-in-law Cut, my aunt Lydia and my uncle Alfredo, and my cousins Paula (and Dave, Adrianna, and Leo) and Marina (and Jason and Aniyah), Joanne, Anthony Jr. and Philip, Roberta and Dario, Patrizia and Stefano, and all the members of my extended family scattered throughout the United States, Canada, Italy, and Sicily. (There are far too many of us to name individually—I think I'm personally related to approximately one of every ten Italians walking this Earth and one of every four Sicilians walking this Earth, without exaggeration.) Quite the motley crew we are . . . and I love you all for it.

To my Rottweiler, Angela—also known as Big Ang, Fat Fat, and Fatty McFatterton—for snoring at my feet as I wrote this book late into the night. (As if you can read this thing.) Thanks for saving my life and my mom's life, literally and figuratively. Sometimes angels come in human form, and sometimes they come in the form of fat Rottweilers who eat too much Italian food. I'm grateful you're the latter. Thanks, Big Ang. Special thanks, too, to Hounds Town Doggie Day Care in Island Park, New York, for keeping her amused five days out of the week while I toiled away at this book.

To my friends in real life: Douglas Friday, Robyn Smith-Kaiser (and Larry Kaiser, and Maverick, and of course, CharStar the Little Rock Star), Marabelle Blue, Jenny "Devil Doll" Gonzalez (and Eric Blitz), Philip Richards (and Jeanne "Panini" Pinnieri-Richards), Ray Monell, Cymande Russell (and Akira), Sesh Foluke-Henderson, Taalib "Ghetto Philosopher" Wheeler (and Goddess Queen Nefertari), Dr. JonPaul Higgins (and Jonathan Ray), Shaun Lally, Gerard "HipHopGamer" Williams (and RedInfamy), Walter "Lucky Church" Simons (and Vivian Veng), Jasmine O'Day (and Jessica O'Day), Patricia Kuneff, Chrissy Melchiore, and all the people whose names I'm forgetting right now (but whom I will remember when the book comes out and gladly add a follow-up post on my website or something). I love you guys, and that's not something I say lightly.

To Christen Karniski and Deni Remsberg of Rowman & Littlefield, for seeing this vision and believing in my ability to deliver above and beyond all expectations. Here's to success with this book and many, many more.

To all the people I work and have worked with, whom I love and respect and appreciate forever, and whose continued support means the world: Richard Willis Jr. and Bryan Ransom. The Metropolitan Opera. *Teen Vogue. Vogue Italia.* VH1. *XXL Magazine. The Source Magazine. LatinTRENDS Magazine. Go! NYC Magazine.* Interactive One. *Vibe. Blasting News. The Inquisitr. Contrast Magazine.* Kool G Rap. G-Unit. Curtis "50 Cent" Jackson (so much love and respect for this man!). Lloyd Banks. Tony Yayo. Kidd Kidd. Mike Styles. The G-Unit Riders. Michael Maddaloni. Chris Lanston. Nassau Community College. Hofstra University. Dr. Kenneth Lampl. WLIR-FM. WBAB-FM. Malibu Sue. Rob Rush. Andre Ferro. Jon Daniels. Keith "Fingers" Steele. Joe Rock. Vinnie "The Chainsaw" Graziano. Amanda Elsheikh. Scott Church. Michael Donati. Sarah Squeaky. Alan Davis. Renee Graziano. Karen Gravano. Big Ang Raiola (God rest your beautiful soul). *Good Times Magazine. Long Island Entertainment Magazine* (RIP). *The Inside Connection* (RIP). Splash News. PR Photos. FlashCity (RIP). WENN. SIPA. Ariel Publicity. John Gilbert Young. Anita Gordy (RIP to the beautiful Ryan). Sam Felipe. The list goes on, and I'm sure I'm forgetting people along the way, but again, you are loved and respected and appreciated. Thanks for believing in the talents of a nerdy Sicilian girl with too many books, too many records, too many smart-assed remarks, and too many crazy dreams—and for making all of them come true and even giving me dreams I never thought I could have and making *them* come true. Y'all are awesome, and I sincerely hope the Universe blesses you and provides for you for all the days of your life.

To the professional places I currently call home: FinTech TV, all the Blavity properties, and Mozell Entertainment/Ransom Notice/Pop Icon Clashes. Thank you, all, for the faith you put into me and my work every day. I hope I make you glad, every day, that you hired me.

And finally, I'd like to thank every one of you for reading this book. May you all have the guts to chase your dreams wherever they may lead you, to live your life out loud, to *never* dim your light—and most of all, to speak out against injustice and bad behavior when you see it, no matter what it costs. I appreciate you all.

Don't talk about it. Don't tweet about it. Don't wish about it.

Be about it, and then *do* it. Period.

NOTES

INTRODUCTION

1. Corinne Heller, "Betty White Dead at 99: Ryan Reynolds and More Celebs Mourn Beloved Actress," *E! News*, December 31, 2021, www.eonline.com/news/1314861 /betty-white-dead-at-99-ryan-reynolds-and-more-celebs-mourn-beloved-actress.

2. Dustin Fitzharris, "Catching up with the Golden Girls' Susan Harris," *Out*, February 6, 2015, www.out.com/entertainment/television/2010/10/03/catching-golden -girls-susan-harris.

I. A BRIEF HISTORY OF THE GIRLS

1. Nicholas Fonseca,"Bea Arthur: 'Golden Girls' Memories," EW.com, April 24, 2009, www.ew.com/ew/article/0,,1100651,00.html.

2. Diamond died in May 1985, just a few months before *The Golden Girls*—the show on which her infamous sketch was based—debuted on NBC.

3. At the time, Roberts was known for her role as Mildred, the wisecracking secretary, on *Remington Steele*, which starred Stephanie Zimbalist and a pre-007 Pierce Brosnan.

4. Fonseca,"Bea Arthur: 'Golden Girls' Memories."

5. Anita Gates, "Austin Kalish, a Writer of 'Maude' Abortion Episode, Dies at 95," *New York Times*, October 8, 2016, www.nytimes.com/2016/10/08/arts/television/aus tin-kalish-dead.html.

6. Rue McClanahan, *My First Five Husbands . . . and the Ones Who Got Away* (New York: Random House, 2007).

7. "Rue McClanahan," Television Academy Interviews, February 22, 2019, https:// interviews.televisionacademy.com/interviews/rue-mcclanahan.

8. "Rue McClanahan," Television Academy Interviews.

9. In the season 1, episode 26 episode, "The Way We Met," Dorothy and Blanche are arguing on the couch about watching *Another World*. As can be expected, Blanche wants to watch the soap opera, but Dorothy does not. Many fans of the show believe that this is a tip of the hat to McClanahan's past on the once-beloved soap opera.

10. *Torch Song Trilogy* also featured a then-unknown actor named Matthew Broderick, who played a teenager in the plays.

156   NOTES

11. David Vergun, "Before Stage and Screen, Bea Arthur Shined as a Marine," U.S. Department of Defense, October 13, 2021, www.defense.gov/News/Feature-Stories/Story/Article/2803048/before-stage-and-screen-bea-arthur-shined-as-a-marine/.

12. Kali Martin, "Bea Arthur, US Marine," The National World War II Museum, April 11, 2018, www.nationalww2museum.org/war/articles/bea-arthur-us-marine.

13. Piscator, like Bertolt Brecht, was a proponent of epic theater, which is when the sociopolitical elements of the story are emphasized over the more emotional aspects, which can be seen as "manipulating" the audience. With such an impressive mentor, then, it's no wonder that Arthur's regal appearance—and subsequent career—featured biting commentary and liberal politics over emotionally overwrought scenes.

14. In 2017, a book anthology confirmed that despite George Lucas's best efforts to make the *Star Wars Holiday Special* little more than a 1970s fever dream, the film was not only classified as canon, but Arthur's character of Ackmena was a queer woman who had a wife named Sorschi—thereby once again solidifying Arthur's status as a queer icon (Joe Schmidt, "Star Wars Book Confirms 'Holiday Special' Character as Canon and Gay," Comicbook.com, October 24, 2017, https://comicbook.com/starwars/news/star-wars-holiday-special-bea-arthur-ackmena-canon/).

15. "Rue McClanahan," Television Academy Interviews.

16. "Rue McClanahan," Television Academy Interviews.

17. Sean Daly, "Why Bea Arthur Wanted to Quit 'Golden Girls' and More Secrets from behind the Lanai," *Fox News*, April 4, 2016, www.foxnews.com/entertainment/why-bea-arthur-wanted-to-quit-golden-girls-and-more-secrets-from-behind-the-lanai.

18. United Press International, "'Girls' Prompts $5-Million Suit," *Los Angeles Times*, July 5, 1986, www.latimes.com/archives/la-xpm-1986-07-05-ca-20405-story.html.

2. GRANDMAS GONE WILD

1. The "tradwife" movement—a portmanteau of "traditional" and "wife"—can be considered a 1950s housewife cosplay, at best. Omnipresent (or seemingly so) on Instagram, members of the tradwife movement endorse a "traditional" role for women in marriage, with the husband managing everything about finances and a job and the wife being taken "under his wing" like a particularly submissive apprentice or a child. Despite its carefully curated image, with the likes of Katie Couric touting its values, the tradwife movement is quite sinister and noxious in its modus operandi. Its repugnance is not because the women are choosing to be "traditional"—to the contrary, women are free to choose the lifestyle they please—but because the tradwife movement is rooted in white supremacy, the alt-right, and the more fringe elements of the Republican Party. Critics of the movement have noted its rise has coincided with the decline in American birth rates—especially of white children—and the movement's insistence on white women having white babies suggests that the messaging isn't as subtle as it seems at first glance. Plus, as we see later in this chapter, the "1950s housewife" trope is a stereotype that has no basis in reality (Katie Couric, "The Real Tradwives of 2022: Why More Young Moms Are Becoming Traditional Housewives," Katie Couric Media, April 9, 2022, https://katiecouric.com/culture/what-is-a-tradwife/; Catherine Rottenberg and Shani Orgad, "Tradwives: The Women Looking for a Simpler Past but Grounded in the Neoliberal Present," *The Conversation*, February 11, 2022, https://theconversation.com/tradwives-the-women-looking-for-a-simpler-past-but-grounded-in-the-neoliberal-present-130968).

2. "Women in the 1950s," Eisenhower Presidential Library, accessed August 8, 2022, www.eisenhowerlibrary.gov/research/online-documents/women-1950s.

3. Asha C. Gilbert, "'He Stays': Betty White Refused to Remove Black Dancer from Her Show in 1954," *USA Today*, January 5, 2022, www.usatoday.com/story/entertainment /celebrities/2022/01/01/betty-white-black-dancer-arthur-duncan/9067252002/.

4. Weber's most infamous work was a film called *Where Are My Children?* which was about a doctor who performed illegal abortions in a small town. Screenings for the film were consistently sold out, and at the Boston premiere more than twenty-five hundred people reportedly waited in line to catch a screening.

5. Jill S. Tietjen and Barbara Bridges, "The Women Hollywood Forgot," *The Helm*, June 11, 2021, https://thehelm.co/hollywood-herstory-book/.

6. The 2007 television show *Mad Men*, starring Jon Hamm as Don Draper, frequently referenced these types of social mores—although the show was set in 1960 at the start of the series, very little had changed since the late 1950s.

7. Kate Moore, "The American History of Silencing Women through Psychiatry," *Time*, June 22, 2021, https://time.com/6074783/psychiatry-history-women-mental-health/.

8. In the 1950s, more working-class and poor women died from illegal abortions than the total number of Americans who perished in the Vietnam War. Rich women, however, had the funds and the means to go to private clinics to get a "procedure" without much fanfare in all fifty states, if that's what they so chose—and if they chose to keep the out-of-wedlock child, that too was quite alright, although not exactly preferred, especially if the father of the child was of a lower economic caste ("Mrs. America: Women's Roles in the 1950s," PBS, accessed February 4, 2022, www.pbs.org/wgbh/americanexperience /features/pill-mrs-america-womens-roles-1950s/).

9. This phenomenon, too, was often a function of financial means. Poorer families often would push the "shotgun wedding" or adoption, whereas richer families had more options at their disposal.

10. "Mrs. America: Women's Roles in the 1950s."

11. "Women in the 1950s."

12. "Women's Earnings: The Pay Gap (Quick Take)," *Catalyst*, June 30, 2022, www .catalyst.org/research/womens-earnings-the-pay-gap/.

13. "Psychiatry: The Wife Beater & His Wife," *Time*, September 25, 1964, http:// content.time.com/time/subscriber/article/0,33009,876203,00.html.

14. *That Girl* is considered the forerunner to *The Mary Tyler Moore Show*, though the latter was far more popular than the former.

3. BACK IN ST. OLAF

1. The actual town is called St. Olaf Township, Minnesota, and it was established in 1870. Named after Olaf II of Norway, St. Olaf Township was originally called Oxford Township, and it kept that name until 1869. As of the 2020 census, the population of St. Olaf Township was 395 people ("Total Population in St. Olaf Township, Otter Tail County, Minnesota," U.S. Census Bureau, accessed August 8, 2022, https://data.census.gov/cedsci /all?q=st+olaf+township+minnesota+population).

2. "Betty White Called 'C' Word by 'Golden Girls' Star Bea Arthur," TMZ, April 11, 2022, www.tmz.com/2022/02/10/betty-white-c-word-golden-girls-bea-arthur/.

3. Megan Garber, "The Sly Sunniness of Betty White," *The Atlantic*, January 2, 2022, www.theatlantic.com/culture/archive/2022/01/betty-white/621144/.

4. The name "Henny Penny" comes from the Americanization of the Norwegian phrase *høne pøne*, which means "fine hen."

5. "History of Measles," Centers for Disease Control and Prevention, November 5, 2020, www.cdc.gov/measles/about/history.html.

6. "Just Say No," History.com, May 31, 2017, www.history.com/topics/1980s /just-say-no.

7. Brian Mann, "There Is Life after Addiction: Most People Recover," NPR, January 15, 2022, www.npr.org/2022/01/15/1071282194/addiction-substance-recovery-treatment.

8. To this day, some people believe that addiction is a disease that can be cured. Contrary to this erroneous belief, the disease can be treated and managed successfully but never cured (Mann, "There Is Life after Addiction").

9. Erin Clements, "5 'Golden Girls' Episodes Where Betty White Shines as Rose," *Today*, December 31, 2021, www.today.com/popculture/tv/betty-white-golden-girls -episodes-rcna10209.

10. It's unclear whether this is a tradition from the "old country" or from a small town in the United States, but as a rule, arranged marriages aren't a part of American culture. And though it's possible that arranged marriages may have been performed in Sweden in the past, they were outlawed as of 2009 (David Landes, "'Outlaw Forced Marriages in Sweden,'" *The Local*, June 2, 2009, www.thelocal.se/20090602/19820/).

11. The line is from "Reluctance" by Robert Frost, and it's from the final stanza of the poem, which reads in full: "Ah, when to the heart of man / Was it ever less than a treason / To go with the drift of things / To yield with a grace to reason / And bow and accept the end / Of a love or a season?"

12. The words "shade" and "reading" have entered common parlance in the twenty-first century, but prior to *RuPaul's Drag Race*, the terms were used almost exclusively in queer Black and Latino communities, especially in New York City. Although there is a lot of nuance behind both "shade" and "reading" and their respective meanings—and the cult classic documentary, *Paris Is Burning*, goes into detail about those nuances courtesy of the late, great Dorian Corey—in a nutshell, "shade" refers to a subtle insult that's more contextual than anything else, and "reading" refers to a direct insult. To put it in the context of *The Golden Girls*, Blanche's backhanded "Southern belle" compliments are considered shade, whereas Sophia's direct Sicilian-grandmother-style insults are considered reading.

13. Ybarra v. Illinois 444 U.S. 85 (1979).

14. Blanche's reasoning is that she won the tickets, whereas Dorothy's reasoning is that it's her mother who is bailing them out. Rose, however, insists that she deserves to keep her ticket because "I lost Butter Queen! Haven't I suffered enough?" That line draws uproarious laughter from the audience because Rose had regaled those in the holding cell with her story of losing a coveted beauty pageant title back in St. Olaf.

4. GYPSIES, TRAMPS, AND SLUTS

1. Slut-shaming is "embarrassing, insulting or otherwise denigrating a girl or woman for her real or extrapolated sexual behavior, including for dressing in a sexual way, having sexual feelings and/or exploring and exhibiting them" (Emily Lindin, "6 Ways You

May Be Slut Shaming without Realizing It," *Teen Vogue*, June 3, 2016, www.teenvogue.com/story/slut-shaming-subtle-ways-unslut.

2. This seems to be a direct swipe at the United Daughters of the Confederacy, an organization founded in 1894 that, among other things, believes in the "Lost Cause of the Confederacy," which suggests that the Confederate side of the Civil War was fighting for a just cause and it had *nothing* to do with slavery. Perhaps unsurprisingly, this belief is dismissed as the pseudohistorical nonsense that it is.

3. This was in season 1, episode 11 of *The Golden Palace* titled "Camp Town Races Aren't as Fun as They Used to Be," in which a then-unknown Don Cheadle—who played Roland Wilson, the manager of the hotel—schooled Blanche on the real history of the Confederate flag and what it meant to a Black man like him. It's worth tracking down this episode to listen to Cheadle's monologues, because they're not only shockingly prescient, but they're still relevant today.

4. Douglas Martin, "Rue McClanahan, Actress and Golden Girl, Dies at 76," *New York Times*, June 4, 2010, www.nytimes.com/2010/06/04/arts/04mcclanahan.html.

5. Erin Donnelly, "We Figured out How Many Men 'The Golden Girls' Dated," Refinery29, August 31, 2015, www.refinery29.com/en-us/2015/08/93152/golden-girls-how-many-dates.

6. Tracie Egan Morrissey, "Rue McClanahan: An Appreciation of the Original Jezebel," *Jezebel*, June 3, 2010, jezebel.com/rue-mcclanahan-an-appreciation-of-the-original-jezebel-5554762.

7. "Summary of Major Provisions of the Department of Education's Title IX Final Rule," U.S. Department of Education, June 28, 2021, www2.ed.gov/about/offices/list/ocr/docs/titleix-summary.pdf.

8. The title of this episode is based on a song in the film *A Star Is Born* called "The Man That Got Away," which is best known for being performed by gay icon Judy Garland in the film. The final stanza of the song's lyrics references a woman looking for the man who got away, which precisely describes Blanche, especially in this episode. Though she yearns for her dead husband, George, she's pining over Ham, "the man that got away."

9. *The Golden Girls* was frequently successful at casting veterans and legends from the stage and the small screen for memorable guest parts, and the role of Ham Lushbough was no exception. In this case, John Harkins brought the character to life. The veteran of the Actors Studio was best known for his television roles on *Dark Shadows* and *Cagney & Lacey* and for his roles in such films as *Absence of Malice* (opposite Paul Newman) and *Six Weeks* (opposite Mary Tyler Moore and Dudley Moore). Sadly, however, Harkins died in 1999 at the age of sixty-six.

10. John Schuck brought the character of Gil Kessler to life. Schuck, at the time, was best known for his role as Captain Waldowski in the film *MASH*; today, he's best known for his role on *Law & Order: Special Victims Unit* as Chief Muldrew, the chief of detectives. As of 2022, Schuck is alive and still working as an actor.

11. Paul Schotsmans, "Bereavement: Reactions, Consequences and Care," *Health Policy* 5, no. 1 (1985): 86–88, https://doi.org/10.1016/0168-8510(85)90071-5.

12. This is a continuity error—in the season 2, episode 6 show called "Big Daddy's Little Lady," Blanche's father Curtis (aka Big Daddy) says that Blanche's mother's name is Elizabeth Ann Bennett.

13. This is seen, correctly, as a swipe at the Daughters of the American Revolution, who believe in ahistorical pseudohistory about the American Civil War (which they call "The War of Northern Aggression").

14. Kamille Santana, "Can You Trust At-Home Pregnancy Tests?" UHealth Collective, August 5, 2022, https://news.umiamihealth.org/en/can-you-trust-at-home-pregnancy-tests/.

15. Alma Gottlieb, "Menstrual Taboos: Moving beyond the Curse," in *The Palgrave Handbook of Critical Menstruation Studies*, ed. Chris Bobel, Inga T. Winkler, Breanne Fahs, Katie Ann Hasson, Elizabeth Arveda Kissling, and·Tomi-Ann Roberts (Singapore: Palgrave Macmillan, 2020), 143–62. https://doi.org/10.1007/978-981-15-0614-7_14.

16. This comment is in reference to the "B" story line in the episode, in which Sophia decides to throw a wake for herself after she and Rose attend an Irish wake and have the time of their lives. As it turned out, someone began dancing with the corpse at one point during the wake, which Rose found "surprisingly touching."

17. This is the second time that Arthur sang "Hard-Hearted Hannah" on television. The first time she sang it was on season 2, episode 10 of *Maude* called "Maude's Musical," which originally aired on November 13, 1973.

18. There's no way that a story line about saving a southern plantation—where these were countless abuses involving slavery and the mistreatment of Black Americans victimized as part of the transatlantic slave trade—would fly in the twenty-first century.

19. Best known for his role on *The Carol Burnett Show*, Lyle Wesley Waggoner was also known for his role as Steve Trevor—and later, Steve Trevor Jr.—in the *Wonder Woman* television series opposite Linda Carter's titular character. In his later years, Waggoner founded a company called Star Waggons, which rented luxury trailers to studios. Waggoner died of cancer in March 2020, just before the COVID-19 pandemic went into full swing.

20. In earlier episodes of *The Golden Girls*, it was revealed that George died in a horrific car crash. In this episode, it's presumed that the accident featured a crash test dummy in place of George, or perhaps another person's body in place of George's, or maybe the accident never really happened at all.

21. It's unclear why Blanche is confused about George's misrepresentation of the truth—because in the season 5, episode 18 show called "An Illegitimate Concern," George's love child—the product of a secret affair he had with a woman in Dallas during a business trip—is revealed. So it's not as if George *never* lied to Blanche prior to this.

5. SHADY PINES, MA

1. Mayerene Barker, "Match Arranged in Sicily Stands Test of Time: Couple Chalks up 80 Years of Marriage," *Los Angeles Times*, January 13, 1987, www.latimes.com/archives/la-xpm-1987-01-13-me-4196-story.html and Gaia Zol, "Arranged Marriage in Italy: The Disappearance of Saman," Life in Italy, August 4, 2021, https://lifeinitaly.com/she-refuses-the-arranged-marriage-then-she-disappears/.

2. In today's parlance, Phil would be classified as "gender fluid" or simply "queer." But in the 1980s, this was the best way they could describe Phil's non-heteronormative gender expression.

3. Ebbets Field was a Major League Baseball field located in the Flatbush section of Brooklyn. It was demolished in 1960 and replaced with the Ebbets Field apartments, which are known as the Jackie Robinson apartments today, named in honor of the most famous and groundbreaking Brooklyn Dodger to ever grace Ebbets Field.

4. Wini Breines, "Domineering Mothers in the 1950s: Image and Reality," *Women's Studies International Forum* 8, no. 6 (1985): 601–8, www.sciencedirect.com/science/article/abs/pii/0277539585900998.

5. Peg Streep, "Is It Always a Turf War? Adult Daughters and Their Mothers," *Psychology Today*, June 25, 2014, www.psychologytoday.com/us/blog/tech-support/201 406/is-it-always-turf-war-adult-daughters-and-their-mothers.

6. Streep, "Is It Always a Turf War?"

7. Veteran actor Bill Dana brought Uncle Angelo to life. Like Bea Arthur, Bill Dana was a World War II veteran who went on to act in such TV shows as *Get Smart* and *St. Elsewhere*. Dana died in 2017.

8. Naomi Gerstel, "Divorce and Stigma," *Social Problems* 34, no. 2 (April 1987): 172–86.

9. Stephanie Kirchgaessner, "Pope Reforms Catholic Church's Marriage Annulment Process," *Guardian*, September 8, 2015, www.theguardian.com/world/2015/sep/08/pope -radically-reforms-catholic-churchs-marriage-annulment-process.

10. While Dorothy and Sophia are dealing with family, Blanche and Rose get bit parts as nuns in the local production of *The Sound of Music*—and to keep up the jig, they wear their nun habits around Uncle Angelo, referring to themselves as "Sister Rose" and "Sister Blanche." This also prompts Blanche to hold up her bra and utter the classic line, "we're here . . . collecting *lingerie* . . . for needy sexy people," as she struggles to come up with an excuse on the spot.

11. Though it's a common stereotype that Sicilian men are insanely devoted to their mothers—often holding their mothers in the same regard as the Virgin Mary herself—it's a stereotype that happens to be true.

12. A 2019 FBI report revealed that xenophobic violence against Latino Americans rose more than 21 percent in 2018, when the Trump administration began its no-tolerance policy against refugees from Central America. That same year, a gunman named Patrick Crusius, a devout Trump supporter and far-right extremist in El Paso, Texas, began targeting Mexicans and was involved in a mass shooting that killed more than twenty-three Latinos and injured twenty-three more. It remains the most deadly hate crime against Latinos in modern American history. Brad Brooks, "Victims of Anti-Latino Hate Crimes Soar in U.S.: FBI Report," Reuters, November 12, 2019, www.reuters.com/article/us-hatecrimes-report /victims-of-anti-latino-hate-crimes-soar-in-u-s-fbi-report-idUSKBN1XM2OQ.

13. "Know Your Rights," American Civil Liberties Union, August 26, 2022, www .aclu.org/know-your-rights/immigrants-rights.

14. "Rita Moreno," Television Academy Interviews, September 4, 2020, https://inter views.televisionacademy.com/interviews/rita-moreno.

15. Prominent voice actor Lloyd Bochner brought Patrick Vaughn to life. Bochner's early career involved roles in such television shows as *The Six Million Dollar Man* and *Dynasty* (where he played Cecil Colby), but he's perhaps best known for his voiceover work on various *Batman* cartoons, where he voiced Mayor Hamilton Hill for such shows as *Batman: The Animated Series*, *The New Batman Adventures*, and the video game *Batman: Vengeance*. Bochner died in 2005.

16. The aging hippie in question, Jimmy, was brought to life by veteran character actor Martin Mull. At this point in television history, he was best known for his roles on *Mary Hartman, Mary Hartman* and *Laugh-In*. Today, however, he's best known for his roles on *Two and a Half Men, Roseanne*, and *Sabrina the Teenage Witch*. As of 2022, Mull is still acting steadily, though he's not as prolific as he once was (which is perhaps understandable, given his advanced age).

17. I. Boyd, G. J. Rubin, and S. Wessely, "Taking Refuge from Modernity: 21st Century Hermits," *Journal of the Royal Society of Medicine* 105, no. 12 (2012): 523–29, https://doi.org/10.1258/jrsm.2012.120060.

18. Veteran character actor Richard Roat brought Kendall Nesbitt to life, though to fans of *The Golden Girls*, he may look familiar, as he played Rose's boyfriend Al (who subsequently died of a heart attack after spending the night in her bed). Roat's impressive career included appearances on *Night Court, Days of Our Lives*, and *Cold Case*. Roat died on August 5, 2022.

19. Claire Sewell, "Interview with Jim Colucci," The Golden Girls Fashion Corner, April 23, 2020, https://goldengirlsfashion.com/2020/04/23/interview-with-jim-colucci/.

20. Christopher Rudolph, "Go behind the Scenes of 'The Golden Girls' Emotional Series Finale," *Logo TV*, May 19, 2017, www.logotv.com/news/wsed1t/the-golden-girls-series-finale.

21. Julie Miller, "The Queen Mother Loved the Golden Girls So Much That She Requested a Live Performance from the Cast," *Vanity Fair*, April 29, 2014, www.vanityfair.com/hollywood/2014/04/queen-elizabeth-golden-girls.

22. Barbara Babcock brought Charmaine Hollingsworth to life. A veteran of stage and screen, Babcock starred in such television shows as *The Law & Harry McGraw, Murder, She Wrote*, and *Dr. Quinn: Medicine Woman*. She was also named one of *People*'s 50 Most Beautiful People in 1994. Though largely retired from acting, Barbara Babcock is still alive as of this writing.

23. Marian Mercer brought Magda—and her thick Czech accent—to life. Mercer was perhaps best known for her role as Eve Leighton on *St. Elsewhere*, but she also had roles on sitcoms like *It's a Living* and *Empty Nest*, in the latter of which she played Ursula Dietz, Charlie Dietz's equally annoying and overbearing mother. Mercer died in 2011.

24. Alex Galloway, "The Six Most Important Girl Code Rules," The Tack Online, November 6, 2018, https://bvtack.com/31324/feature/the-six-most-important-girl-code-rules/.

25. Henry Darrow brought Fidel Santiago to life. He was born Enrique Delgado in New York City, and subsequently played a series of "Latin heartthrobs" on television. He also starred on soap operas like *Santa Barbara* and *The Bold and the Beautiful*. Darrow died in 2021.

26. Cesar Romero was nothing if not a legend—one generation of women knew him as a great "Latin lover" of the big screen, starring in such films as the original *Ocean's Eleven*, and on television as Esteban de la Cruz in the original *Zorro* television show. A different generation of women—nerds, blerds, and comic book fans—knew him as the Joker in the *Batman* television series (opposite Adam West as Batman). Romero died in 1994.

27. On *The Golden Girls* season 2, episode 23, Sophia tells Dorothy that she had a dream where she was on an island with Cesar Romero wearing nothing but a loincloth. "Dorothy, you know that blue washcloth in my bathroom? That's how big Cesar's loincloth was. Good night."

28. Though residential police stakeouts may be common in small towns, they are rare in large cities like New York, Los Angeles, and—yes—Miami. There are several reasons why this is so, but the top three reasons are: liability (if someone in the residence gets hurt, both the city and the police department can be sued), perception (it doesn't take much to arouse neighbors' suspicions), and bias of the residence's owner (having something like that happen in your house can be very exciting and something that an owner would be eager to share with friends and family, which easily compromises the safety of the cops on the job). What's more, on the rare occasions that a stakeout *does* occur in a residential home, the call would come from someone of a much higher pay grade than a senior and a rookie detective. Put simply, this scenario would never happen in the first place—though, again, no one would ever watch *The Golden Girls* and think it was a police procedural.

29. Wiretapping is used at the *federal* level, not at the state level, and Florida doesn't allow wiretapping, because it's a two-party consent state (meaning that both parties in a conversation must consent to recording a conversation or it's inadmissible). What's more, wiretapping is one of the most sensitive techniques that law enforcement uses, and it must be done under highly controlled circumstances (for example, a federal judge must be allowed to monitor how it's used) or it will be inadmissible in court. Finally, the crime must be a serious one for the FBI to sign off on its use—things like counterterrorism efforts, the global illegal drug trade, and human trafficking are all crimes that would be appropriate to use a wiretap for—so it's highly unlikely that this would qualify. "Digital Media Law Project," accessed September 9, 2022, www.dmlp.org/legal-guide/florida-recording-law.

30. Veteran comedic actress Nancy Walker brought Angela to life. The daughter of a vaudevillian family, Walker—born Anna Myrtle Swoyer—had an impressive resume that included credits on such television shows as *Columbo*, *McMillan & Wife*, and *Rhoda* (another spin-off of *The Mary Tyler Moore Show*, which featured the late, great Valerie Harper in the title role). Walker died of lung cancer in 1992, at the age of seventy.

31. A Pulitzer Prize–winning play, *Long Day's Journey into Night* was written by Eugene O'Neill sometime between 1939 and 1941 and published posthumously in 1956. Considered his magnum opus, *Long Day's Journey into Night* was a semiautobiographical play that dealt with O'Neill's family and their various foibles thanks to drug addiction, promiscuity, and mental illness.

32. There's another continuity error in this episode: when Sophia asks Angela about the rest of the family in Sicily, Angela has only one word: "Dead." But in the season 3, episode 17 show called "My Brother, My Father," Uncle Angelo—Sophia's brother—is introduced, proving that not everyone in the family was "dead."

33. The face cream in question—Porcelana—is still on the market today, though it isn't as popular as it once was. Its main ingredient is hydroquinone, which is known as a skin lightening agent. Though elder folks of a certain age used Porcelana to bleach dark spots due to sun exposure, Sophia's comment about "having more brown skin than the Temptations" because Angela used up all her skin-lightening cream wouldn't fly in the twenty-first century, and rightly so.

34. Sophia threatens to kill Angela when she arrives, to which Angela quips, "What are you gonna do? Make me eat your ziti?" This is only one of many quips that the two fire at one another, with the funniest being when Sophia says, "You can run, but you can't hide!" Angela replies, "Run? I can barely walk!" Sophia quips, "Fine! Rub it in!" implying that Angela's inability to walk was due to a particularly raucous lovemaking session with Tony DelVecchio.

35. These days, one needs only to click on a game show's website to request tickets to the show. But before the Internet, game shows used to advertise their studio addresses in the middle of the show, inviting viewers to mail a self-addressed stamped envelope to the address for the tickets they desired.

36. Then, as now, last-minute flights and hotel bookings are extremely expensive, which makes one wonder both how the Girls managed to afford it on semiretirement incomes *and* how they justified the cost, knowing that their winnings may not have covered it.

37. This, again, is illustrative of the times that the Girls lived. The twenty-first century is a world where Kim Kardashian was able to build an entire mainstream career off one sex tape with Ray J. But the 1980s was a world in which an aspiring starlet's entire career could be destroyed if nude—or seminude—photos were leaked to the press. Vanessa Williams

lost the Miss America crown because of it, and *Wheel of Fortune* host Vanna White came under fire for it. Just a few months before this episode was taped, seminude photos that White had taken before she got the *Wheel of Fortune* gig were published in *Playboy*, which is what Blanche references with her "sleazy girlie magazine" comment. In 2017, White told *Fox News* that she did the photos against her better judgment because she was too embarrassed to ask her parents for rent money and she said she regrets the photos to this day. "Never do anything that you don't want to do. Listen to your instincts and follow it," she said to the outlet (Stephanie Nolasco, "Vanna White Dishes on 'Wheel of Fortune's' Lasting Success, Playboy Regrets," Fox News, March 29, 2017, www.foxnews.com /entertainment/vanna-white-dishes-on-wheel-of-fortunes-lasting-success-playboy-regrets).

38. Before the game show goes to commercial break, Guy Corbin—played by James MacKrell—makes a hand gesture that, as it turns out, is a nod and a wink to White's late husband, Allen Ludden. It was the same gesture that Ludden would make on *Password* and *Password Plus*—on which White was a frequent guest—to introduce each new password that appeared on the screen.

39. This is another continuity error: Dorothy has two children, Gloria has one child, and Phil—it's later revealed—has ten children (who all live in a trailer park). This means that Sophia is a grandmother of thirteen, not six.

40. Though largely ahead of its time, the AMC Pacer was produced from 1975 until 1980 and was one of the first small-sized cars to hit the market. It's worth remembering that, at the time, big boatlike cars that guzzled gas like water were all the rage, and the Pacer was a "futuristic" answer to those large cars. Unfortunately, the car didn't perform very well on the road, and by 1980, AMC stopped producing the car altogether.

41. These days, plane rides on most airlines include personalized television screens at each seat. But in the 1980s, many long-haul flights—such as the one from Miami to Los Angeles—featured a movie on the big screen that passengers had the option of watching if they purchased a headset that looked a lot like a toy stethoscope.

42. Today, people don't "out" others out of a social politesse. But back in the 1980s, outing someone could have dire consequences—including social ostracization and legal issues (especially in states that arbitrarily applied sodomy laws to entrap gay people "caught in the act" of a consensual love affair)—so one's sexuality was kept secret for his or her protection.

43. Rose's response: "I could have looked it up!"

44. "Gay panic" was a nonsense defense used by Jonathan Schmitz, the man behind the infamous "Jenny Jones murder." In 1995, Schmitz became a household name when he shot Scott Amedure in cold blood after Amedure confessed his love for Schmitz on *The Jenny Jones Show*. Schmitz was released from prison in 2017. Bernadette Giacomazzo, "This Man Killed His Friend Because He Admitted His Attraction to Him on 'The Jenny Jones Show.'" All That's Interesting, May 3, 2022, https://allthatsinteresting.com /jonathan-schmitz.

45. Sophia's initial response: "I know you don't get many dates but stick to what you know. At your age, it's very difficult to break into something new. Good night."

46. Louis Peitzman, "Classic Gay TV: The Golden Girls, 'Isn't It Romantic?'" *Logo TV*, September 12, 2012, www.logotv.com/news/edodez/classic-gay-tv-the-golden -girls-isnt-it-romantic.

47. The St. Valentine's Day Massacre occurred in 1929 and resulted in the murder of seven members of Chicago's North Side Gang. The seven members—all of whom were Irish—were shot by four assailants, two of whom were dressed as police officers when they

committed the murders (though the murderers themselves weren't police officers). Though it was never proven, it's widely believed that Al Capone—who headed up the rival South Side Gang, also known as the Chicago Outfit—was responsible for the hit.

INTERLUDE: AN ODE TO "EBBTIDE'S REVENGE"

1. The most infamous mother of the House of LaBeija was Pepper LaBeija, who appeared in the documentary *Paris Is Burning* and was considered "the last remaining drag queen of the Harlem drag balls."

2. The most infamous father of the House of Ninja was Benny Ninja. A self-taught vogue dancer who was given the title by the late great Willi Ninja, the mother of the House of Ninja, Benny Ninja also appeared in the documentary *Paris Is Burning* and was known as the "godfather of voguing."

3. The most infamous member of the House of Xtravaganza was Venus Xtravaganza, a transgender performer who was murdered in 1988. Her body was found under a bed in the Duchess Hotel—and her murder remains unsolved to this day.

4. The term "Latino" wasn't officially adopted by the U.S. Census until 1997. Prior to that, the term "Hispanic" was used, and it was meant to denote persons whose primary language was Spanish, not English. Today, "Hispanic" specifically denotes someone whose familial origins are in Spain (i.e., European), whereas "Latino" is a catchall term referring to Spanish-speaking peoples from the Caribbean, Central America, and South America (i.e., not European). Put another way, "Hispanic" means "from Spain," and "Latino" means "conquered by Spain." But outside the United States, "Latinos" do not refer to themselves as such. Rather, they identify themselves by their country of origin (i.e., Mexican, Guatemalan, Salvadoran). Even today, the word "Latino" sparks debate among those who fall under the catchall term, with some being fine with it, and others preferring to identify themselves by their country of origin. It goes without saying that the term "Latino" doesn't take one's cultural origins into account, as Puerto Ricans aren't like Dominicans, who aren't like Mexicans, who aren't like Salvadorans, and so on. Evelyn G. Aleman, "The Term 'Latino' Describes No One," *Los Angeles Times*, April 10, 1999, www.latimes.com /archives/la-xpm-1999-apr-10-me-26028-story.html.

5. Riki Anne Wilchins, "A Note from Your Editrix," *In Your Face*, 1995.

6. Frank Yemi, "Kenny Niedermeier Has an 'Ex-Wife'—Here's How the 90-Day Fiancé Star's Family Came to Be," Monsters and Critics, November 8, 2021, www.mon stersandcritics.com/tv/reality-tv/kenny-niedermeier-has-an-ex-wife-heres-how-the-90 -day-fiance-stars-family-came-to-be/.

7. One of the longest-running sketch shows in history, *The Benny Hill Show* was popular in both Britain and the United States. It aired from 1955 until 1989 and featured a brand of slapstick comedy that combined burlesque and double entendres. Hill's sexual innuendo was significantly toned down for American audiences, though unedited episodes can be found easily today thanks to the magic of YouTube.

8. The good father was referring to *Candid Camera*, a hidden camera television show that ran from the 1948 until 2014 (though, obviously, not with the same host). One might say that *Candid Camera* was a precursor to shows like *Punk'd* and *Ridiculousness*.

9. "The HIV/AIDS Epidemic in the United States: The Basics," KFF, June 7, 2021, www.kff.org/hivaids/fact-sheet/the-hivaids-epidemic-in-the-united-states-the-basics/.

10. Gregory B. Lewis, "Support for Same-Sex Marriage: Trends and Patterns," *American Sociological Association*, April 22, 2015, www.asanet.org/sites/default/files /handout_lewis_ssm_asa_2015_8-16-15.pdf.

6. THE TOUGH STUFF

1. Katana Dumont, "Monkeypox Reporting Parallels AIDS Coverage in the '80s," *Blavity News & Politics*, August 5, 2022, https://blavity.com/monkeypox-reporting-par allels-aids-coverage-in-the-80s?category1=news.

2. German Lopez, "The Reagan Administration's Unbelievable Response to the HIV/AIDS Epidemic," *Vox*, December 1, 2015, www.vox.com/2015/12/1/9828348 /ronald-reagan-hiv-aids.

3. Mark Morford, "The Sad, Quotable Jerry Falwell," *San Francisco Chronicle*, February 11, 2012, www.sfgate.com/entertainment/morford/article/The-Sad-Quotable-Jerry -Falwell-It-s-bad-form-3302297.php.

4. "Party of Reagan? No, Party of Falwell, Writer Says," NPR, April 26, 2012, www.npr.org/2012/04/26/151444474/party-of-reagan-no-party-of-falwell-writer-says.

5. Justin McCarthy, "Gallup Vault: Fear and Anxiety during the 1980s AIDS Crisis," Gallup, June 28, 2019, https://news.gallup.com/vault/259643/gallup-vault-fear-anxiety -during-1980s-aids-crisis.aspx.

6. Anthony Violanti, "Shocking Words Audiences Seem to Enjoy the Abusive Language of Today's Performers. Andrew Dice Clay Is a Case in Point," *Buffalo News*, February 2, 1990, https://buffalonews.com/news/shocking-words-audiences-seem-to-enjoy -the-abusive-language-of-todays-performers-andrew-dice-clay/article_86b00602-e86f -531b-84ee-846105d00b5e.html.

7. Peter Dreier, "Reagan's Real Legacy," *The Nation*, June 29, 2015, www.the nation.com/article/archive/reagans-real-legacy/.

8. Reagan was perhaps most infamous for "union busting" the air traffic controllers. On August 5, 1981, Reagan began firing more than eleven thousand air traffic controllers, who were part of the Professional Air Traffic Controllers Organization, or PATCO, union, and banning them from working in the field for life. This was just the first of many unions targeted by the administration, further contributing to the wage disparity between the working class and the upper class. "Ronald Reagan Fires 11,359 Air-Traffic Controllers," History.com, February 9, 2010, www.history.com/this-day-in-history /reagan-fires-11359-air-traffic-controllers.

9. Xandi McMahon, "The Non-Consensual Identity Politics of the 'Welfare Queen,'" *Compass*, November 13, 2018, https://wp.nyu.edu/compass/2018/11/13/the-non-consen sual-identity-politics-of-the-welfare-queen/.

10. McMahon, "The Non-Consensual Identity Politics of the 'Welfare Queen.'"

11. Dreier, "Reagan's Real Legacy."

12. Aja Romano, "A History of 'Wokeness,'" *Vox*, October 9, 2020, www.vox.com /culture/21437879/stay-woke-wokeness-history-origin-evolution-controversy.

7. A COMEDIC MASTER CLASS

1. Though Alzheimer's was referenced—but never mentioned by name—in a 1964 episode of *The Alfred Hitchcock Hour* called "The Gentleman Caller" and featured in

episodes of British and Australian television shows, the first American television episode to ever address Alzheimer's directly was a 1987 episode of *Magnum P.I.* called "The Aunt Who Came to Dinner," in which Thomas Magnum (Tom Selleck) has his favorite aunt over as a guest. She spends most of the episode convincing Magnum that someone's out to kill her, and it's only at the end of the episode that her diagnosis is revealed.

2. The same year that this episode aired—1989—Oregon became the first state in the union to introduce an assisted suicide bill. However, in the other forty-nine states, assisted suicide was illegal. Measures to change that first began gaining momentum in the 1990s, and it was called the "death with dignity" movement. As of 2022, eleven states had a "death with dignity" statute in place, meaning assisted suicide is legal in those states. However, Florida (where *The Golden Girls* took place) is not one of those states nor has it ever been. "State Statuses," Death with Dignity, July 7, 2022, https://deathwithdignity. org/states/.

3. Dr. Harry Weston was played by Richard Mulligan, who was the lead character in *Empty Nest*, a *Golden Girls* spin-off that aired from 1988 until 1995. The Girls all appeared in various episodes of the show as their characters from *The Golden Girls*, and Mulligan costarred opposite Dinah Manoff, Kristy McNichol, Lisa Rieffel, and Park Overall.

4. Blanche: "I know what a metaphor is, dear. I'm not a dummy." Rose: "Blanche, what's a metaphor?"

5. It's unclear how this was even possible in the 1980s, considering the Civil Rights Act of 1964 made it illegal to discriminate based on religion, among other things. But as we have already seen, the best *Golden Girls* episodes also have a basis in some sort of absurdity, which makes for an even better payoff.

6. Malina Saval, "Too Jewish for Hollywood: As Antisemitism Soars, Hollywood Should Address Its Enduring Hypocrisy in Hyperbolic Caricatures of Jews," *Variety*, June 21, 2021, https://variety.com/2021/biz/features/jewish-hollywood -antisemitism-hyperbolic-caricatures-casting-jews-hate-crimes-1234997849/.

7. Travis Reilly, "Sarah Silverman on the Uphill Battle for Jewish Actresses, Quarantining with Her New Boyfriend, and the Tragic Death of Her Friend Adam Schlesinger," *Howard Stern*, November 17, 2020, www.howardstern.com/news/2020/11/17 /sarah-silverman-on-the-uphill-battle-for-jewish-actresses-quarantining-with-her-new -boyfriend-and-the-tragic-death-of-her-friend-adam-schlesinger/.

8. Aljean Harmetz, "NBC's 'Golden Girls' Gambles on Grown-Ups," *New York Times*, September 22, 1985, www.nytimes.com/1985/09/22/arts/nbc-s-golden-girls-gam bles-on-grown-ups.html.

9. Roisin O'Connor, "Seth Rogen Says Antisemitic People 'Thrive' in Hollywood," *Independent*, August 3, 2020, www.independent.co.uk/arts-entertainment/films/news/seth -rogen-jewish-antisemitism-hollywood-mel-gibson-a9652336.html.

10. An a capella version of the song was sung toward the end of the episode; Cynthia Fee, who sang *The Golden Girls* theme song, "Thank You for Being a Friend," provided the vocals.

11. "Veteran Homelessness," National Coalition for Homeless Veterans, February 4, 2021, https://nchv.org/veteran-homelessness/.

12. Megan Rosenfeld, "A Pregnant Pause for Chung?" *Washington Post*, July 31, 1990, www.washingtonpost.com/archive/lifestyle/1990/07/31/a-pregnant-pause-for-chung /0faaf6f0-16a4-4c81-bc1a-cde8e151d504/.

13. Husna Haq, "Interracial Marriage: More Than Double the Rate in the 1980s," *Christian Science Monitor*, June 4, 2010, www.csmonitor.com/USA/Society/2010/0604 /Interracial-marriage-more-than-double-the-rate-in-the-1980s.

14. In January 2021, "Mixed Blessing" was pulled from most streaming services— including Hulu—because of this scene. As of August 2022, the episode has been restored to Hulu.

15. Also known as myalgic encephalomyelitis, chronic fatigue syndrome was first recognized as a disease by the Centers for Disease Control in 1987. It's a complex disease whose exact mechanisms still aren't known in the twenty-first century. Women are more likely to get the disease than men, and it affects white people more than Black and Latino people.

16. Vidya Rao,"'You Are Not Listening to Me': Black Women on Pain and Implicit Bias in Medicine," *Today*, July 27, 2020, www.today.com/health/implicit-bias -medicine-how-it-hurts-black-women-t187866.

17. At the end of the episode, Dorothy encounters Dr. Budd—and his blonde date—at a celebratory dinner and laces into him for being dismissive of her. The monologue earned loud whooping applause from the studio audience.

18. Eliza Strickland, "'Yuppie Flu' Isn't Just in the Head: Chronic Fatigue Syndrome Linked to Virus," *Discover*, October 9, 2009, www.discovermagazine.com/health /yuppie-flu-isnt-just-in-the-head-chronic-fatigue-syndrome-linked-to-virus.

19. Strickland, "'Yuppie Flu' Isn't Just in the Head."

20. Stacey Wilson Hunt, "The Golden Girls Creators on Finding a New Generation of Fans," *Vulture*, March 3, 2017, www.vulture.com/2017/03/the-golden-girls-creators-on -finding-new-fans.html.

21. Emily Paulsen, "Recognizing, Addressing Unintended Gender Bias in Patient Care," Duke Health Referring Physicians, 2022, https://physicians.dukehealth.org/articles /recognizing-addressing-unintended-gender-bias-patient-care.

22. Diane Shipley, "30 Years Ago, 'The Golden Girls' Treated Sick Women Like We Matter," Bitch Media, August 7, 2019, www.bitchmedia.org/article/the-golden-girls -chronic-fatigue.

23. "Types of HIV Tests," Centers for Disease Control and Prevention, June 22, 2022, www.cdc.gov/hiv/basics/hiv-testing/test-types.html.

24. Mark Morford, "The Sad, Quotable Jerry Falwell," *San Francisco Chronicle*, February 11, 2012, www.sfgate.com/entertainment/morford/article/The-Sad-Quotable -Jerry-Falwell-It-s-bad-form-3302297.php.

25. Robert Moritz, "Life Is a Scream for Betty White," *Parade*, October 31, 2010, https://parade.com/132208/robertmoritz/betty-white-goes-wild/.

26. Barbara Fletcher, "What 'The Golden Girls' Taught Us about AIDS," NPR, July 22, 2014, www.npr.org/2014/07/22/333759394/what-the-golden-girls-taught-us-about-aids.

8. THE END OF AN ERA

1. Sean Daly, "Why Bea Arthur Wanted to Quit 'Golden Girls' and More Secrets from behind the Lanai," Fox News, April 4, 2016, www.foxnews.com/entertainment /why-bea-arthur-wanted-to-quit-golden-girls-and-more-secrets-from-behind-the-lanai.

2. Erin Clements, "Inside the Emotional 'Golden Girls' Finale on Its 30th Anniversary," *Today*, May 9, 2022, www.today.com/popculture/tv/golden-girls-series -finale-30th-anniversary-rcna27079.

3. That viewership was the highest on record for the show.

4. Bea Arthur's last-ever appearance as Dorothy Petrillo Zbornak Hollingsworth was on November 6, 1992, in "Seems Like Old Times, Part 2."

5. Laughing Place Disney Newsdesk, "Fathom Events to Celebrate Nearly 40 Years of 'The Golden Girls' This September," Laughing Place, August 13, 2021, www.laughingplace.com/w/news/2021/08/13/fathom-events-to-celebrate-nearly-40 -years-of-the-golden-girls-this-september/.

9. FRIENDS OF DOROTHY

1. "This Alien Legacy: The Origin of Sodomy Laws in British Colonialism," Human Rights Watch, April 29, 2015, www.hrw.org/report/2008/12/17/alien-legacy/ori gins-sodomy-laws-british-colonialism.

2. Jill Cowan, "Bayard Rustin, Gay Civil Rights Leader, Is Pardoned in California," *New York Times*, February 5, 2020, www.nytimes.com/2020/02/05/us/bayard-rustin-par don.html.

3. "Bowers v. Hardwick (1986)," Legal Information Institute, accessed July 31, 2022, www.law.cornell.edu/wex/bowers_v_hardwick_(1986).

4. L. Frank Baum, *The Road to Oz* (Chicago: Reilly & Britton, ca. 1909), www .gutenberg.org/files/26624/26624-h/26624-h.htm.

5. To see how language evolves over time—even during just a few short decades— all one must do is look at the evolution of the word "queer." The term, during the sixteenth century, meant "strange" or "eccentric." But according to the *Columbia Journalism Review*, "queer" first began to denote "homosexual" in 1894, after the Marquess of Queensbury coined the term, and it began to enter the common parlance in this context in 1914. By 1965, "queer" was almost exclusively used to denote a homosexual, though it was mostly used in a derogatory fashion until the early twenty-first century, when gay rights activists began reclaiming the word, once a slur, as their own for the community.

6. It wasn't a coincidence that the Stonewall Riots and Judy Garland's funeral happened on the same day.

7. Terra Necessary, "So What Does It Mean to Be a 'Friend of Dorothy?'" *Pride*, July 8, 2020, www.pride.com/identities/2020/7/08/so-what-does-it-mean-be-friend-dorothy.

8. Parker's husband, however, called himself "queer as a billy goat," so it's possible that he identified more as gay than bisexual.

9. "Why Gen Z Is More Likely Than Millennials to Identify as LGBTQ+," YPulse, March 17, 2022, www.ypulse.com/article/2022/03/17/why-gen-z-is-more-likely-than-mil lennials-to-identify-as-lgbtq/.

10. This means that evangelicals—the "heart" of the Moral Majority—are and always have been a *minority*, and their numbers are decreasing as time goes on. And it's their diminishing numbers that make their demands to rule the majority even more curious— what *is* the endgame here, anyway?

11. "Why 'The Golden Girls' Are Still Golden," NPR, February 1, 2022, www.npr .org/transcripts/1074829590.

12. Logan Raschke, "Why 'The Golden Girls' Helps Me Cope," *Daily Eastern News*, June 19, 2020, www.dailyeasternnews.com/2020/06/19why-the-golden-girls-helps-me-cope/.

13. Seth Abramovitch, "How Bea Arthur Gave Back to the Gays Who Loved Her," *The Hollywood Reporter*, September 26, 2016, www.hollywoodreporter.com/tv/tv-news /bea-arthur-lgbt-teen-homeless-932269/.

14. Sara Kettler, "How Bea Arthur and 'Maude' Changed the Way Women Were Portrayed on Television," Biography, March 16, 2020, www.biography.com/news/maude -abortion-storyline-bea-arthur.

15. Carl Siciliano, "How Bea Arthur Became a Champion for Homeless LGBT Youth," *HuffPost*, July 21, 2016, www.huffpost.com/entry/how-bea-arthur-became-a-c_b _7837174.

16. Mel Gussow, "Theater: Fierstein's 'Torch Song,'" *New York Times*, November 1, 1981, www.nytimes.com/1981/11/01/theater/theater-fierstein-s-torch-song.html.

17. Andrew Belonsky, "Today in Gay History: Estelle Getty Won't Gay Bash," *Out Magazine*, February 6, 2015, www.out.com/entertainment/today-gay-history/2013/07/22 /today-gay-history-estelle-getty-wont-gay-bash.

18. Patrick Ninneman, "Triad Hospice for AIDS Patients Opens," *Greensboro News and Record*, January 24, 2015, https://greensboro.com/triad-hospice-for-aids-patients -opens/article_aa970828-d9c4-591b-93ea-b60e35253155.html.

19. The event, hosted by comedian Judy Gold and former *Queer Eye* cohost Carson Kressley, featured a who's who of celebrities like Cameron Mathison (Drew on *General Hospital*), Cyndi Lauper, Billy Porter (*long* before he became a modern-day meme generator and Gen Z cultural icon), and the Reverend Al Sharpton.

20. Proposition 8, also known as Prop 8, was a California constitutional amendment that banned same-sex marriage. Though the bill initially passed in the November 2008 California state elections, it was overturned in 2013. Proponents of the bill included the Catholic Church, the Knights of Columbus, and Senator John McCain.

21. Robert Moritz, "Life Is a Scream for Betty White," *Parade*, October 31, 2010, https://parade.com/132208/robertmoritz/betty-white-goes-wild/.

22. "Betty White Defends the Gay Community, Talks Sex Drive and Loss of Mickey Rooney," *YouTube*, 2014, www.youtube.com/watch?v=t47r7N2lSjs.

23. October 17 is GLAAD's Spirit Day initiative, when people don purple to stand in solidarity with bullied queer youth.

CONCLUSION

1. Sa'iyda Shabazz, "Why 'The Golden Girls' Stands the Test of Time," Scary Mommy, December 8, 2021, www.scarymommy.com/the-golden-girls-still-relevant.

BIBLIOGRAPHY

Abbott, Jim. "Not Everyone Laughs at Kinison's Gaffes." *Sun Sentinel*, May 24, 1990, www.sun-sentinel.com/news/fl-xpm-1990-05-25-9001100397-story.html.

Abramovitch, Seth. "How Bea Arthur Gave Back to the Gays Who Loved Her." *The Hollywood Reporter*, September 26, 2016, www.hollywoodreporter.com/tv/tv-news /bea-arthur-lgbt-teen-homeless-932269/.

Aleman, Evelyn G. "The Term 'Latino' Describes No One." *Los Angeles Times*, April 10, 1999, www.latimes.com/archives/la-xpm-1999-apr-10-me-26028-story.html.

Barker, Mayerene. "Match Arranged in Sicily Stands Test of Time: Couple Chalks up 80 Years of Marriage." *Los Angeles Times*, January 13, 1987, www.latimes.com/ar chives/la-xpm-1987-01-13-me-4196-story.html.

Baum, L. Frank. *The Road to Oz* (Chicago: Reilly & Britton, ca. 1909), www.gutenberg. org/files/26624/26624-h/26624-h.htm.

Baume, Matt. "Why Do Gays Love the Golden Girls?" The Stranger, January 18, 2022, www.thestranger.com/slog/2022/01/18/65092818/why-do-gays-love-the-golden-girls.

Belonsky, Andrew. "Today in Gay History: Estelle Getty Won't Gay Bash." *Out Magazine*, February 6, 2015, www.out.com/entertainment/today-gay-history/2013/07/22/today -gay-history-estelle-getty-wont-gay-bash.

Bennington-Castro, Joseph. "How AIDS Remained an Unspoken—but Deadly— Epidemic for Years." History.com, June 1, 2020, www.history.com/news/aids-epi demic-ronald-reagan.

"Betty White Called 'C' Word by 'Golden Girls' Star Bea Arthur." TMZ, April 11, 2022, www.tmz.com/2022/02/10/betty-white-c-word-golden-girls-bea-arthur/.

"Betty White Defends the Gay Community, Talks Sex Drive and Loss of Mickey Rooney." *YouTube*, 2014, www.youtube.com/watch?v=t47r7N2lSjs.

Bonner, Jeanne. "Hollywood's Struggle to Deal with AIDS in the '80s." CNN, June 2, 2016, www.cnn.com/2016/06/01/entertainment/80s-hollywood-aids-crisis.

"Bowers v. Hardwick (1986)." Legal Information Institute. Accessed July 31, 2022. www .law.cornell.edu/wex/bowers_v_hardwick_(1986).

Boyd, I., G. J. Rubin, and S. Wessely. "Taking Refuge from Modernity: 21st Century Hermits." *Journal of the Royal Society of Medicine* 105, no. 12 (2012): 523–29, https://doi.org/10.1258/jrsm.2012.120060.

Breines, Wini. "Domineering Mothers in the 1950s: Image and Reality." *Women's Studies International Forum* 8, no. 6 (1985): 601–8, www.sciencedirect.com/science/article /abs/pii/0277539585900998.

"A Brief History of TV Couples Sleeping in the Same Bed." MeTV, January 10, 2022, https://metv.com/lists/a-brief-history-of-tv-couples-sleeping-in-the-same-bed.

Brooks, Brad. "Victims of Anti-Latino Hate Crimes Soar in U.S.: FBI Report." Reuters, November 12, 2019, www.reuters.com/article/us-hatecrimes-report/victims -of-anti-latino-hate-crimes-soar-in-u-s-fbi-report-idUSKBN1XM2OQ.

Cantor, Muriel G. "The American Family on Television: From Molly Goldberg to Bill Cosby." *Journal of Comparative Family Studies* 22, no. 2 (1991): 205–16, https://doi .org/10.3138/jcfs.22.2.205.

Carlson, Michael. "Obituary: Estelle Getty." *Guardian*, July 23, 2008, www.theguardian .com/culture/2008/jul/24/television.television.

Clements, Erin. "5 'Golden Girls' Episodes Where Betty White Shines as Rose." *Today*, December 31, 2021, www.today.com/popculture/tv/betty-white-golden-girls -episodes-rcna10209.

———. "Inside the Emotional 'Golden Girls' Finale on Its 30th Anniversary." *Today*, May 9, 2022, www.today.com/popculture/tv/golden-girls-series-finale-30th -anniversary-rcna27079.

Collins, Glenn. "In 'Safe Sex,' Harvey Fierstein Turns Serious." *New York Times*, April 5, 1987, www.nytimes.com/1987/04/05/theater/in-safe-sex-harvey-fierstein-turns-se rious.html.

Colucci, Jim. "The Golden Girls Proved Its Fearlessness Yet Again When It Tackled HIV/ AIDS." Vulture, February 17, 2017, www.vulture.com/2017/02/the-golden-girls -streaming-aids-hiv-fearless-book-excerpt.html.

Couric, Katie. "The Real Tradwives of 2022: Why More Young Moms Are Becoming Traditional Housewives." Katie Couric Media, April 9, 2022, https://katiecouric.com /culture/what-is-a-tradwife/.

Cowan, Jill. "Bayard Rustin, Gay Civil Rights Leader, Is Pardoned in California." *The New York Times*, February 5, 2020, www.nytimes.com/2020/02/05/us/bayard-rustin -pardon.html.

Daly, Sean. "Why Bea Arthur Wanted to Quit 'Golden Girls' and More Secrets from behind the Lanai." Fox News, April 4, 2016, www.foxnews.com/entertainment /why-bea-arthur-wanted-to-quit-golden-girls-and-more-secrets-from-behind-the-lanai.

"Digital Media Law Project." Digital Media Law Project. Accessed September 9, 2022. www.dmlp.org/legal-guide/florida-recording-law.

Donnelly, Erin. "We Figured out How Many Men 'The Golden Girls' Dated." Refinery29, August 31, 2015, www.refinery29.com/en-us/2015/08/93152/golden -girls-how-many-dates.

Dreier, Peter. "Reagan's Real Legacy." *The Nation*, June 29, 2015, www.thenation.com /article/archive/reagans-real-legacy/.

Dumont, Katana. "Monkeypox Reporting Parallels AIDS Coverage in the '80s." *Blavity News & Politics*, August 5, 2022, https://blavity.com/monkeypox-reporting -parallels-aids-coverage-in-the-80s?category1=news.

Finn, Natalie. "The Truth about Betty White and the Golden Girls: How the Beloved TV Best Friends Really Got Along." E! Online, December 31, 2021, www.eonline.com /news/1060432/the-truth-about-the-golden-girls-friendship-how-the-devoted-tv -foursome-really-felt-about-each-other.

Fitzharris, Dustin. "Catching up with the Golden Girls' Susan Harris." *Out*, February 6, 2015, www.out.com/entertainment/television/2010/10/03/catching-gold en-girls-susan-harris.

Fletcher, Barbara. "What 'The Golden Girls' Taught Us about AIDS." NPR, July 22, 2014, www.npr.org/2014/07/22/333759394/what-the-golden-girls-taught-us-about-aids.

Fonseca, Nicholas. "Bea Arthur: 'Golden Girls' Memories." EW.com, April 24, 2009, www.ew.com/ew/article/0,,1100651,00.html.

Galloway, Alex. "The Six Most Important Girl Code Rules." The Tack Online, November 6, 2018, https://bvtack.com/31324/feature/the-six-most-important-girl-code-rules/.

Gans, Andrew. "Defying Inequality Benefit, Hosted by Gold and Kressley, Presented Feb. 23 at the Gershwin." Playbill, February 23, 2009, https://playbill.com/article/defying-inequality-benefit-hosted-by-gold-and-kressley-presented-feb-23-at-the-gershwin-com-158243.

Garber, Megan. "The Sly Sunniness of Betty White." *The Atlantic*, January 2, 2022, www.theatlantic.com/culture/archive/2022/01/betty-white/621144/.

Gates, Anita. "Austin Kalish, a Writer of 'Maude' Abortion Episode, Dies at 95." *The New York Times*, October 8, 2016, www.nytimes.com/2016/10/08/arts/television/austin-kalish-dead.html.

Gerstel, Naomi. "Divorce and Stigma." *Social Problems* 34, no. 2 (April 1987): 172–86.

Giacomazzo, Bernadette. "This Man Killed His Friend Because He Admitted His Attraction to Him on 'The Jenny Jones Show.'" All That's Interesting, May 3, 2022. https://allthatsinteresting.com/jonathan-schmitz.

Gilbert, Asha C. "'He Stays': Betty White Refused to Remove Black Dancer from Her Show in 1954." *USA Today*, January 5, 2022, www.usatoday.com/story/entertainment/celebrities/2022/01/01/betty-white-black-dancer-arthur-duncan/9067252002/.

Gold, Michael. "Looking Out: Betty White Shows Support for Bullied LGBT Youth." *Baltimore Sun*, June 1, 2019, www.baltimoresun.com/features/bs-gm-looking-out-betty-white-lgbt-youth-spirit-day-20131010-story.html.

Gottlieb, Alma. "Menstrual Taboos: Moving beyond the Curse." In *The Palgrave Handbook of Critical Menstruation Studies*, edited by Chris Bobel, Inga T. Winkler, Breanne Fahs, Katie Ann Hasson, Elizabeth Arveda Kissling, and Tomi-Ann Roberts, 143–62. Singapore: Palgrave Macmillan, 2020. https://doi.org/10.1007/978-981-15-0614-7_14.

Gussow, Mel. "Theater: Fierstein's 'Torch Song.'" *New York Times*, November 1, 1981, www.nytimes.com/1981/11/01/theater/theater-fierstein-s-torch-song.html.

Haider, Arwa. "The Golden Girls: The Most Treasured TV Show Ever." BBC, April 1, 2020, www.bbc.com/culture/article/20200401-the-golden-girls-the-most-treasured-tv-show-ever.

Hammond, Kristyn. "American Women in the 50s." The Classroom, November 5, 2021, www.theclassroom.com/american-women-50s-9170.html.

Handelman, David. "The Devil and Sam Kinison." *Rolling Stone*, June 25, 2018, www.rollingstone.com/culture/culture-news/the-devil-and-sam-kinison-63844/.

Haq, Husna. "Interracial Marriage: More than Double the Rate in the 1980s." *Christian Science Monitor*, June 4, 2010, www.csmonitor.com/USA/Society/2010/0604/Interracial-marriage-more-than-double-the-rate-in-the-1980s.

Harmetz, Aljean. "NBC's 'Golden Girls' Gambles on Grown-Ups." *New York Times*, September 22, 1985, www.nytimes.com/1985/09/22/arts/nbc-s-golden-girls-gambles-on-grown-ups.html.

Heller, Corinne. "Betty White Dead at 99: Ryan Reynolds and More Celebs Mourn Beloved Actress." E! Online, December 31, 2021, www.eonline.com/news/1314861/betty-white-dead-at-99-ryan-reynolds-and-more-celebs-mourn-beloved-actress.

Hill, Erin. "Betty White Was Supposed to Play Blanche! Take a Look Back at the Beloved Star's Famous Golden Girls Role as Rose—Plus, Fun Facts about the Show." *Parade*, December 31, 2021, https://parade.com/52981/erinhill/surprising-secrets-of-the-golden-girls-castmates-revealed/.

"History of Measles." Centers for Disease Control and Prevention, November 5, 2020, www.cdc.gov/measles/about/history.html.

"The HIV/AIDS Epidemic in the United States: The Basics." KFF, June 7, 2021, www.kff.org/hivaids/fact-sheet/the-hivaids-epidemic-in-the-united-states-the-basics/.

Hunt, Stacey Wilson. "The Golden Girls Creators on Finding a New Generation of Fans." *Vulture*, March 3, 2017, www.vulture.com/2017/03/the-golden-girls-creators-on-finding-new-fans.html.

Jacobs, Leonard. "'Golden Girls: Live!' Sent to Shady Pines." *Backstage*, March 25, 2013. www.backstage.com/magazine/article/golden-girls-live-sent-shady-pines-36221/.

"Just Say No." History.com, May 31, 2017, www.history.com/topics/1980s/just-say-no.

Kalish, Nancy. "1950's Birthparents and Lost Loves: Some Similarities." *Psychology Today*, May 31, 2013, www.psychologytoday.com/us/blog/sticky-bonds/201305/1950s-birthparents-and-lost-loves-some-similarities.

Kettler, Sara. "How Bea Arthur and 'Maude' Changed the Way Women Were Portrayed on Television." Biography, March 16, 2020, www.biography.com/news/maude-abortion-storyline-bea-arthur.

Kirchgaessner, Stephanie. "Pope Reforms Catholic Church's Marriage Annulment Process." *Guardian*, September 8, 2015, www.theguardian.com/world/2015/sep/08/pope-radically-reforms-catholic-churchs-marriage-annulment-process.

"Know Your Rights." American Civil Liberties Union, August 26, 2022, www.aclu.org/know-your-rights/immigrants-rights.

Korn, Steven. "Beatrice Arthur, 'Golden Girls' Star, Dies at 86." EW.com, December 20, 2019, https://ew.com/article/2009/04/25/beatrice-arthur/.

Lacey, Liam. "Who Controls Hollywood?" *Globe and Mail*, July 18, 2014, www.theglobeandmail.com/arts/film/who-controls-hollywood/article19670867/.

Landes, David. "'Outlaw Forced Marriages in Sweden.'" *The Local*, June 2, 2009, www.thelocal.se/20090602/19820/.

Laughing Place Disney Newsdesk. "Fathom Events to Celebrate Nearly 40 Years of 'The Golden Girls' This September." Laughing Place, August 13, 2021, www.laughingplace.com/w/news/2021/08/13/fathom-events-to-celebrate-nearly-40-years-of-the-golden-girls-this-september/.

Lewis, Gregory B. "Support for Same-Sex Marriage: Trends and Patterns," American Sociological Association, April 22, 2015, www.asanet.org/sites/default/files/handout_lewis_ssm_asa_2015_8-16-15.pdf.

Lindin, Emily. "6 Ways You May Be Slut Shaming without Realizing It." *Teen Vogue*, June 3, 2016, www.teenvogue.com/story/slut-shaming-subtle-ways-unslut.

Little, Becky. "How Gary Hart's Sex Scandal Betrayed His Character." History, November 7, 2018, www.history.com/news/gary-hart-scandal-front-runner.

Lopez, German. "The Reagan Administration's Unbelievable Response to the HIV/AIDS Epidemic." *Vox*, December 1, 2015, www.vox.com/2015/12/1/9828348/ronald-reagan-hiv-aids.

Mann, Brian. "There Is Life after Addiction: Most People Recover." NPR, January 15, 2022, www.npr.org/2022/01/15/1071282194/addiction-substance-recovery-treatment.

Martin, Douglas. "Rue McClanahan, Actress and Golden Girl, Dies at 76." *New York Times*, June 4, 2010, www.nytimes.com/2010/06/04/arts/04mcclanahan.html.

Martin, Kali. "Bea Arthur, US Marine." The National WWII Museum, April 11, 2018, www.nationalww2museum.org/war/articles/bea-arthur-us-marine.

Martinez, Kiko. "Ahead of San Antonio Gigs, Andrew Dice Clay Says He's 'Grandfathered in' When It Comes to Cancel Culture." *San Antonio Current*, August 10, 2021, www.sacurrent.com/arts/ahead-of-san-antonio-gigs-andrew-dice-clay-says-hes-grandfathered-in-when-it-comes-to-cancel-culture-26882964.

McClanahan, Rue. *My First Five Husbands . . . and the Ones Who Got Away*. New York: Random House, 2007.

McMahon, Xandi. "The Non-Consensual Identity Politics of the 'Welfare Queen.'" *Compass*, November 13, 2018, https://wp.nyu.edu/compass/2018/11/13/the-non-consensual-identity-politics-of-the-welfare-queen/.

Miller, Julie. "The Queen Mother Loved the Golden Girls So Much That She Requested a Live Performance from the Cast." *Vanity Fair*, April 29, 2014, www.vanityfair.com/hollywood/2014/04/queen-elizabeth-golden-girls.

Moore, Kate. "The American History of Silencing Women through Psychiatry." *Time*, June 22, 2021, https://time.com/6074783/psychiatry-history-women-mental-health/.

Morford, Mark. "The Sad, Quotable Jerry Falwell." *San Francisco Chronicle*, February 11, 2012, www.sfgate.com/entertainment/morford/article/The-Sad-Quotable-Jerry-Falwell-It-s-bad-form-3302297.php.

Moritz, Robert. "Life Is a Scream for Betty White." *Parade*, October 31, 2010. https://parade.com/132208/robertmoritz/betty-white-goes-wild/.

Morrissey, Tracie Egan. "Rue McClanahan: An Appreciation of the Original Jezebel." *Jezebel*, June 3, 2010, https://jezebel.com/rue-mcclanahan-an-appreciation-of-the-original-jezebel-5554762.

"Mrs. America: Women's Roles in the 1950s." PBS. Accessed February 4, 2022. www.pbs.org/wgbh/americanexperience/features/pill-mrs-america-womens-roles-1950s/.

Necessary, Terra. "So What Does It Mean to Be a 'Friend of Dorothy?'" *Pride*, July 8, 2020, www.pride.com/identities/2020/7/08/so-what-does-it-mean-be-friend-dorothy.

Ninneman, Patrick. "Triad Hospice for AIDS Patients Opens." *Greensboro News and Record*, January 24, 2015, https://greensboro.com/triad-hospice-for-aids-patients-opens/article_aa970828-d9c4-591b-93ea-b60e35253155.html.

Nolasco, Stephanie. "Vanna White Dishes on 'Wheel of Fortune's' Lasting Success, Playboy Regrets." Fox News, March 29, 2017, www.foxnews.com/entertainment/vanna-white-dishes-on-wheel-of-fortunes-lasting-success-playboy-regrets.

"Number of Jews in the World." World Population Review. Accessed August 2, 2022. https://worldpopulationreview.com/country-rankings/number-of-jews-in-the-world.

O'Connor, Roisin. "Seth Rogen Says Antisemitic People 'Thrive' in Hollywood," *Independent*, August 3, 2020, www.independent.co.uk/arts-entertainment/films/news/seth-rogen-jewish-antisemitism-hollywood-mel-gibson-a9652336.html.

Parascandola, Rocco. "Exclusive: NYPD Takes Fresh Look at '90s Transgender Murders in Harlem." *New York Daily News*, April 9, 2018, www.nydailynews.com/new-york/nyc-crime/nypd-takes-fresh-90s-transgender-murders-harlem-article-1.2590002.

"Party of Reagan? No, Party of Falwell, Writer Says." NPR, April 26, 2012, www.npr.org/2012/04/26/151444474/party-of-reagan-no-party-of-falwell-writer-says.

Paulsen, Emily. "Recognizing, Addressing Unintended Gender Bias in Patient Care." Duke Health Referring Physicians, 2022, https://physicians.dukehealth.org/articles/recognizing-addressing-unintended-gender-bias-patient-care.

Peitzman, Louis. "Classic Gay TV: The Golden Girls, 'Isn't It Romantic?'" Logo TV, September 12, 2012, www.logotv.com/news/edodez/classic-gay-tv-the-golden-girls-isnt-it-romantic.

Perlman, Merill. "How the Word 'Queer' Was Adopted by the LGBTQ Community." *Columbia Journalism Review*, January 22, 2019, www.cjr.org/language_corner/queer.php.

Press, Andrea. "Gender and Family in Television's Golden Age and Beyond." *The Annals of the American Academy of Political and Social Science* (September 2009): 139–50.

"Psychiatry: The Wife Beater & His Wife." *Time*, September 25, 1964, http://content.time.com/time/subscriber/article/0,33009,876203,00.html.

Rao, Vidya. "'You Are Not Listening to Me': Black Women on Pain and Implicit Bias in Medicine." *Today*, July 27, 2020, www.today.com/health/implicit-bias-medicine-how-it-hurts-black-women-t187866.

Raschke, Logan. "Why 'The Golden Girls' Helps Me Cope." *Daily Eastern News*, June 19, 2020, www.dailyeasternnews.com/2020/06/19/why-the-golden-girls-helps-me-cope/.

Reilly, Travis. "Sarah Silverman on the Uphill Battle for Jewish Actresses, Quarantining with Her New Boyfriend, and the Tragic Death of Her Friend Adam Schlesinger." *Howard Stern*, November 17, 2020, www.howardstern.com/news/2020/11/17/sarah-silverman-on-the-uphill-battle-for-jewish-actresses-quarantining-with-her-new-boyfriend-and-the-tragic-death-of-her-friend-adam-schlesinger/.

"Rita Moreno." Television Academy Interviews, September 4, 2020, https://interviews.televisionacademy.com/interviews/rita-moreno.

Rogers, Nicole. "It's Show Time: TV Grandmas Turn the Rocking, Knitting Stereotype on Its Ear." *Wisconsin State Journal*, December 20, 2011, https://madison.com/entertainment/television/its-show-time-tv-grandmas-turn-the-rocking-knitting-stereotype-on-its-ear/article_d3ce2dcf-4f28-5403-ab2f-cf37daf4e193.html.

Romano, Aja. "A History of 'Wokeness.'" *Vox*, October 9, 2020, www.vox.com/culture/21437879/stay-woke-wokeness-history-origin-evolution-controversy.

"Ronald Reagan Fires 11,359 Air-Traffic Controllers." History, February 9, 2010, www.history.com/this-day-in-history/reagan-fires-11359-air-traffic-controllers.

Rosenfeld, Megan. "A Pregnant Pause for Chung?" *Washington Post*, July 31, 1990, www.washingtonpost.com/archive/lifestyle/1990/07/31/a-pregnant-pause-for-chung/0faaf6f0-16a4-4c81-bc1a-cde8e151d504/.

Rottenberg, Catherine, and Shani Orgad. "Tradwives: The Women Looking for a Simpler Past but Grounded in the Neoliberal Present," *The Conversation*, February 11, 2022, https://theconversation.com/tradwives-the-women-looking-for-a-simpler-past-but-grounded-in-the-neoliberal-present-130968.

Rudolph, Christopher. "Go behind the Scenes of 'The Golden Girls' Emotional Series Finale." *Logo TV*, May 19, 2017, www.logotv.com/news/wsed1t/the-golden-girls-series-finale.

"Rue McClanahan." Television Academy Interviews, February 22, 2019, https://interviews.televisionacademy.com/interviews/rue-mcclanahan.

Salguero, Gabriel. "Evangelicals Are Not a Monolith." *New York Times*, June 1, 2016, www.nytimes.com/roomfordebate/2016/03/07/what-does-it-mean-to-be-evangelical-today/evangelicals-are-not-a-monolith.

Santana, Kamille. "Can You Trust at-Home Pregnancy Tests?" UHealth Collective, August 5, 2022, https://news.umiamihealth.org/en/can-you-trust-at-home-pregnancy-tests/.

Saval, Malina. "Too Jewish for Hollywood: As Antisemitism Soars, Hollywood Should Address Its Enduring Hypocrisy in Hyperbolic Caricatures of Jews."

Variety, June 21, 2021. https://variety.com/2021/biz/features/jewish-hollywood-anti semitism-hyperbolic-caricatures-casting-jews-hate-crimes-1234997849/.

Schmidt, Joe. "Star Wars Book Confirms 'Holiday Special' Character as Canon and Gay." Comicbook.com, October 24, 2017, https://comicbook.com/starwars/news /star-wars-holiday-special-bea-arthur-ackmena-canon/.

Schmidt, Samantha. "Arrested for Having Sex with Men, This Gay Civil Rights Leader Could Finally Be Pardoned in California." *Washington Post*, February 5, 2020, www .washingtonpost.com/history/2020/01/21/bayard-rustin-gay-pardon/.

Schotsmans, Paul. "Bereavement: Reactions, Consequences and Care." *Health Policy* 5, no. 1 (1985): 86–88, https://doi.org/10.1016/0168-8510(85)90071-5.

Sewell, Claire. "Interview with Jim Colucci." The Golden Girls Fashion Corner, April 23, 2020, https://goldengirlsfashion.com/2020/04/23/interview-with-jim-colucci/.

Shabazz, Sa'iyda. "Why 'The Golden Girls' Stands the Test of Time." Scary Mommy, December 8, 2021, www.scarymommy.com/the-golden-girls-still-relevant.

Shewfelt, Raechal. "'The Golden Girls' Finale Was One of TV's Most Watched Ever, and the Show Is Still Going Strong." Yahoo, May 9, 2022, www.yahoo.com/entertain ment/the-golden-girls-finale-30th-anniversary-225633717.html.

Shipley, Diane. "30 Years Ago, 'The Golden Girls' Treated Sick Women Like We Matter." Bitch Media, August 7, 2019, www.bitchmedia.org/article/the-golden-girls -chronic-fatigue.

Shoemaker, Terry. "Understanding Evangelicalism in America Today." *The Con-versation*, March 2, 2022, https://theconversation.com/understanding-evangelicalism -in-america-today-164851.

Siciliano, Carl. "How Bea Arthur Became a Champion for Homeless LGBT Youth." *Huff Post*, July 21, 2016, www.huffpost.com/entry/how-bea-arthur-became-a-c_b_7837174.

Sit, Ryan. "Trump Told Not Everyone on Welfare Is Black: 'Really? Then What Are They?' He Responded: Report." *Newsweek*, May 25, 2018, www.newsweek.com /donald-trump-welfare-black-white-780252.

"State Statuses." Death with Dignity, July 7, 2022, https://deathwithdignity.org/states/.

Streep, Peg. "Is It Always a Turf War? Adult Daughters and Their Mothers." *Psychology Today*, June 25, 2014, www.psychologytoday.com/us/blog/tech-support/201406/is -it-always-turf-war-adult-daughters-and-their-mothers.

Strickland, Eliza. "'Yuppie Flu' Isn't Just in the Head: Chronic Fatigue Syndrome Linked to Virus." *Discover Magazine*, October 9, 2009, www.discovermagazine.com/health /yuppie-flu-isnt-just-in-the-head-chronic-fatigue-syndrome-linked-to-virus.

"Summary of Major Provisions of the Department of Education's Title IX Final Rule." The U.S. Department of Education, June 28, 2021, www2.ed.gov/about/offices/list/ocr /docs/titleix-summary.pdf.

"This Alien Legacy: The Origin of Sodomy Laws in British Colonialism." Human Rights Watch, April 29, 2015, www.hrw.org/report/2008/12/17/alien-legacy/origins -sodomy-laws-british-colonialism.

Tietjen, Jill S., and Barbara Bridges. "The Women Hollywood Forgot." *The Helm*, June 11, 2021, https://thehelm.co/hollywood-herstory-book/.

"Total Population in St. Olaf Township, Otter Tail County, Minnesota." The United States Census Bureau. Accessed August 8, 2022. https://data.census.gov/cedsci/all ?q=st+olaf+township+minnesota+population.

"Types of HIV Tests." Centers for Disease Control and Prevention, June 22, 2022, www .cdc.gov/hiv/basics/hiv-testing/test-types.html.

United Press International. "'Girls' Prompts $5-Million Suit." *Los Angeles Times*, July 5, 1986, www.latimes.com/archives/la-xpm-1986-07-05-ca-20405-story.html.

Vergun, David. "Before Stage and Screen, Bea Arthur Shined as a Marine." U.S. Department of Defense, October 13, 2021, www.defense.gov/News/Feature-Stories /Story/Article/2803048/before-stage-and-screen-bea-arthur-shined-as-a-marine/.

"Veteran Homelessness." National Coalition for Homeless Veterans, February 4, 2021, https://nchv.org/veteran-homelessness/.

Violanti, Anthony. "Shocking Words Audiences Seem to Enjoy the Abusive Language of Today's Performers. Andrew Dice Clay Is a Case in Point." *Buffalo News*, February 2, 1990, https://buffalonews.com/news/shocking-words-audiences-seem-to-enjoy-the -abusive-language-of-todays-performers-andrew-dice-clay/article_86b00602-e86f -531b-84ee-846105d00b5e.html.

"Why an Episode of the Golden Girls Was Removed in 2020." CBC/Radio Canada, January 7, 2021, www.cbc.ca/radio/undertheinfluence/why-an-episode-of-the-golden -girls-was-removed-in-2020-1.5864445.

"Why Sodomy Laws Matter." American Civil Liberties Union. Accessed July 31, 2022. www.aclu.org/other/why-sodomy-laws-matter.

"Why 'The Golden Girls' Are Still Golden." NPR, February 1, 2022. www.npr.org /transcripts/1074829590.

Wilchins, Riki Anne. "A Note from Your Editrix." *In Your Face*, 1995.

"Women in the 1950s." The Eisenhower Presidential Library. Accessed August 8, 2022. www.eisenhowerlibrary.gov/research/online-documents/women-1950s.

"Women's Earnings: The Pay Gap (Quick Take)." *Catalyst*, June 30, 2022, www.catalyst .org/research/womens-earnings-the-pay-gap/.

Wong, Curtis M. "Shelter for Homeless LGBTQ Youth, Named for 'Golden Girls' Star, Opens in NYC." *HuffPost*, December 6, 2017, www.huffpost.com/entry /bea-arthur-residence-lgbtq-youth_n_5a283792e4b0c2117627e650.

Ybarra v. Illinois 444 U.S. 85 (1979).

Yemi, Frank. "Kenny Niedermeier Has an 'Ex-Wife'—Here's How the 90 Day Fiance Star's Family Came to Be." Monsters and Critics, November 8, 2021, www.monster sandcritics.com/tv/reality-tv/kenny-niedermeier-has-an-ex-wife-heres-how-the-90 -day-fiance-stars-family-came-to-be/?fr=operanews.

Zol, Gaia. "Arranged Marriage in Italy: The Disappearance of Saman." Life in Italy, August 4, 2021, https://lifeinitaly.com/she-refuses-the-arranged-marriage-then-she -disappears/.

INDEX

AAVE. *See* African American Vernacular English

abortion, illegal, 15, 16, 157n4, 157n9; 1950s deaths from illegal, 157n8

absurdity, 29, 37, 86, 118

"The Accurate Conception," 123–25, *124*

"The Actor," 78

"Adult Education," 46–48

The Adventures of Ozzie and Harriet, 14

African American Vernacular English (AAVE), 107

"aging hippie," 79, 161n16

aging theme, 55–56

AIDS Project Los Angeles White Party, 144. *See also* HIV/AIDS

airplanes, movies on, 90, 164n41

The Alfred Hitchcock Hour, 166n1

Ali Forney Center, 143–44

All in the Family, 2, 5, 9

Alzheimer's disease, 109–11, 166n1

AMC Pacer, 90, 164n40

Americana, 118, 167n10

animal activism, 56

anti-Semitism, 112–15, 167n5

Arnaz, Desi, 5, 14

arranged marriage, 36, 158n10

Arrested Development, 20–21

Arthur, Beatrice (nee Frankel), *3, 63, 67*; birthplace of, 7; on Broadway, 8; casting of, 9; death of, ix, x, xi; "Dorothy bashing" and, 133; Dorothy Zbornak character and, 8; film roles of, 8–9, 156n14; finale tears of, 82;

Findlay-Zbornak similarity and, 69; Harris script and, 3; as Jewish, 114; LGBTQIA activism of, 143–44; as marine, 8; *Maude* role of, 2; name change of, 8; as queer icon, 156n14; role hesitation of, 69; songs sung by, 57, 160n17; thorny relationship between White, B., and, 27–28; vampy character played by, 41. *See also* Dorothy Zbornak

artificial insemination, 123–25, *124*

Asian doctor, episode with, 127

assisted suicide, 111–12, 167n2

The Atlantic, 28

"The Auction," 106

Aurthur, Robert Alan, 8

Babcock, Barbara, 162n22

Ball, Lucille, 5

Bartlett, Bonnie, 113

Baum, L. Frank, 141

BDSM, 18

Bea Arthur Residence, 144

Beacon Place, 144

"Bedtime Story," 26

The Benny Hill Show, 97, 165n7

Berlin, Irving, 57

The Beverly Hillbillies, 21

Bewitched, 19, 118

Bible, on menstrual period, 56

"Big Daddy's Little Lady," 64, 69–70

bigotry, in comedy, 104

Bitch, 128

Black, Jack, 135
blackface (mud masks) scene, 126, 168n14
Black-ish, 20, 134
Blacks: historical misconceptions about,
126–27; "woke" and, 107
Blanche Devereaux (GG character):
backstory and disparities, 41, 43, 44;
center of attention loved by, 56–58;
character of, 46, 58; Confederacy
and, 53–55; Confederate flag and, 43,
159n3; conservatism, 1980s and, 107,
123; death of husband, 160n21; depth
of character, 58–59; Dorothy's beauty
acknowledged by, 58; dream of dead
husband, 59–60, 160n21; family of, 43;
gay brother visit with fiancé, 120–22;
healthy sexuality and boundaries for,
47–48, 49; husband's brother and,
50–51; last appearance of, 137; married
men avoided by, 51–52; McClanahan
in real life *vs.*, 42; mother called
"Samantha Rocquet" by, 43, 159n2;
multilayered character of, 51; number
of relationships, 45; promiscuity, 44;
real life of McClanahan disparity with,
43; rejection by Lushbough, 48–49,
159n9; as Republican, 43; as sex-
positive role model, 41, *42*, 45–46;
sexual harassment episode, 47–48;
"slut" insult to, 45; as southern belle,
43, 50; southern heritage and, 53–55;
top ten best episodes with, 46–60;
unworthy men category and, 45;
widowhood and, 50–51
"The Bloom Is off the Rose," 64
Bostwick, Barry, 135
Bowers v. Hardwick, 140–41
Breines, Wini, 66
Bretzfield, Nancy, 9–10
"Bringing up Baby," 44
Broadway: Arthur roles on, 8; McClanahan
roles on, 5
Brochner, Lloyd, as Vaughn, Patrick, 78,
161n15
"Brother, Can You Spare That Jacket?,"
106, 118–20, 167n10
"Brotherly Love," 107–8
Butter Queen, 40

Campanella, Joseph, 87
"Camp Town Races Aren't as Fun as They
Used to Be," 159n3
Candid Camera, 97, 165n8
CARE Act, 102
"The Case of the Libertine Belle," 79–80
casting, *Golden Girls*, 4–9, 28; guest stars
on, 159n9
Catholicism, divorce law and, 71
Centers for Disease Control and
Prevention (CDC), 30, 131
CFS. *See* chronic fatigue syndrome
Chandler, Raymond, 80
Cheadle, Don, 54, 159n3
"Cheaters," 65
"The Cheese Man" (character), 25, 37
Cherry, Marc, 26–27, 37
Chicago Seven, 79
"The Chicken and the Egg," 137
"Chicken Little" fairytale, 158n4. *See also*
"Henny Penny--Straight, No Chaser"
Christianity: evangelical, 142; Republican
Party and, 103
chronic fatigue syndrome (CFS), 126–28;
ME and, 168n15
Chung, Connie, 123
civil rights movement, 139–40
Clay, Andrew Dice, 104, 143
Clooney, George, 66, 87
Cole, Nat King, 57
Colucci, Jim, 32, 133
comedy: bigotry in, 104; culture, mistakes
and, 49, 122
"The Competition," 68
Confederacy, 43, 53–55, 159nn2–3
conservatism, 1980s, 107, 123
continuity errors, 25, 159n12, 163n32,
164n39
corpse, dance with, 57, 160n16
costar relations, 27–28
COVID, 131
cross-dresser, 62, 160n2
Czechoslovakia, 84

Daily Eastern News, 143
Dana, Bill, 72, 161n7
Darling, Candy, 144
Darrow, Henry, 162n25

ABOUT THE AUTHOR

Bernadette Giacomazzo is an editor, writer, photographer, publicist, and pop culture commentator with an entertainment industry career spanning more than two decades. Her work has been featured in more than one hundred print and digital publications, including *People*, *Teen Vogue*, *Us Weekly*, the *Los Angeles Times*, the *New York Post*, and more. In addition to being the senior search engine optimization manager at Blavity, Giacomazzo is the CEO and founder of G-Force Marketing and Publicity, which has been featured in *The Hollywood Reporter* and has worked with blue-chip clients across a large swath of the entertainment industry. She lives in Atlantic Beach, New York.

OTHER BOOKS BY THE AUTHOR

Swimming with Sharks: A Real-World, How-to Guide to Success (and Failure) in the Business of Music (coauthored with M. J. Deskovic)

The Gathering, book 1 of The Uprising series

In Living Color: *A Cultural History* (Rowman & Littlefield)

Aquarius Rising (Nightingale & Sparrow Press)

Coming Soon

Kings and Queens, book 2 of The Uprising series

Rise River Rise, book 3 of The Uprising series

Honor Thy Father, book 4 of The Uprising series

Vector Prime, book 5 of The Uprising series

The Final Battle, book 6 of The Uprising series

My Life on the Press List: Life Lessons Learned from the Front Row Seats (memoir)

Printed in the USA
CPSIA information can be obtained
at www.ICGtesting.com
LVHW041423261023
761444LV00003B/5